Yukon was part wolf, part Alaskan mala-mute, and completely wild when R. D. Law-rence found him, but Lawrence swore he would win the animal's trust without vio-lence.

Though an old Indian thought Lawrence was crazy, and the wolf dog was confused by the unaccustomed kindness, slowly they began to share experiences. They hunted, trapped, and hauled wood through the frozen forests of British Columbia. They sur-vived a blizzard and a tornado. And as they explored many thousands of wilder-ness miles, an ancient chord was struck, establishing a friendship so strong that Yukon would fight against insurmountable odds to save his master's life.

"FASCINATING . . . HEROIC."
Sacramento Bee

"A REMARKABLE STORY . . . LAWRENCE COM-BINES ADVENTURE WITH A KEEN APPRECIATION OF THE NATURAL BEAUTY OF THE LAND."
Publishers Weekly

The
NORTH
RUNNER

R. D. Lawrence

BALLANTINE BOOKS • NEW YORK

Library of Congress Catalog Card Number: 78-23576

ISBN 0-345-33202-4

This edition published by arrangement with
Holt, Rinehart and Winston

Manufactured in the United States of America

First Ballantine Books Edition: November 1980
Fifth Printing: December 1988

First Canadian Printing: November 1980
Fourth Canadian Printing: June 1983

Map by Rafael Palacios

For Joan,
in fond memory;
for Sharon,
with love.
For a great dog,
in tribute.

I am grateful to the Canadian Horizons Program
of the Canada Council for assistance given me
when I returned to northwest British Columbia in
1972 to do further research on this book.

R. D. LAWRENCE
Watson Lake, Yukon Territory,
March 1978

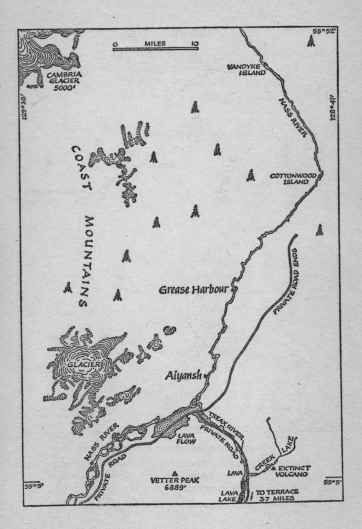

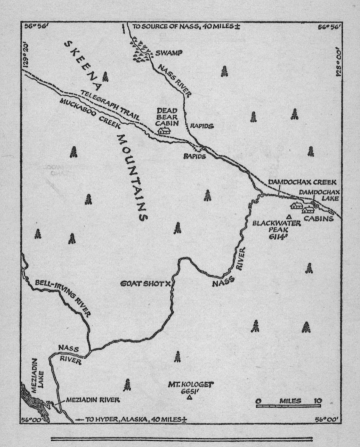

Map details show land topography as it was in 1959. Today, the road from Terrace, British Columbia, reaches northward to join the Alaska Highway near Watson Lake, Yukon Territory.

Chapter 1

The yellow eyes bored into mine as the lips parted, wrinkled, and drew back into a silent snarl, showing the great fangs and the moist cavern of the mouth. He was without a doubt the most ill-kept, the most beaten-up, and the *biggest* sled dog that I had ever seen, and he was probably the most dangerous. His entire bearing bristled with threat, but it was the almond-shaped wolf eyes that most clearly signaled his aggressiveness; this dog was wild, he would not hesitate to go for the throat at the slightest opportunity. He stood, quietly sinister, his great paws planted solidly on the bottom of the truck box, and returned my gaze, holding my eyes where another dog would have averted his glance.

I stood looking into the creature's face during those first few moments of our meeting, and my initial reaction to him made my scalp prickle and almost caused me to take a step backward. For a time we remained staring at each other while Alfred, the Ojibway Indian who had brought the dog in hopes of sell-

1

ing him to me, hovered nearby with a stout club in his hand.

I needed a lead dog for my team, but this monster spelled trouble. This one was a rebel with a mind of his own, as ready to take punishment as he would be quick to dish it out, a creature more wolf than dog who had learned early to hate man. No, he wasn't for me, I decided after I had finished my inspection, had noted the heavy chain with which Alfred had secured him to one of the sides of the Ford pickup truck, and had noted also the open cut on the dog's left shoulder and the large scabbed-over wound on his right foreleg. I was about to turn away and refuse the offer, but I hesitated, paused to have a second look, moving closer, but being careful not to get within reach of the gaping mouth that was so well filled with strong white teeth. There was something about the animal that touched me; he was so damned *primordial!* Half starved so that his ribs and hips were easily noticeable despite the heavy coat of fur, injured, scarred, evidently brutalized since puppyhood, the dog yet had dignity, and the strength of him showed in every line.

He stood chest-high to me from his place on the truck's platform, which was not a good angle from which to view him for the first time, for with his head held high, he looked directly into my face; this intensified the sense of danger that he carried like a banner. Not once did he move; he stood rock still with his eyes fixed on mine while the autumn breeze ruffled his unkempt fur and fanned to my nostrils the rank dog smell of him. I noticed his lips moving again. They were coming together slowly, losing their wrinkles and covering the big tusks, closing the mouth. So we faced each other for some little time of mutual appraisal. I spoke to him then as though he were another person.

"You're a wild-looking son of a bitch, dog, but I'll be darned if I don't like the looks of you."

Exactly those words, no more, no less; I can quote them verbatim twenty years later because that evening, during supper, I wrote them down, wondering just why I had spoken in the first place and why I said what I did.

At the sound of my voice the dog raised his tail slightly and pricked up his ears; I have never been sure, but it seemed to me that there was the merest nuance of a wag in the movement. I fervently hoped so, because by now I had determined to buy him, albeit against my better judgment. I turned to Alfred, prepared to drive a hard bargain.

"He's not pretty, Alfred, that's for sure . . . and he looks as though he'd rather tear my throat out than lift his leg against a tree. . . ."

"He's a good dog, pulls good," Alfred interrupted in his soft voice. "You carry a club, he's OK. He knows what a club's for, that dog."

"How much?" I asked bluntly, already sorry that I had admitted aloud my liking for the gaunt wolf-dog. I needn't have worried. Alfred, whom I had helped out of a bind in early summer and who had since become a friend, was obviously anxious to turn the dog into "cash money" with which he could go to town and buy a fresh supply of cheap wine, for good fellow though he was, he had an affection for the bottle that was eventually to run him into serious trouble with the law.

"Would fifteen dollars be too much?" he asked pleadingly.

I offered him twenty dollars, but I attached one condition to my generosity: He was to remove the dog from the truck and lead him to an unused shed on my property and there tie him up securely. I had no intention of using a cudgel on this animal, yet it was obvious that a club was going to have to be used to get him from the truck to the shed without damage to our persons. So I wanted the Indian to do it. He knew how, and the dog was used to such treatment from him, whereas I hoped that if the animal never saw a club in my hand, I could win him over more readily, especially if I kept him tied in the shed, fed him well, and treated him gently—but from a safe vantage, naturally.

The deal was made, the money changed hands, and the transaction was properly sealed with a toast from a bottle of red "screech" that Alfred had in the glove compartment of his wreck, a ceremony I could easily have done without but in which I had perforce to participate in order to observe the rules of backwoods etiquette. After his second pull at the wine (I managed to get by with one small one) Alfred wiped the bottle neck on the sleeve of his bush jacket, screwed the cap back on, and returned the half-empty quart to its hiding place. Then he belched pleasurably, hefted his club, and approached the truck, brandishing the weapon in front of the dog's face.

The Indian did not climb in over the lowered tailgate as I had expected and feared he would do, thereby exposing himself to attack while he scrambled up. Instead, he stood on the running board of the old truck, brandishing the club in his right hand and mouthing curses at the dog; a moment later he cocked one leg up and over the side and followed through with the rest of his body, never once bending down and always keeping the cudgel at the ready.

The animal backed up warily but didn't take his eyes off the Indian's face. It was like watching a trained boxer, dancing and weaving in front of his opponent while waiting to read in his eyes advance notice of a blow. The dog moved lightly, his fangs bared once more, but now he snarled lustily, a malevolent, deep-throated rumble uttered not as a threat, but rather as a certain promise of what would happen if the man dropped his guard for even one second. Alfred knew his animal too well to take chances, the club never wavered. Using his left hand, he unfastened the chain and unwound it the two turns it had been wrapped around a two-by-four wooden upright. With the speed and dexterity of practice, he slid his hand along the chain until it was some eighteen inches from the collar, at which point he closed his grip, extended his left arm stiffly away from his body, threatening all the time with the club, and then started to pull the animal toward the tailgate.

The dog continued to growl, mouth agape, lips peeled back to their fullest extent so that his formidable, inward-curving tusks were revealed fully: two-inch-long fangs within jaws powerful enough to crush the leg bone of a moose.

Before he brought him to the homestead, Alfred had told me that the dog's grandmother had mated with a timber wolf and that one of her litter, who was to become the big dog's father, was bred to a bitch that was half wolf. The lupine heritage was easy to note in the dog, not just in his size and looks, but also in his manner, especially in the way that he moved, fluidly, catlike; but until I actually saw him, I suspected the Indian had been exaggerating somewhat in the hope of arousing my interest. I knew now that if anything, the reverse was true, that the Ojibway had underplayed the dog's wolfishness for fear that I might not want to buy him.

Earlier, while we were discussing the dog and before I had stood back to get a good look at him, Alfred told me that the animal was nearly three years old, but whether this was fact or fiction was impossible to determine because of the dog's condition. Some time was to elapse before I judged that the Indian's age estimate was probably correct.

Alfred heaved, and the captive moved forward while putting up enough resistance to show that he was acting under duress. Quite evidently he knew from past experience that he stood no chance against the raised club and that so long as Alfred held the weapon ready, the dog would do as he was urged; but somehow he did it with dignity. Watching intently, I felt all my sympathy go out to this magnificent beast, even to the extent that I found myself hoping that Alfred would slip up, just once, and that the dog would have a chance to attack, though I quickly put this thought away. I had often felt the same way as a child in Spain when I was taken to a bullfight—always I hoped the bull would win. Now I stood aside and was filled with admiration for this creature, for his courage and his intelligence. Despite his fierceness, he appealed to me; I felt that we would be able to establish a close relationship once he came to live on the homestead.

When he had got the animal to the very edge of the tailgate and already overbalanced, Alfred jumped to the ground, pulling the dog with him and turning quickly to threaten even more vigorously with the club. The dog didn't change his attitude or his manner. Growling in the same tone and with the same volume, yellow eyes still turned upward, fixed on the Indian's face, he went along, while I followed behind thoughtfully. In the shed I watched to make sure that Alfred fastened the chain securely to a stout wooden upright that had once been used as part of a stall, and when he was done, I ushered him out of the shed and closed the door. As we walked away, I could hear the prisoner lunging at the chain.

Alfred, now being rich, was anxious to drive the twenty-seven miles to town to spend some of his wealth. This suited me; I wanted to feed the dog, give him water, and spend a little time with him to try to show him that a club would never become part of our relationship. If ever an animal needed a friend, it was this one, but I knew that I would have to earn his confidence.

The other dogs were in the barn, loose in the empty hay-storage section, and they knew instantly that a stranger had arrived, no doubt hearing his growls and almost certainly scenting his formidable rankness, so redolent of an old and often-used wolf den. Now, as I waved Alfred off, the ruckus from the barn was formidable; the huskies howled wolfishly, and the collie bitch barked hysterically. I yelled at them to shut up, but they would not be pacified until I prepared for them an extra feed of dog meal mixed with scraps of cooked moose offal.

When peace was restored in that quarter, the new dog's rations were prepared: raw moose meat scraps, a couple of good, big marrow bones, some dog meal, and a liberal helping of "gravy" from the cooked offal. About to take the dishpan to him, I remembered the worm powder and mixed a larger-than-prescribed dosage in the food, for the newcomer would be full of roundworms and tapeworms, not to mention such things as liver flukes, about which I could do nothing but hope that the animal's constitution would withstand the inroads of these trematodes. All wild canids are hosts to these parasites, which are acquired, in most cases, from eating their prey's offal; that is why one should cook this before feeding it to dogs. Native huskies and malamutes, whose rations are meager at the best of times, are also fed raw fish, which are hosts to the flukeworm.

The dog was lying down, broad head resting on his front paws, ears pricked forward, and eyes focused on the opening door; he didn't move when I entered the shed until his keen nose picked up the smell of the food. It was intriguing to note how quickly the scent of the meat reached him and to watch the wet pink tongue fall out of the wide jaws and pass over the upper lip. With nostrils twitching, he jumped to his feet, tail coming up, eagerness showing in eyes that were warily expectant. Because I had already learned that animals, especially wild ones, feel more comfortable with slow, purposeful movement, I walked toward him at an easy pace, talking continuously and trying to make my voice sound as reassuring as possible. He moved to meet me, advancing almost to the full extent of the nine-foot chain. I stopped half a yard from him and lowered the dish to waist level, but held it out of his reach until I had a chance to see how he was going to react.

He didn't appear to be hostile, yet it was obvious that suspicion struggled against the pull of hunger. He couldn't conceal his desire, but he held it in check, too wary to trust anybody, even the bearer of such a tantalizing aroma. I backed away slightly so that I could bend down and place the dish on the floor without coming into range of those big fangs, which were readily visible despite the fact that he wasn't snarling. As the dish slid toward him, the slaver flowed out of his mouth, actually dripping onto the floorboards, and his entire body quivered with appetite. Never was there a hungrier dog; the poor beast seemed to be actually starving!

Ravenous he was, yet he did not attack the food as one might have expected, as a house dog would have done, gulping and snapping and swallowing whole the pieces of meat. Instead, he sniffed at the dish almost suspiciously for several seconds, drooling continously, then picked up one of the bones and retreated with it to the corner he had evidently selected as his resting place. There he dropped it on the floor, smelled it again, licked it, and turned and padded back to the dish. Meanwhile, he had almost ignored me, except for a fast glance or two, just to make sure that no hostile moves were made, that this unexpectedly succulent meal was not about to be snatched from his very jaws.

Back at the food, he picked out the second bone, hesitated with it gripped between his teeth while he sniffed the dish, dropped it between his front legs, and bent his muzzle to the feast. He took big mouthfuls, but he chewed everything thoroughly, if rapidly, a purposeful, controlled way of eating calculated to ingest the most in the shortest time and in the most efficient manner. This surprised me at the moment, but months later, after I had learned much about the ways of the wolves, I witnessed precisely the same eating habits displayed by these animals and learned that this is the way of the wild dogs, who must chew their food well so that none of it is wasted during the digestive process, to be lost as lumps in the feces. So efficiently does a wolf chew its food, and so effective is its digestion, that its winter scats contain hardly anything but fur and bits of bone, indigestible substances bound by waste juices into the characteristic oblongs. Between spring and late autumn, if game is plentiful on their range, wolves feed rather more wastefully, and their scats will tend to resemble those deposited by well-fed (overfed, really) dogs. When game is scarce in winter or at any time of the year and the wolves must go days without eating, the food is chewed thoroughly by the powerful jaws; a rather marvelous, natural thriftiness is programmed in the breed, the mechanics of which elude me as yet even if the way in which it is accomplished is perhaps simple enough: It seems that in the face of hardship, wolves feel impelled to chew more, and being the possessors of such incredibly powerful jaws and teeth, they can easily crush the heaviest bones and extract from them every last ounce of protein.

The dog was eating in such a fashion, hungrily, yet unhurriedly, his attention centered partly on the food and partly on me. Watching him, I wondered how long it would be before he trusted me enough to allow himself to be handled, so that his injuries could be treated. They certainly needed attention! The scabbed place appeared to be festering, and the more recent cut, deep and angry-looking, would soon start to suppurate unless it received some quick first aid. And his coat was in deplorable condition; it was dry and brittle, filthy and matted with his own feces, tick-ridden, and no doubt full of fleas.

I felt now that once I could get him cleaned up and fed him plenty of nourishing food, he would become a great lead dog. But it was going to take time to put meat back on his bones and to give him the energy he would need to handle a loaded sled while maintaining his place as team leader.

It was probable that his last good meal had been at his mother's dugs when he was a blind puppy. He had known nothing but abuse since he first began to move around the shack where his master lived. But he was big and strong and had the will to survive. All might yet be well, if I could find a way to communicate with him.

When he had almost finished the contents of the dish, I went to get a pail of water. I returned to find him lying down in the corner, chewing on the first moose bone. He looked up when I entered but continued his attack on the bone, and the way that his jaws and teeth demolished the femur confirmed the initial impression of savage strength that had so impressed

9

me. I put the water down where he could get at it, then moved back a little ways and squatted down, talking the while and being rewarded by an occasional glance from those yellow eyes or by the flick of the ears.

Occasionally he would pause in his crunching, pin the bone to the floor with one paw while he thrust his tongue into the marrow cavity, licking the gray substance with relish before cracking another section and repeating the procedure. In about ten minutes the bone was demolished, its splinters littering the floor; he rose, stretched, sniffed once in my direction, and walked to the water pail. He lapped noisily, watching me and listening to my voice. Done, he turned around, picked up the other bone from where it lay near the dish, and carried it to his corner, there to flop down and to begin to chew.

I rose quietly and went to get the dish. It had been moved deeper inside the circumference of the chain and was now about five feet from where the dog was feding. I bent down, reached with my left hand, and was about to grasp the pan.

He was unbelievably fast! Before my fingers touched the dish, he was on his feet and moving, a low growl rising in his throat. My senses registered the danger, but my reflexes were too slow to deal with it. When his teeth fastened on the heel of my hand, I actually heard his two tusks click as they came together inside my flesh.

I was too stunned to react quickly. For a second or two it seemed as though we both were frozen into immobility; there was no pain, but I watched with a sense of unreality as my blood ran out between the two big fangs, staining them pink because the redness was diluted by the saliva that bathed the teeth. It is amazing how much detail the senses can absorb in a split second of time: the smell of him, the malevolence in the eyes, the way the upper and lower fangs had grasped my hand, almost missing their target, but getting enough of my meat between them to punch two deep holes.

I couldn't quite believe that it was happening, and because of this, I didn't panic, I didn't lash out with my free hand, I just remained still. I believe it was my passivity more than anything else that made him let go without shaking and ripping and perhaps taking another slash or two. When he freed his hold, he backed up, still growling, while he looked expectantly into my face, believing, no doubt, that he was now going to get a thorough drubbing with a club.

I cannot claim that what happened next occurred as a result of my valor. For the next few moments my actions were dictated by some unknown, subconscious reasoning at the hub of which was a feeling that it was vitally important for me not to show hostility to the dog while demonstrating that I was not afraid of him. Instead of backing off, as sanity dictated, I got to my feet and stepped forward, looking full into his eyes. He didn't budge, and he returned my stare; but he stopped growling, and by the set of his ears I knew he was listening to my voice. I stooped, having to move my body to the side so as not to brush against his head, and I reached down with the bitten hand and picked up the dish, straightened again, stood absolutely still, and then turned my back on him and walked to the door. I turned again, paused, and spoke to him.

"That's the last time you're going to bite me, you hear!" I spoke gruffly, but I didn't raise my voice. He stood as before, eyeing me fixedly. I left.

In the house, I looked at the wounds, squeezed them to make them bleed, then washed them with soap and water and poured strong iodine over each fang hole, working it in as deeply as I could. By the time that this operation was concluded I had an urge to cut a club and to go beat the hell out of the dog, but the ugly desire faded as the pain caused by the tincture subsided and I regained composure. If there had been a doctor near, I would have gone for a tetanus shot; as it was, I left the wounds uncovered, letting them bleed and trusting to my body's natural abilities to deal with infection, which it had always done most effectively. When my emotions were properly under control I went to the meat larder, a roughly built wooden hut near the house where the butchered moose hung; I cut three smallish pieces of meat and went with them to the shed.

The dog was lying down again when I entered his quarters, one paw draped loosely over the remains of the second bone. Holding the meat in my right hand, I moved to within six feet of him, talking softly. He stayed where he was, but he watched me alertly. I extended the bitten hand and held it palm outward, almost like a peace sign, so that he could scent the blood and watch it as it dripped onto the boards; then I shook the hand, spraying blood toward him, and he jerked his head to the side when a drop or two hit his muzzle.

"See that, you son of a bitch? Do you?" I made my voice gruff again.

His expression didn't change. He looked at the hand, sniffed at it, but soon swiveled his eyes back to mine. Now he evidently picked up the scent of the moose meat, for he looked at my right hand expectantly, ears stiffly alert. He got onto all fours and took a step toward me.

I switched back to gentle talk, uttering the first nonsense that entered my head, for it was the tone of voice that mattered, not the words, and he raised his head as he worked his nostrils, siphoning the aroma of fresh moose meat. I tossed the first piece to him, and he snapped it up before it hit the floor, chewed it, swallowed, and looked for more. I suppose I wasn't quick enough with the second piece, for he moved forward again, stopping two feet from me. It was hard not to back away. I gave him both pieces of meat at once, letting them drop out of my open hand; he fielded one in midair, chewed, swallowed, and bent his head to pick up the other. When he had finished eating, he turned and went to lie down in his corner, the first time that he had fully exposed his back in my presence.

Resting his head on the floor between his front paws, he licked his lips a couple of times, yawned, and closed his eyes. I grinned and uttered a few more quiet words, and he half opened his eyes to watch me leave the shed.

Alfred brought the dog to my homestead on November 12, 1955, almost eleven months after I had arrived in the northern Ontario backwoods and eighteen months from the date when I had climbed down the gangway of the immigrant ship that carried me from England to Quebec City. During the first half of my life in the New World events were routine once the bloom of strange surroundings had worn off, and one evening of crisp, colorful autumn, when walking through a piece of suburban woodland, I suddenly realized that the real purpose of my departure from Europe had not been achieved; I had simply exchanged metropolitan London for metropolitan Toronto, routine was once more becoming the norm, people in bunches, like animated bananas, were again giving me mental indigestion.

It was true that many of the reasons that led to emigration from Europe did not exist in Canada, but the inner restlessness, the extreme distaste for crowds rushing and pushing like ants erupting from a disturbed hill continued to irritate the invisible tender places that I carried somewhere inside my head. There was no peace to be had in Toronto, and peace was what I wanted, with time to think, alone, somewhere where the banging and clanging of humanity on the move could not intrude.

The civil war in Spain had found me in the summer of 1936 at a camp for boys on the shores of the Mediterranean when I was not yet fourteen years old. A little more than three years later, as a teenager who was trying to continue an interrupted education while odd-jobbing for a living, World War II arrived to give me a new uniform, a new cause, and final proof that mankind had gone quite mad. Afterward, still limping from a shrapnel injury and the possessor of a pension that was just enough to buy me two ounces of pipe tobacco a week (which a grateful government referred to euphemistically as an allowance), I tried to settle in London, grubbed through its streets on assignments, wrote pointless articles, and at last decided that a new start in a new land had to be made. In 1954, accompanied by envious sighs from colleagues who were equally free to do what I was doing but who had already succumbed to postwar routine, I shook the soot of London from my heels.

Now the less black, but equally abrasive, atmosphere of Toronto had to be dusted off. I returned to my lodgings that evening, collected my few belongings, packed them in the car, and paying the rent a week in advance in lieu of notice, set out for the north in the middle of a light snowfall. Three days and twelve hundred eventful, fascinating miles later found me parked tight against a fourfoot snowbank reading a dilapidated, crudely lettered FOR SALE sign posted on a rotting fencepost in front of a deserted log house. There was no address on the sign, but inquiries at a general store in a hamlet four miles away elicited the name and address of the owner, now an old man living in a city seventy-two miles to the south. This was it, the place I had unknowingly been looking for, two hundred acres, forty of them cleared, the rest forested, mingling with thousands of wilderness miles. The nearest human was more than a mile away, the nearest town, population nine hundred, was twenty-seven miles south-west; no telephones, no power lines, but unlimited peace spiced by the sounds of the northland, the bird calls, the often-heard howl of the timber wolf, the sudden snort of a startled white-tailed deer. Eight hundred dollars changed hands over a couple of signatures in a law office, and before Christmas I was settled on the old homestead. Winter came and logging and hunting for the pot and days of wandering through the white-topped land and nights of sound, nightmare-free slumber and dawns the like of which I had never before experienced and an appetite, a gusto for simple food that made breakfast a feast, lunch an event, and dinner a gourmet's delight. And then came Sussie, a bitch dog, gaunt, starving, a waif of the north, mostly collie, but mixed up with some other breed.

She came to the back door and scratched, whining, and when I opened, she entered as though she belonged there. After she had eaten, she curled up by the fire, thumped her matted tail twice in gratitude, and fell into a deep sleep from which she didn't awaken for four hours. She was my first dog, a good companion. Next came Rocky, a true dog of the north, lean, wolfish, with tightly curled tail and the yellow eyes of the wild ones, eighty-five pounds of sled-puller who more than repaid me the thirty-five dollars he cost. Then the sled, a U.S. Army war surplus vehicle that was strong and well designed and cheap, if rather heavy. Its weight suggested a third dog and so Sooner was added. I had hoped he was going to be the leader; he was older, seemed wiser than Rocky, if not quite as big, but it turned out that he would sooner eat than pull, thus his name. He ran if sandwiched between the other two, he had to, but his heart was never really in it. All in all, it was an indifferent collection of dogs that pulled the sled through the latter part of my first winter in the backwoods. That was why, at the end of the next summer, I began asking around, looking for a suitable team leader.

The night of the big dog's arrival, after supper, I was not at all sure that I had found what I was looking for. Washing up one-handed, feeling the throb of the bite, which by then I had covered, I was most conscious of the work that lay ahead. There was the winter fuel to cut, a proper stall to build for the cow, a warm henhouse for the twelve hens and one rooster, and then a winter of logging, cutting pulpwood logs by hand to sell to the paper mill in the distant city, my only immediate source of revenue already half committed to pay for trapline supplies for my newly acquired line, which I hoped would furnish spring and summer income after the furs were marketed. And to this had been added the need to tame the wild dog.

After the dishes were done and stacked, I made coffee and sat for a time sipping from the mug and

debating my next moves. It was then that the idea
came; if the dog was to be gentled and used on the
trail, the sooner it was done the better. Why not spend
the night with him in the shed? Pouring the remaining
coffee into a thermos, I opened the tin of oatmeal
cookies I had baked the previous day and packed a
dozen in a paper bag. With these things and my
sleeping bag and a kerosene barn lantern, I went to
the shed.

In the yellow glow of the lantern the big dog looked
more savage than usual, but he did not show actual
hostility or rise from his corner when I entered the
shed. His ears moved at the sound of my voice, and
his eyes were fixed on me, watching as I put down
my things, unrolled the sleeping bag, and settled it
just out of his reach. The lantern was left burning
that night, hanging from a nail on one of the rafters,
not for the dog's benefit, certainly, but for mine, to
let me see what was going on at all times and to allow
me to watch him for a while before I settled down to
sleep.

Sitting on the bedroll, back against the wall, I
poured a cup of coffee, fished out a cookie from the
bag, and munched between sips, now and then speaking to the dog and watching him intently. He couldn't
make out what was going on. This was most likely the
first time that a human had lain close to him at night,
and he must have found it puzzling. He was also
interested in the cookie, sniffing toward my hand and
watching my mouth as I chewed. I tossed a whole one
to him; he smelled it, picked it up, and ate it, rising
to come forward even as he was swallowing. He ate
three more while I finished the coffee and he was still
standing expectantly when I slipped into the sleeping
bag.

The wilderness has the power to exert enormous influence on the mind of a man freshly arrived from civilization, especially if he lives alone and has but little
contact with other people; some that I have known
could not take the solitude, the absence of comfort and

reassurance offered by the presence of other humans.

Such men have become effete in terms of personal survival in the face of natural challenges, the city is too much with them, and they don't last. There are also those who go too far the other way, becoming misanthropes uncomfortable in the presence of more than one companion; these are the withdrawers, and they are found sprinkled loosely wherever there is a forest or a jungle, like seeds that have lost the ability to germinate in cultivated soil. But between the quitters and the lone stayers, there is a third kind—indeed, there may be more than that, for all I know—in whom the wilderness acts as a catalyst and who, after they have experienced both the wild and the civilized, begin to form new values, to explore unknown pathways, and to realize that nature is an endlessly patient teacher with an infinite capacity to stimulate thought and to sharpen the hunger for knowledge.

That is how the wilderness affected me, and I say it humbly, taking no credit for it because the process began without my conscious awareness. Even when I did start to realize that my philosophies had altered radically, I did not pause to consider the whys and wherefores of the thing; I was too busy, too stimulated and interested to spend time pursuing that concept.

After almost a year of living within the solitude of a northern forest, I started to become aware that human speech, for all its marvels, is neither the only nor necessarily the best way for communication, that there is a wild, sensory kind of communion that is wholly trustworthy and completely honest. Those who are expert in its pactice cannot be cheated, nor can it serve *their* purpose to cheat.

Humans can lie to each other most convincingly; in some cases maliciously, in others feeding so-called white lies to their interlocutors for a variety of valid or invalid reasons. But the wild ones never lie, and not having the gift of tongues, as we know it, they have become masters of observation and are additionally so finely tuned to their environment that they can at once note even the most tenuous sensory influences. Some

17

of the ways by which animals can pick up and transmit messages are too hidden to define, yet they are there, of that I am convinced; others are the result of their wonderful powers of observation coupled with an inherent ability to interpret quickly the signals picked up by all their senses, whereas civilized man, surrounded by the safety of his inventions, long ago allowed many of these faculties to become dulled, using them only marginally, even losing some of them altogether. As a result, humans rely heavily on speech and on the written word, by these means being uniquely able to enrich their culture greatly, to benefit from the experience of others, and to project themselves far into the future. But what a pity that these inventive gifts could not have progressed side by side with our inherited, wild perceptiveness! Perhaps then man would not rely quite so heavily on speech and on the written word, would not be able to lie as easily, and silence in the presence of others would not become as embarrassingly painful as it now does in the absence of love or hate. Love, it seems to me, sharpens all our senses; so does hate, I think, but I cannot really speak to that because I have never been able to muster enough anger in order to develop hate. Some people, of course, have retained the gift of silent communication; they are the fortunate ones.

Be that as it may, whether it came about through ESP or through some other kind of special magic we each carried in our beings, the big dog and I *communicated* that night. For about an hour I sat propped against the wall, puffing silently on my pipe or sipping hot coffee, feeling that I no longer needed to resort to speech because we had become attuned to each other, managing in some way to achieve understanding. Occasionally the yellow eyes would swivel to my face, but now their expression no longer signaled hostility. Several times he dozed off only to awaken the moment I moved, to look at me for a second or two, then to return his head to its place between his paws. The autumn night got chilly, crystaled by the first frosts of the dying year. To keep warm, I slid into the bag;

when my eyes got heavy, I shuffled down, burrowing like some animal in its den, concealing even my head.

I thought at first I had been awakened by a dream. Befuddled with sleep as I was, eyes open, but unseeing because my head was still buried inside the bag, the sensation of someone having shaken my shoulder was strong, but I knew it was unreal because I was alone with the dog inside the shed. Yet even as I began to stick my head out, my shoulder was shaken again. I was unprepared for what met my gaze. The sturdy furred legs and chest of the dog were very close to me, and when I looked up, it was to see his massive head poised not *quite* over mine. His jaws couldn't reach me, for he was at the extent of his chain, but his paws could. As I moved, he lifted one front foot and pawed again, his thick, blunt nails scratching the bag, and he was whining!

Evidently I had turned over in my sleep, rolling, bag and all, toward his corner of the shed, a lot closer to him than I would have dared to get while awake.

It must be remembered that I had just awakened from a deep sleep, that this enormous creature had bitten through my hand not long ago, and that now, standing over me with jaws agape, even though he was not snarling and showed no outward hostility, he looked like something I *should* have seen in a dream, in a nightmare, rather, a sort of sleep-phantom incarnate.

Reflex made me roll away too quickly, causing him to jump back and snarl. It did no good that I realized my error immediately and that I tried to make it up to him; clearly he had interpreted my sudden, injudicious move as a manifestation of aggression; I had betrayed his trust. He did not seem to be as hostile as yesterday, but he wouldn't respond after I had gathered my wits, crawled out of the sleeping bag, and walked toward him talking quietly, and he wouldn't allow me to get near him. Standing close to the wall, he snarled deeply, showing his formidable teeth. When

I halted, he stopped snarling and covered his fangs, but he watched intently.

Outside, dawn was arriving, a faint luminescence that filtered through the one small window that had been set high into the east wall; it could hardly be called light, and it did little to aid the flickering lamp that was going out for want of oil. The low flame gave some light, but it also intensified the shadows, denying a really clear view of the dog; he *seemed* to be listening to me, but I could have been mistaken. About the only thing that was reasonably certain just then was his silence; at least he wasn't growling, and his teeth were covered, for even in that gloom his tusks became whitely visible when he bared them.

I was angry with myself for missing the opportunity to win his trust, and because of his mood, I felt it would be better to go have breakfast and return later with food for him. Perhaps then I could make up the lost ground, going back when my self-annoyance was spent and I could again approach him in a relaxed frame of mind.

It was full daylight when I revisited him after an absence of two hours, carrying a dish of meat and dog chow. He was in the act of rising, ears pricked, already siphoning the aroma of the food, and he was wagging his tail, half wagging, really, as though he were embarrassed at showing emotion. I walked up to him and bent to put the dish down, and he dipped his muzzle into it before my hand was withdrawn. I left silently.

The other dogs had to be fed, the cow milked, and the chickens inspected and counted, for there was a hungry bobcat living nearby who had already tried to get his talons in the Rhode Island Red rooster.

It was while I was feeding the team that I got the idea. When chores were done, I would take Sussie to the shed, fuss over her, and let her and the newcomer become acquainted, for male dogs will not attack a female; after that I would call Sussie to me, allowing the big dog to see how she trusted me and delighted in being caressed.

Milking the cow and thinking about the scheme, I suddenly realized that the dog had no name. Alfred, when asked, had merely shrugged, shaking his head as though to say that naming a dog was a frivolous waste of time. No doubt the animal had been called many things, none of them complimentary. As my fingers worked the milk out of the cow's teats so that it hit the pail with the forceful, musical cadence that is so pleasantly restful, my mind was searching for a suitable name, and presently the white, frothy milk suggested one.

Watching as the alternate jets dimpled the surface of the pail's contents, making new bubbles, I thought of snow, and mountains in the far north, and although I had not then been there, the Yukon Territory, photographs of which I had seen but recently in a magazine, came to mind. Yukon . . . the name suited him; he was as wild as the northland and as rugged as the mountains; the name conjured excitement, the dog *was* exciting.

Sometime later I called Sussie, stopped Rocky and Sooner from sneaking out of the barn behind her, and led the collie to the shed. I am sure she knew where we were going. Sniffing intently, she paused impatiently while I opened the door; then she eagerly popped into the building. By the time I followed the two were nose to nose, Sussie showing in her stance that she wasn't going to fall all over this scruffy stranger, but coy enough to invite his attention. Yukon was holding himself tall, tail up high, wagging vigorously, ears forward, and (I swear to it!) an inane smile on his face. He didn't so much as glance in my direction, but now pranced as well as his chain would allow, darting forward only to be brought up short.

Sussie, the flirt, backed away, wagging her tail sedately, but at the same time showing her teeth in a refined, silent snarl. This, as no doubt the bitch intended, aroused Yukon the more. He whined, scratched at the boards with one paw, straining at the chain until he actually coughed.

Stepping back to the far wall, I called Sussie in the

tone reserved for commands, firm, definite, but not un-kindly. As always, she came; I spoke to her affec-tionately, rubbing her belly, which she loved, then scratching her neck and head, while I talked as much for Yukon's benefit as for hers.

Sussie loved every second of the act, but the big lummox at the other end of the shed sounded as though he was going to choke himself to death; he coughed and spluttered and tried to whine all at the same time, jumping against the chain, wagging his tail profusely, pleading with the collie to come back to him. What I did next made me feel a little guilty, and sorry for Yukon, but I sensed it to be the right move.

Still caressing Sussie, I led her to the open door and took her outside, being careful to place us at an angle that allowed Yukon to witness events. I invited the bitch to play, fooling with her, and she ran around me in circles, barking ecstatically and coming in every now and then for more patting and scratching. De-spite the noise she was making, I could hear Yukon whine, gag, scratch, and jump; then he sat and started to howl, the song of the wolf, beginning deep, rising slowly, and fading into a contralto moan. Sussie halted in her tracks, looked toward the shed, then scampered toward it, entered immediately and going up to Yu-kon, who forthwith tried to hang himself anew. In the meantime, Rocky and Sooner picked up the big dog's howl and now Sussie joined in, so perforce, Yukon sang once more, howling louder than any of the oth-ers. The concert, if such it could be termed, continued for several minutes inside the shed and for half an hour in the barn.

Yukon and Sussie fell silent. Now the bitch moved close to the dog and allowed herself to be well and truly sniffed. When I went into the building, Yukon was much too busy to devote any attention to me, but when I called Sussie again, he repeated his previous antics. A little at a time I edged closer to him, Sussie at my side. The last step had to be taken, the one that would put me in range of the dog's fangs. And suddenly the big head was under my left hand while Sussie's smaller and finer pate was under my right. My fingers caressed both dogs, but my eyes were glued on Yukon. Right then I knew with certainty that I had nothing more to fear from him; friendship had developed.

Chapter 2

Wolves have had the power to excite me ever since I first made contact with them in the backwoods of Canada almost a quarter of a century ago, but whereas the initial emotions they conjured resulted from ignorance of the species and from the fear of them instilled into me as a child by wildly irrational tales, the excitement they stimulated later, when I got to know them intimately, was pleasurable: the sort of warm, wonderful thrill that comes when one is privileged to observe at firsthand some great and breathtaking piece of art.

Because there was so much of the wolf in Yukon, it was he who first taught me about his kin, especially about the relationships that exist in the pack, whose members form bonds so strong that they make pale by comparison the interactions that occur in human communities. The pack is paramount, its rules are inflexible, but good for all; it inspires deep loyalties, fierce, unselfish love; it protects the weak and teaches tolerance and responsibility to the strong. It is the ideal society.

Of course, members of a pack sometimes compete for position, but whether they win or lose, the fighting that may ensue during the contest is nearly bloodless and rarely leads to killing. Even when it does, such killing is accidental, the result of an unfortunate move by one or the other of the combatants—and the loser does not lose in the sense that humans view the term, but simply returns to his place within the pack's hierarchy and picks up where he, or she, left off, without shame or ostracism. The leader, be it male or female, continues to lead, and the challenger, having properly obeyed the drives of ambition, continues to follow, developing the strength, character, and knowledge that may in the future cumulate to produce a new leader, because, of course, every leader born will one day be deposed, if only by death.

Until the morning when Yukon put his massive head under my hand, the dog had never acknowledged any leadership but his own and had, in fact, not really belonged to a pack because he was kept tied up whenever he was not working. Without understanding these things at the time, I sensed them, realizing that the events preceding the start of our friendship had been, as far as Yukon was concerned, a leadership contest. He viewed me as he did all humans, as a threat, and he was determined not to capitulate, taking his lumps, licking his wounds, submitting only to the unbreakable chain, and biding his time, waiting for the moment when he could either escape his imprisonment or kill the cause of it. Then he was confronted with kindness and good treatment, and he was confused and uncertain. Uncertainty for him had always ended in the certainty of ill treatment, so he reacted as he had always done—he fought. But when his opponent didn't fight back, he became puzzled, remaining on his guard, continuing to show hostility, yet interested enough in this sudden change of environment and of human contact to observe with the inherent capabilities of his wild ancestors. And when, probably despite himself, he literally bit the hand that fed him, he had no means of knowing that this action would not result in an unmerciful beating.

But instead of the club, he was given good meat, and the new human showed no anger and no fear. The big dog must have been completely mystified, while the comfort of a full belly, coupled with continuing kindness began to break down his hostilities.

If I am accurate in this assessment, the contest for leadership was probably won during that first night, while I was asleep and Yukon felt himself alone. Anger and brutality he could deal with, but the treatment he had received since Alfred tied him in the shed was something quite beyond his understanding. He liked it, yet he distrusted it because it was unknown. Later, as I was preparing to spend the night with him, talked to him, and shared the cookies with him, he experienced companionship. Now, if there is one thing a wolf cannot stand, it is loneliness. These animals are socially programmed, they need companionship just as humans need it; they are nothing without it. The "lone wolf" concept is fallacy, stemming perhaps from the occasional sighting by our remote ancestors of a lone wolf temporarily separated from the pack for anyone of a variety of reasons.

Having now tasted companionship of this kind for the first time since he was removed from his mother, Yukon became lonely when I slipped all the way down into the sleeping bag and it was probably for this reason that he pawed me at dawn. What followed reawakened his hostility, but when Sussie came in, showed her trust in me and her affection, Yukon voluntarily joined our "pack," electing me its leader forthwith.

Stroking the two dogs in the shed that morning, I was at first conscious of little else but the pleasure of gaining Yukon's friendship and trust, but when my fingers began to encounter the wood ticks, the singles, some of them as big and as black as ripe grapes, and the clusters of smaller ones, I was reminded of the dog's distress and of the need to care for him.

This made me realize that I was now faced by a

major decision: I *had* to accept the dog's trust without allowing myself to feel any concerns for my safety. The three of us stood almost at the limit of Yukon's chain, and standing as I was, I could quickly move out of his reach if he should decide to turn on me, perhaps taking a slash or two from those quick and deadly fangs, but avoiding serious injury. But could he be trusted all the way? Could I place myself in a position from which there was no escape if he attacked? Even as I silently formulated these questions, I knew what I must do. I simply had to give this gaunt and savage beast my full trust; anything less would be quickly detected by him. The writing of it fills more time than the doing of it. To help me take that last, decisive step, I concentrated on the dog's deplorable condition and, feeling pity for him, wanted to comfort him.

I squatted between the two dogs, Sussie on my right, Yukon on my left, leaned my head against his vermin-infested face, and slid my arm around his shoulders and patted his side. Yukon pushed hard against me; Sussie, a bit jealous, lifted her head and licked my face. Suddenly Yukon's slobbery tongue passed across my forehead, and my cheek was moved back to rest on his shoulder by the upward jerk of his head. Seconds later both dogs were vying for my affections; they pushed me backward to a sitting position, rubbed against me, licked wherever they could find flesh, whined. In another moment I would have been pushed flat on my back. I judged it was time to stand.

Talking softly, caressing each animal, I walked to where the chain was fastened, undid it, coiled two-thirds of it around one hand, and moved to the doorway. Yukon walked beside me, never once tugging at the chain. Sussie changed sides and trotted beside him. I was taking them both to the house.

Yukon hesitated for just an instant when confronted by the open door of my dwelling and by the unknown within but Sussie slipped inside, and as I moved, the dog walked with me. Clear of the entrance, I closed the door and called Sussie, who had immediately gone to sniff at the cast-iron cooking range where I kept the large pot of offal. Again I petted her with one hand while caressing Yukon's head with the other, but I stopped soon and reached out with both hands and undid his heavy leather collar to take it off him.

I went into the living room, and both dogs ran in after me. Yukon suddenly became aware that he was no longer controlled by the chain and that the accustomed pressure of the collar was missing from his neck, where after such long use it had worn the hair down almost to the skin. He began to roll on the floor, rubbing himself against the bare boards, turning over and over, kicking his legs in the air, and moving his head from side to side. Sussie thought this was a fine game. She ran to him, jumped over him, barking almost hysterically and the house seemed to become full of dogs as the two dashed at full speed between the kitchen and the living room. Now and then Sussie hit a chair; once she brushed against my legs and almost knocked me off my feet. But Yukon avoided every obstacle with the catlike grace that I had found so remarkable.

This seemed like a good time to quiet them down with a feed, although Sussie didn't need one and might get spoiled a little; Yukon certainly needed feeding! My normal practice was to give the dogs a little gravy each morning, just a taste apiece, and a good meal each evening, varying the quantity of this to conform to the size and weight of each dog. Yukon's arrival had upset this schedule slightly, especially in Sussie's case, but this was her reward for acting as a sort of canine bellwether.

The two were still rushing around the house when I went to get their food ready. Sussie's dish received only a token share; Yukom's was filled with a mixture of dog meal and about half the carcass of a groundhog I had shot two days before, minus the offal.

It took them a few seconds to realize that more food had arrived. Yukon, as might be expected, was the first to know. He stopped practically in midstride and walked quickly into the kitchen, the by-now familiar look of expectancy on his face, his tail wagging quickly, held high. Sussie ran, catching up to him before he reached me. Holding a dish in each hand, I stopped, spreading my arms wide so that each dog went for the appropriate dish. Two mouths dipped into the food before the containers touched the floor.

Sussie wasn't very hungry, being already replete with breakfast; she toyed with her meal. Not so Yukon. His feeding was as before, controlled, purposeful, but steady. Even so, he still had food in his dish when the bitch licked hers clean and went over to nose at his. I expected trouble, but before I could decide what I would do if there was a fight, Sussie stuck her nose down, sniffed, and lost interest. No growl came from Yukon; he didn't so much as look at her.

In my hurry to complete chores that morning, I had not properly cleaned out the cow's stall or let the chickens into the yard so that they could scratch, take dust baths, and cram insects into their crops, thereby saving on the bought feed; leaving the two dogs in the house, I went to do these things.

It is disconcerting to discover in the privacy of a rural outhouse that a wood tick has made a cozy home for itself within the wrinkles of the body's last outlet. Reaction to such a discovery must surely vary with individual temperament and probably ranges from mild revulsion to an instant attack of the screaming meemies; to describe my own feelings when finding that a member of the family *Ixodes ricinus* had set up housekeeping in that intimate region of my anatomy after it had been unceremoniously ousted from Yukon's hide is difficult at this time. I know I jumped up from the seat with considerable alacrity, clutched my clothing to me, and hobbled as fast as I could manage to the house, there to be greeted profusely by the bug's former host, who was unable to understand the antics of his recently acquired friend; my inner feelings are harder to describe.

In the porch hung a round galvanized washtub that

also did duty as a bathtub, and after I had filled a large pot full of water and placed it on the cookstove to heat, I carried the tub into the kitchen and put it near the stove in readiness. All this while fighting to control an urge to pluck the revolting beast from its unorthodox locale.

Those who have not experienced a close, unwilling association with wood ticks may wonder why I did not, indeed, pluck out the bloody-minded monster upon the instant of discovery; well, let me tell you about *Ixodes ricinus*. . . .

These armored, crablike vampires are called mites and have been assigned to the superfamily Ixodoidea, which includes some very nasty members, most of which, the gods be praised, sit expectantly in the steamy jungles of the Amazon and central Africa. But this does not mean that their North American relatives are harmless. If they do nothing else, they can take up to half a teaspoonful of blood if allowed to suck their fill, but some members of the clan are carriers of dangerous viruses that produce such diseases as Rocky Mountain spotted fever, tularemia, and encephalitis.

Ixodes had a flat, scaly red-brown body, shaped like a tiny bladder, on the upper, pointed end of which are mouthparts full of minute barbs with which the tick tears open the skin of its victims; it is such an expert with these little scalpels that it is rarely felt by the host during the time it is mining through the hide. Besides the barbs, the wood tick has two sucking tubes which it inserts into the wound, after which it anchors itself with the quills and begins to suck blood out and to pump in ixodin, a liquid substance that dilutes the blood and prevents it from coagulating. If one plucks it from the skin, the mouthparts break off and remain buried and must be removed surgically or they will cause infection within a couple of days; additionally, by grasping the tick with the fingers, the victim is liable to squeeze its stomach contents out through the sucking tubes into the wound, adding to the subsequent infection. It is *not* a good idea to pluck the beast out by force!

One mama bug lays some three thousand eggs, from which hatch an army of little ones measuring about one millimeter in length, replicas of the old lady, except that they have only three legs a side, instead of four as do the adults. As is the case with mosquitoes, the female of the species does all the bloodsucking, and they begin young. When they emerge from the egg, they cling to low vegetation, waiting there to pounce on the first small animal that happens to brush against their perches. The girl bugs spend between three and five days frolicking on their first victims, having a nip or two, and gathering their strength for the next stage of their nefarious lives. When ready, they drop off, burrow into the earth, and shed their first skins and grow two more legs. Now, fully adolescent, the buglets emerge aboveground, find shelter in rotten wood, in tree bark, or even on the ends of low branches, and wait again, this time for a moose, or a bear, or a human, or whatever. . . .

For all that it is so revolting, I confess that *Ixodes* is also interesting, having among other abilities the fortitude to go hungry for up to four years. Now that's patience and endurance! I plucked one mama off a cow once, a fat bug, looking rather like a big black olive, and because I wanted to photograph it, I put it into an empty glass bottle, stuck it on one of the rafters of the barn, then promptly forgot all about it. A *year and a half later,* while whitewashing the barn in late spring, I found the bottle, remembered Mama *Ixodes,* and wondered about her. Taking the bottle into the sunlgiht, I upended it. Out came a flaky, red-brown scale with legs, as thin as a piece of writing paper. What I thought was a very dead bug lay upside down on my hand; about to let the thing drop onto the ground, I saw the legs begin to move. Less than a minute later mama bug was back in business, crawling along my palm looking for a place to sharpen her scalpels. Sticking the brute between my thumbnails, I squeezed, failed to hear or feel that satisfying click that tells you when a nasty little bloodsucker has been killed quite dead, and uncovered the beast; undeterred by the pressure, the tick began to crawl off the nail, looking for blood. I cut it in two with a pen-knife.

In any event, when the tick finds her second victim, she sucks her fill during several more days of feasting, drops off once more, gains additional strength and stature, and reaches marriageable age: afterward she produces her three thousand eggs and performs the first and last good deed of her life; she dies.

In the backwoods and in the mountains where these unpleasant beasts are found, practically everybody has a pet method for removing ticks from the body. Some claim that the bug will back out if one holds the end of a lighted cigarette just in front of it: others swear by kerosene: some say that vinegar will do the job. I tried all these methods. My ticks up and died when I put a cigarette near their noxious heads, leaving me the job of chopping them out of my skin (fortunately these had sucked themselves into accessible parts of my anatomy). Vinegar did no more than make the bugs a little active, scrabbling their eight legs over my skin. Kerosene, apart from stinking, took a long time to have effect, and as often as not, it killed the tick while it was still buried. For a time I obtained excellent results by poking a needle just under my skin in the exact center of the bug's twin feelers and bodily hoisting out the parasite. This is an effective method when the tick is accessible or when one has an able assistant to operate on the unreachable parts. But the best method of all, the mama tick's true Achilles' heel, is to choke her out. The brute is air-breathing: although her "lungs" are not like ours, she must suck in oxygen: anoint her liberally with butter, Vaseline, dubbin, or axle grease and she backs out of her burrow, gasping for air, within a minute or two.

While the water was heating, I grabbed the butter container and went upstairs to my bedroom, shutting the door on Yukon, who wanted to join in the fun. Off came all my clothes: I checked myself carefully, looking for more of the same, searching the accessible parts first, then looking with the aid of a hand mirror. There were no more. I buttered the bug as no other of its kind has ever been buttered; came a time of waiting, an awkward time, for the mirror was necessary to see when she began to move. At last she emerged, panting, to be firmly grasped and incinerated by a well-applied match: I am not a sadist, but I did enjoy watching her curl up, sizzle gently, and inflate like a miniture balloon before she burst with a tiny, satisfying pop. After going downstairs, I soaped vigorously, rinsed, and dressed.

The afternoon previous to the wood tick episode I attended to Yukon's needs, feeling confident that he would now allow me to do so. Earlier that day, accompanied by Sussie, who was never inclined to stray far from my side, I had taken both dogs for three short walks in the immediate area of the house and outbuildings, against all of which Yukon painstakingly left his sign. I was a little nervous as I opened the door on the first walk, worried in case he would run away, but at no time did he do more than trot to the nearest building, tree, or other solid object to cock his leg up and deposit his mark, returning to my side after each event, looking proud. And every time he came back I patted his head and praised him, as I did all the dogs when they curbed their inordinate desire to hunt and remained with me during exercise walks. After the third outing, in the middle of which Yukon went dry but continued to lift his leg symbolically, I set about preparing to doctor his injuries and to commence delousing him. But first Sussie needed attention. She had almost certainly acquired a number of Yukon's bugs, and I didn't want her taking them back to the other dogs, which were as free of vermin as it is possible to keep such animals during the snowless time. Once the cold sets in, and provided that the animals are dusted with flea powder occasionally and their sleeping places are disinfected every now and then, fleas and lice disappear and the wood ticks go to ground for the winter or spend it in some other fashion, probably as clusters of eggs in the cracks of bark or rotten wood. It was, in fact, rather late in the season even then for ticks, but Yukon had no doubt acquired them earlier, before the frost, and had been rearing them in the comfort of his thick fur.

When Sussie was done and back in the barn, Yukon's medication and bug treatment were readied. Butter wouldn't do to rub on him, he would simply lick it off, but I had bought a jar of greasy medicated ointment with which to treat minor injuries; it would do admirably and offered the added advantage of its disinfectant properties. For his injuries I used permanganate of potash, an excellent antiseptic. I began preparations.

Yukon lay on his side, fully stretched out near the south window of the living room, watching me occasionally and thumping his tail on the floor when I spoke to him, but evidently quite enjoying his leisure. I put a chair beside him; he showed little interest, merely raising his head when he saw me approaching with the bowl of permanganate solution and a roll of cotton batting. His keen nose soon told him that the bowl did not contain food, and he dropped his head again.

As luck would have it, the open cut was uppermost; it would be easy to get at if he stayed where he was. I squatted beside him, spoke to him gently, and stroked his head, then ran my hand over his massive chest and continued to move it slowly down toward the cut. Now the big head raised itself again, but he was merely interested, watchful. I touched the edges of the nasty wound as gently as possible, pushing the lips together and noting that the lower end had already become infected, was showing the yellow of pus. At that, Yukon stretched his neck and licked my hand, then licked the wound and my fingers. Taking a previously prepared wad of cotton soaked in the purple solution, I applied it to the cut. Again Yukon licked, but the acrid taste of the antiseptic made him stop at once; he opened and closed his mouth noisily, drooling, moving his tongue in and out of his mouth, and making little wet sounds as he tried to rid himself of the bitter taste. Yet he remained docile while I bathed the wound again and again, dried it at last with a fresh wad of cotton, and applied a liberal coating of salve for good measure. When it was done, Yukon leaned over, sniffed once, and turned his head away, avoiding the combined smells. He licked my hand as I patted him once more.

Now he had to be moved so that the scabbed-over injury could be attended to. I don't know exactly what he weighed at the time, but thin as he was, I judged he would scale at least a hundred pounds, perhaps more; on this account alone, I wasn't anxious to wrestle him over, for even a skinny hundred-pound wolf-dog has enough strength to outclass the average man. It was going to be necessary to coax him. I began to stroke his belly, and he at once lifted his back leg, and as the stroking continued, he did the expected: he rolled onto his back. I kept rubbing, edging my hand across his body to stroke his flank, pulling him toward me gently. Again he cooperated, rolling onto his opposite side and exposing the big scab that, on closer inspection, wasn't as bad as I had thought. But I treated it in any event, first with the permanganate, then with the ointment. The next task was to get him up on all fours. I stood up, backed to the middle of the room, and called him, slapping my thigh with one hand, using his new name. It was easy. He rose immediately and loped to me, raising his head so that it could be scratched.

So far he had been trusting and docile, but when the flea powder was added to his treatment, he didn't like it and tried to avoid it, for which I couldn't much blame him; I loathed the smell of the stuff myself, and *my* nose was not nearly as sensitive as his. Sneezing loudly, he backed away, undecided whether to growl or not while curling his upper lip into a sort of half snarl. I kept at it, following him around the room, rubbing the powder in with one hand and talking continuously, trying hard not to raise too much dust. Working along his body, I eventually reached the root of his tail, a spot that always seems itchy in all canids. I scratched hard; he liked that, standing quietly and arching his back to help my fingers dig deeper. But when I tried to do the tail itself, he wouldn't let me. He growled loudly and showed his teeth. I was sure he was bluffing and called him on it.

"Now cut that out!" My voice wasn't raised, but I made it gruff, as I had done after he had bitten me. He stopped growling and covered his teeth, but he gave me a long, hard stare. I reached for his tail, and he snarled once more, and I spoke gruffly again; this time he let me take hold of it, and I shook some powder into the matted fur, only half doing the job, for I didn't want to press my luck.

The ticks came out next. He was full of them, had even dropped some on the floor where he had been lying; they were of assorted sizes and were crawling aimlessly, seeking a new host. They would be dealt with later, when I sprayed both rooms with insecticide.

Unexpectedly the job of daubing ointment on the bloodsuckers was made easier by the ticks themselves, for only the larger ones, the adults, were dug in. The small ones were still ambulatory and already appeared to be suffering from the effects of the flea powder. Once more Yukon objected to his treatment, moving away, growling halfheartedly, and now and then showing his teeth. I ignored him, I *knew* he wouldn't bite. It was rather wonderful; yesterday he would have torn me to pieces, today he protested but did not attempt to snap. I was at once elated and moved by his acceptance of me.

Yukon looked odd when the last tick had been anointed; wherever the grease had been applied it made his fur darker, each blob glistening and matting the hairs together, and by the way his nose was twitching, he wasn't any too happy about the strong, germicidal odor. To make up for the indignities of the treatment, I gave him several small pieces of meat, and while he was eating them, I got the cow's currycomb, intending to give him a good grooming just as soon as the ticks began to back out of his skin. I hoped he would enjoy the experience.

An hour later the job was done. He loved every minute of it, even suffering his tail to be combed and brushed and exhibiting considerable curiosity over the great tangled balls of old fur that littered the floor. It would be a pity to burn his wool, for washed and dried, it would make excellent pillow stuffing, but inside each football-sized mound were entrapped fleas, ticks, and other assorted vermin, most of them already moribund, but probably the progenitors of many eggs that adhered to the hairs.

At first I was too busy cleaning up the mess, sweeping the floor, and squirting insecticide on it to pay much attention to the dog, who disappeared upstairs as soon as he got the first whiff of the spray gun, but when the rooms had been tidied up and the supplies were put away, I opened the windows to get rid of the smell and called him down. Now I was able to appreciate the result of my labors, and I could hardly credit the transformation.

Yukon had evidently indulged himself by rolling and then giving himself a good shaking; his once dirty, tangled fur was now sleek and glossy and fluffed out, and his mane, a thick roach of black hair that began atop his shoulder blades and extended along the neck, stood out magnificently; the white on his chest was almost milky; his tail looked twice its former size. He advanced toward me, holding his head up and his tail high, and his slant eyes were full of joie de vivre. He was no longer the same dog! Even his personality seemed to have changed, and the pride that I had earlier glimpsed in him despite his deplorable condition was now clearly evident.

He came up to me, rose lightly on his hind legs, and put one great front paw on each of my shoulders. Slap! His long pink tongue splashed against my chin and traveled upward to end wetly at my hairline. As I went to wipe the slaver off my face, Yukon pivoted with the grace of a ballerina, dropped onto all fours, and began to run at speed through the house, tearing along into the kitchen, back to the living room, and galloping upstairs, sounding like a minor avalanche.

For the next week he remained in the house when he wasn't out with me and Sussie, and if I wondered on occasion how he would react when the time came to put him in the barn with the other dogs, I was so busy looking after him and attempting to make up for the neglect of all the other animals that the thought caused no great concern. As it turned out, keeping him with me continuously during those first days was, I believe, largely responsible for the strong bonds that were to grow between us. We did all things together, and it was amazing to note how quickly he staked his claim to the homestead, becoming aggressively jealous of any extraneous influences that intruded on his new domain, such as the male pileated woodpecker that came morning and evening to chisel into a dead tamarack that stood behind the barn; Yukon's one ambition was to chase that bird into the next county.

Yet he accepted the domestic animals. I wondered what his reactions would be when he met the chickens, but apart from a few cursory runs at them, when each bird would flap away, squawking furiously, he didn't molest them.

At first the cow was a problem. As far as I am aware, the dog had never seen one before, and he exhibited the inherent curiosity of his kind. He didn't attempt to attack her, but he paid her so much attention, circling her, sniffing at her feet, and sometimes prancing in front of her, that *she* became aggressive toward him until she learned that no matter how she charged, he was never there when her head came down to deliver the toss. After that she gave up, ignoring him studiously, and because of this, he quickly lost interest in her.

On the fourth night, while he was lying at my feet, he suddenly lifted his head and whoofed softly, looking at me. I supposed that he wanted to go outside and wet a tree, and I rose and opened the door for him. In a flash he was on the porch, rooting around it wildly but silently. Seconds later a strong, fetid stench assailed my nose and filled the kitchen, and I heard a series of small and vicious squeaks. Soon after that Yukon trotted back into the house with the body of a weasel (*Mustela rixosa*, or least weasel), an animal some nine inches long that was in the middle of exchanging its brown coat for the ermine white of winter. It was dead, of course, and since its fur was not in its prime, there was nothing I could do with it except to take it from his mouth and throw it on the manure pile behind the barn, then open all the windows to get rid of the stink. That the dog allowed me to take away his prize was remarkable and told me more than anything else how much he trusted me. Not that he would have eaten the animal, for the weasel tribe is palatable to a carnivore only in face of extreme hunger, but he had been intent on bringing it indoors and playing with it, which was *not* a good idea.

This incident made me realize how extraordinarily keen were the dog's perceptions; it was the first of many such demonstrations that I was to witness, all of which caused me to regret the atrophy of my own puny senses and then, in time, taught me how to sharpen some of them, though no human can ever hope to attain sensorial parity with a dog, let alone a wolf-dog.

Chapter 3

It may be that in its madness the bull moose was simply running in the wrong direction, but sight of the phantasmagorical creature charging directly at me was too much for a nervous system that had for some time been calmly and pleasantly relaxed. If only my legs could have obeyed my mind, I would have tried to escape in panic; as it was, the conscious me seemed powerless to order its muscles to unfreeze.

I stood as though rooted in the ground, staring at the grotesque, staggering giant that was coming closer and closer, clearly aware that I was behaving foolishly, but unable to do anything about it, while each hair on the nape of my neck erected itself stiffly and my heart raced wildly.

Forgotten was the Lee-Enfield rifle hanging from its sling over my shoulder; forgotten, too, was the dog straining against his lead.

In my mind there was room only for the ragged and emaciated moose that continued to run toward me, eyes showing white, head held high and tilted backward so that its single antler was almost touching one shoulder.

The whole creature was awesome, but it was the long, stiltlike legs moving jerkily and unsteadily that commanded the most attention and inspired the greatest fear. Each limb pumped like a faltering piston, yet each thudding "stroke" relentlessly ate up ground, while the condition of the gashed, bloody, and mud-stained legs exaggerated the menace of the pointed hooves and heightened the impression of power generated by the animal. Sick though it obviously was, it could yet smash its way through the area of first-growth spruce and snap some of the younger trees like so many dry sticks.

Now it was no more than twenty feet away, moving awkwardly and without the grace and majesty normally displayed by the bull of the species, yet traveling with enough speed to precipitate its bulk on top of me within a few seconds. And I just stood there like a fool, stunned into immobility.

Yukon, fortunately, was made of sterner stuff. He lunged forward, pulling the lead out of my hand in the same instant that he emitted one deep growl, like the single peal of thunder that presages the coming of a storm. Then, in silence, hackles raised to their fullest, tail curled into a tight spiral, he charged the moose; I had it in me to thrill at the sight of that magnificent dog as he went to do battle. His lean and wolfish body moved with the fluid grace and incredible agility of the hunting carnivore, every line of him charged with feral menace. He was a swift and as sure and as indomitable as the wild dogs whose bloodline he shared.

One counts time in heartbeats during such occasions. For two (or was it three?) beats I remained immobile, my fear strangely gone, all my faculties attuned to the dog and to the behemoth that would not turn from the straight-line course it had chosen. Even now, more than twenty years later, every detail of the primordial encounter returns with clear and sharp imagery, as though projected in moving color inside the theater of the mind: I see forest, green, brown, and butter yellow, in places daubed deep purple by the shadows, and the frowning, leaden sky that had been gold and cerulean dressed the wilderness in somber hues. And I see the moose coming closer and the dog gathering himself for the last grandiose leap.

High into the air he went, body stretched out fully, tail uncurled by the momentum streaming behind like a furred banner, the muscles and sinews on his haunches clearly evident despite their covering of hair. The red-brown moose and the black-brown dog came together, and the hunting fangs closed on the pendulous nose of the crazed deer. With a sound like that of a sack of wet sand falling onto a flat surface, dog and moose collided and went down in a melee of thrashing limbs.

At last I came out of my spell. It took but a split second to remove the rifle from my shoulder, work the bolt to put a round into the breech, and take aim. But now that I had passed from craven immobility into a state of hot-blooded belligerence, I couldn't shook without hitting the dog, whose initial nose hold was shaken loose by the fall, but who instantly secured a fresh grip on the bull's neck, a solid, meat-destroying bite that let blood out and prevented the big deer from regaining its feet, yet could not stop the frantic beast from kicking wildly or from jerking its head violently in order to try and dislodge its attacker. The two animals were moving so quickly and so erratically that I couldn't risk a shot, even after I had advanced to within a couple of paces of the battle.

I began to worry about Yukon. The long legs of the moose were lethal weapons, each tipped by sharp, body-destroying hooves; they were flailing wildly, coming too close to the dog. One kick, and Yukon would be severely injured, perhaps disemboweled. I took a step closer, tried to call him off, but it is doubtful that he heard, and even if he had, he was too close to the primeval to respond to human voice.

For what seemed like a long time, but in reality could not have been longer than three or four seconds, I stood almost on top of the struggling animals, trying ineffectually to get a clear shot. When my chance came, I almost missed it. Heaving mightily, the bull shook his head, and the weight of Yukon, anchored by his teeth in the deer's throat, ripped the meat and allowed the animal to scramble groggily to its feet.

Yukon was flung clear, but he was leaping back to attack when I poked the rifle forward (there was no need to aim at that distance) and fired it one-handed. The moose dropped as though poleaxed, shot through the brain. Yukon, already launched into space, sailed over the carcass to land lightly several yards away and to turn around and come tearing back to worry his fallen adversary.

Injudiciously I moved forward to pick up his lead and drag him away, forgetting that new death must always struggle briefly with old life before claiming its own. The legs of the moose kicked violently, powered by the last contractions of the nervous system; one of the pointed hooves grazed my left thigh, scraping off a round patch of skin and throwing me backward, but Yukon, elastic as a rubber band, dodged and jumped clear.

Give that dog credit! Instead of returning to the dead animal, he came to me, to lick my face and dance around me as I stood up. After taking hold of his lead and picking up the rifle from where it landed when I fell, I led him away from the still-quivering carcass and tied him to a tree, despite his tugs and yelps of protest, for he wanted to return to the moose and no doubt take a snack from its body. This I would not allow him to do. The animal was obviously ill and could not be utilized as food for either the dogs or myself.

Leaving an unhappy dog pulling fretfully at his lead and whining disconsolately, I walked back to the dead beast and examined it with care, but not before ensuring that its strictures were ended. The bullet had struck on the side of the head, just below the right ear, making a tiny, neat hole which was now filled with lymph and slowly oozing blood; it seemed almost impossible that compared to the creature's bulk, such a small bit of metal could have ended its life with such instant finality, whereas the gory gashes made by Yukon's fangs, four on the nose and an indeterminate number on the neck, looked much more lethal with the slow, hot blood spreading over a wide area of throat and nostrils.

The moose was woefully thin, its dark coat dry and ragged, the hair actually scraped away in many places; one antler, the right one, had been snapped off, leaving about three inches of jagged stump protruding from the top of the head, like the trunk of a dead and sere sapling snapped off close to the ground, clear evidence that the animal must have charged into trees or rocks while in the grip of its suffering. The body, like the legs, was badly lacerated; these injuries were so obviously caused by the sharp branches through which the moose had blundered that in several places thick slivers were embedded under its hide, especially on the distended paunch, where an inch-thick bone-dry cedar branchlet some seven inches long had worked its way so far under the skin that only about half an inch could be seen protruding from the wound. It was a pitiful sight; I was glad the slim bullet had quickly ended its tortures.

Wondering about the cause of the animal's distress, I recalled being told by a neighbor that moose sometimes poisoned themselves by eating a species of vetch, a member of the large *Astragalus* genus. This plant, also known as locoweed worked slowly and eventually led to a condition that was known as the blind staggers, a term that, when I remembered the bull's behavior, was certainly apt enough.

My neighbor also said that moose were "fearless" of man when poisoned by this plant and that the animals would sometimes charge a human. It seemed that I now had been given firsthand proof of this, but I wasn't entirely convinced that the bull had really intended to attack. I retained the feeling that it was running blindly, irritated beyond endurance, a mindless, purposeless frenzy that caused it to stampede.

I recalled Yukon's alert behavior some minutes before the animal emerged with suddenness from the dense forest; the dog pulled at the lead, looking toward the place where the bull eventually appeared; I remembered, also, that I myself became aware of the crashing noises it was making a moment or two before sight of the demented creature brought me to an abrupt stop. Now I checked the wind; it was blowing toward me, what there was of it, and this ruled out the possibility that our scent had alerted the animal to our presence and led it to us.

If these things were not enough to confirm my belief that the animal's "charge" was accidental, the way in which it traveled gave further credence to my view. I recalled how the eyes were upturned into their sockets, so that the pupils must have been at least partly hidden, as well as directed upward, and how its head was flung back, oddly twisted to one side. No wonder its body and legs became so badly lacerated as it dashed blindly through the trees!

I could not, of course, be absolutely certain, but the more I reflected on the incident, the more I felt I was right in thinking that Yukon and I just happened to be in the bull's way and that if instead of stopping and turning myself into a latter-day version of Lot's wife, I had quickly stepped aside and put a tree between the blundering giant and us, it would have passed us by without even realizing that we were there. By allowing myself to go into such a deep funk, I had to assume entire responsibility for the danger in which we had found ourselves, for I had let my emotions take control of my reason. In future, I admonished myself sternly, I would retain my cool when confronted by new and unexpected situations, yet I had the uneasy feeling that such good advice was easier to give than to heed.

Thinking about these things, I became almost totally oblivious to all else until Yukon recalled me to the realities of the moment by yelping loudly and lunging at his lead, reminding me that he was the hero of the hour. Without my overdramatizing the affair, it is safe to say that the dog had saved me from injury, perhaps had even saved my life, for I really don't think I would have had the wit to avoid the moose or, more to the point, to shoot it immediately. If for no other reason, he deserved a reward of some kind, but there *was* another reason, an important one. The moment that he saw the moose Yukon became a hunting carnivore, a wild predator seeking to bring down its prey. He attacked and became the victor. In a truly natural sense he could now expect to draw his reward from the warm carcass of his victim.

Going to him, telling him he was "a good dog" and all the sort of nonsense we humans resort to when pleased by the behavior of a pet animal, I stroked him, scratched his chest and spent a few moments with him in silent communion. As soon as he settled down, I slipped out of the packsack that contained, among other things, his snack and my lunch and I carried the canvas bag to the moose carcass. After opening the pack, I took out the raw, meaty piece of rib cage brought for Yukon, made a show of drawing my belt knife, and pretended to cut into the dead moose. My stratagem worked. Yukon became suddenly quiet. When I turned around and stood up a few moments later, rib bones in hand, he stood quietly, his attention fixed on the food I carried: his reward, tangible evidence of the success of his hunt.

At that time the dog was still being fed two good meals a day in order to put more meat on his physique, and I knew he wasn't particularly hungry when I gave him the rib bones; nevertheless, he demolished them, eating slowly, licking a great deal, pausing now and then, one big paw draped over his prize, to stare fixedly at the carcass, as though he would have preferred to take his own portion from it.

After watching him a few minutes, I left him to go have a closer look at the moose. If common belief was correct and the blind staggers resulted from eating poison vetch, it was unlikely that the carcass would be harmful to the scavengers of the forest, inasmuch as most of the poison would have been "burned off" the victim and what remained in the tissues would be spread throughout the body. But I couldn't get rid of the presentiment that the bull's condition was due to a disease of some kind, some sort of illness that attacked the nervous system; that would account for the staggering gait, the rolling eyes, the blundering, frenzied way of running. Maybe the illness was induced by a virus or by bacteria, perhaps by a severe parasitic infestation. If any of these were responsible for the behavior I had witnessed, the moose could become a source of infection for a variety of other animals. But how could I dispose of such a huge body?

As I debated the matter, it would have been easy to become convinced that the safety of the wilderness dwellers was none of my affair and that the disposal of this great lump of carrion was rather akin to the problem facing the man who was given a shovel and told to go bury an elephant. But I couldn't shrug off the responsibility that I felt. We, that is, Yukon and the other dogs and I, shared the wilderness with its inhabitants; we all took our living from the same environment, so this alone was of personal concern. And there was another reason that made the health of this forest my business: I could not in all conscience walk away with callous disregard for the suffering of those creatures who would come to eat of the tainted meat, not after seeing how the moose had been tortured by the mysterious ailment.

The only possible means of disposing of so much bulk was fire. There was a lot of deadwood about, and the moose lay in a relatively clear area. Besides, the forest was damp, and this was not the season of bush fires. Yes, I decided, I would burn the carcass, but first I had to take Yukon home. It was necessary to go back in any event to get some tools and to gather containers to hold the tissue samples that I intended to take from the dead animal so I could later submit them to examination under my battered old microscope; perhaps this would provide some sort of clue to the ailment.

The part of the wilderness where the bull lay was about three miles from home. By the time I returned there, carrying bow saw and ax, a number of glass jars with screw-cap lids to hold the samples, and a case of dissecting tools that, together with the microscope, had been purchased in England when I had studied biology, more than two hours had elapsed. Not a long time, perhaps, but already some of the forest's "garbage collectors" had been at work, nipping away with small teeth at various parts of the animal and leaving the telltale signs of their endeavors, little raw patches of flesh, a few minute droppings here and there, and loose, chewed-off hairs. Mice, I thought; but just then a tiny blue-gray creature with a short tail popped out from somewhere under the carcass, a shrew, one of the hungriest carnivores of the forest, capable of eating the equivalent of its own weight in meat every three hours, on the average.

As I watched the small glutton move swiftly through the grass, the ventriloquial voices of a number of ravens drew my attention upward, where, teetering precariously on the flaccid branches of the evergreens, I saw no fewer than ten of the big black carrion lovers. Of course, they were much put out by my arrival, and they wanted to make sure that I knew about their annoyance. Groaning and squeaking and cawing and clacking, they flung multitudinous insults at me as I busied myself cutting firewood; when they realized I was not going to leave them to their anticipated feast, they took to the air, each flinging one last epithet at me before disappearing over the forest.

Working steadily and vigorously, I cut enough deadwood to cover the moose, while at the same time I cleared a circle around the carcass to ensure that the flames would not spread to the adjacent timberline, an almost unnecessary precaution in view of the dampness of the forest, but undertaken for the sake of insurance and peace of mind, for those who dwell in the backwoods soon learn to fear and to respect fire above all other natural forces.

When all the wood was piled convenient to the dead animal, I cut into the carcass, taking tissue samples from the muscles, guts, liver, spinal cord, and brain, each of which was placed in a separate jar, labeled, and capped tightly. Afterward I stacked the wood, placing large, bone-dry logs all around the carcass three logs wide and four layers high, touching the body and leaning toward it; on top of these, piled crossways, more big logs were put until a solid stack was formed. Next came a layer of thick, gum-heavy spruce branches that had been trimmed off the logs, and above these I stacked a trellis of smaller branches, kindling into which were thrust handfuls of birch bark. When the somewhat macabre bonfire was ready, I struck a match and ignited several bundles of birch bark.

The eager flames rushed at the kindling, consumed it in minutes, and began to eat into the branches and logs. The heat drove me away from the pyre. The pungent, sweetish odor of roasting meat filled the clearing; perhaps the aroma was made nauseating by the imagination, but it was certainly quite unlike the savory smell of a joint roasting slowly in the home oven.

It was almost an hour before the first impetus of the flames started to die down to the purposeful, intensely consuming heat of red-hot embers. The bonfire was transformed into an oval, glowing mound some nine feet long, six feet wide, and five or six feet high; cherry red, it was an irresistible furnace generating so much heat that even from thirty yards away it was almost unendurable.

Luckily there was hardly any wind, so the great, roaring flames that had earlier shot up for twenty or thirty feet cast their crackling debris of sparks and fly ash straight into the heavens, or so it seemed, thus ensuring that all embers would be extinguished by the time they descended again onto the autumnal land. Yet I lingered another half an hour, just to make sure that the forest was safe.

Dusk was settling like a vast shroud over the wilderness by the time I got back home to find Yukon amusing himself by chewing pieces from the legs of the kitchen table. Fortunately he was not single-minded about it and had evidently sampled every leg in several places instead of concentrating his work on one particular support, in this way allowing the table to continue to stand even if all its limbs showed the ravages of the dog's powerful teeth.

"Hey! You great *bum!* What d'you think—"

That was as far as I was allowed to proceed with the remonstration before Yukon, not a bit abashed and instantly on his feet, dashed at me, bowing and wagging his tail at one and the same time, and then raised himself on his hind legs the better to hit me in the mouth with a wet, sawdust-laden tongue. My irritation vanished instantly, and even though I would have preferred a different kind of greeting, I could not but feel happy that there was one such as he to welcome me home. To show my appreciation, I punched him, a light blow with closed fist that I knew would precipitate a mock battle. It did. He tried to dodge the blow, failed, and turned swiftly to slam into me with his chest; but I was as wise to his tricks as he was to mine, and I swiveled away from the blow, which, instead of landing fullsquare and knocking me off my feet, merely glanced off my left thigh. The dog's momentum put his tail within reach of my questing hand; I pulled it sharply. As usual he tried to turn and bite, playfully, it is true, but even his "pretend" snaps were not to be courted. As I pulled my hand away swiftly, I made as though to kick him, whereupon he grabbed my pant leg and started to pull me around the kitchen, growling ferociously to the tune of my laughter.

This play ritual had developed within a few days of our friendship and by now had become habit for both of us. If I was clad, as I was that evening, in a pair of heavy wool mackinaw pants already mutilated and patched after daily use outside, the game could begin at once, but if I was dressed in going-out clothes, he was forced to wait until I had changed. This part of the ritual went like this: When I returned from town or from a visit to one of my neighbors of an evening, the dog would greet me first and then seek to initiate a fight. "No! Not yet," I would say. "Wait till I get

into my fighting clothes." It took Yukon no time at all
to learn the meaning of this sentence, not just by ab-
sorbing the sound of the words, but by noting my expression, the way I spoke to him, and the manner in
which I would resolutely march upstairs and begin to
change. And he would wait, always poised at the
bottom of the stairs, from there to charge when I came
down, trying to knock me off balance with his chest
and then, if he failed, to dive for a pant cuff and to
growl and pull.

During those times when he managed to knock me
down, which he did often enough, he would lace into
me, grab whatever part of my clothing his reaching
mouth first touched, only to let go when I threw my
arms around him and wrestled him down beside me.
This was almost his favorite sport. He would struggle
powerfully, using his back legs to kick and claw, his
mouth to grab wherever he could, and his body, so full
of steely muscles, to force me to let go. Now and then
he would draw blood unintentionally; often I would
throw a hard, accidental blow that uncannily would
always land on his rock-hard head, hurting me a lot
more than it hurt him; once he swung his head around
sharply, and one of his long canines hit sideways into
the center of my forehead, punching a fairly deep
hole. I still wear that scar, faded now, resembling a
solitary pockmark.

That evening, tired after the pyrotechnical exertions
in the forest and with barn chores and dog feeding
still to do before I could eat my own supper, I acknowledged defeat by giving vent to a series of low
wolf howls or a reasonable facsimile thereof! This
always stopped Yukon immediately. He would back
off, sit, looking rather worried, and gaze deeply into
my eyes. If I persisted, he showed signs of acute distress and would begin to howl himself, so I didn't often
persist, doing so only occasionally, when some perverse
side of my nature took over. Then I would immediately become contrite and squatting and opening wide
my arms, I would call him to me and he would come
and I would hug him and put my head against his

shaggy coat and we would both enjoy a good love. I did not persist that day. Instead, I spoke the magic word, "supper." While he was eating, I left the house to take care of the rest of my oddly assorted "family."

The incident with the moose occurred about two weeks after Yukon was given his canine beauty treatment and four or five days after he became properly introduced to the other dogs in the barn, a ceremony in which my participation was confined to the opening of the door of the building and being thrust to one side by the dog as he dashed in with tail held high and ears pricked forward.

I followed him and closed the door behind me, but instead of being mobbed by the others, as was their wont upon our meeting for the first time each day, I found myself ignored, an unnoticed spectator in a drama almost as old as life itself, its origins rooted in the social rituals developed by the first wild dogs who roamed in cooperative packs through the silvas of prehistory.

In the center of the barn stood Yukon, virile, keenly alert, his hackles raised, his ears pricked well forward, and his tail arranged in the tight spiral that reflected his feelings of superiority and advertised his desire to respond to any challenge that might be offered.

The other three, scattered in various places on the far side of the barn, faced the newcomer. Sussie was wagging her tail and grinning, confirming her earlier allegiance to Yukon; Sooner stood with drooping tail and ears pegged against the back of his head, his lips peeled back in a facsimile of Sussie's grin, but yet not like her, being more contrived and servile, less open and friendly. He was the smallest of the three males, and clearly, his easygoing nature wanted no part of a leadership trial. For this reason he was signaling his peaceful intentions and his willingness to remain subservient.

Yukon completely ignored Sussie, already aware of her loyalty. He fixed Sooner with an intent, cold stare, and the husky quickly averted his gaze, dropped his tail even lower, almost pressing it under his belly, and bowed by dropping his forequarters and keeping his hindparts raised, retaining this stance after Yukon acknowledged his subservience by looking away.

Rocky was a different kind of dog. Chunky and well muscled, tough and arrogant in his youth, he was used to dominating the others, and he was not about to allow a newcomer to strip him of his power. Even *I* could see that; inevitably, so could Yukon. And Sussie and Sooner became as quickly aware; they edged farther away from "center ring," showing by their manner their reasons for electing neutrality. Sussie walked sedately, tail held fairly high and holding her grin, as though content to wait until her champion established his authority over the brash challenger. Sooner, on the other hand, was anxious to place himself out of harm's way; he almost literally skulked, coming to stand beside me and to lean his body against my right leg.

In the meantime, the rivals stood some distance apart, lips peeled back, hackles raised, already beginning to growl as they stared into each other's eyes. The spectacle presented by the two powerful dogs was intimidating; I remember thinking that I would not wish to face either of them if they behaved toward me as they were doing toward each other. Yukon stood stock-still, seeming to wait for something; Rocky began to move slowly, stiff-legged. I stood irresolutely, worried.

A fight was in the making; there was no doubt as to who the victor would be. Even though he had not yet built up his muscles to prime condition on the plentiful and nourishing food that he was eating, the wolf-dog was a formidable creature that at the time must have outweighed the eighty-five-pound Rocky by a good twenty pounds; and he was taller and longer. It was true that Rocky was a hard, gutsy dog who would probably give a good account of himself, but he didn't have a chance against Yukon.

I asked myself two questions: Would Yukon kill Rocky if he weren't stopped? Could I stop him? I confess I had little appetite for mixing bare-handed in the imminent fray, and I stood there and did nothing while deciding reluctantly that I would have to do *something*. I was about to move, belatedly thinking that if I could interpose myself between the two, a battle might be averted with minimal damage to myself; I was too late. The leadership contest flared into noisy action, subsided momentarily, and began anew.

What happened was this: Even as Rocky took one step forward, Yukon moved swiftly and fluidly. From a standing start he surged ahead, covered the distance between his adversary and him, and smashed his big chest into Rocky's right shoulder, a tremendous, battering blow that flung the malamute off his feet and fetched him up against the barn wall with a loud thump, winded once by contact with Yukon's chest and a second time when he hit the logs. It was a simple, but effective, attack that the big dog no doubt calculated would end the fight before it really began. But Rocky was not going to relinquish his leadership quite so easily.

Still snarling loudly and showing fangs, he was trying to get to his feet when Yukon moved again, reached him, and grasped his entire neck in his mouth, securing a hold behind the head. I was sure the wolf had surfaced in the dog and that Rocky's neck was about to be broken, but before I could run to them to intervene, the big dog surprised me by releasing his opponent and backing up to his original place in the center of the barn.

From a human point of view, Yukon's behavior was sporting and honorable, and of course, that's exactly how I saw it at the time. Many years were to pass before I gained enough experience and knowledge of dogs and wolves to put the matter in its proper perspective.

Sporting or not, Rocky was not yet done. Showing no sign of submission, perhaps snarling more viciously than earlier, he jumped to his feet and rushed at Yukon, seeking to fasten his teeth on the big dog's throat only to find that his adversary was on the alert and more than willing to meet the attack halfway.

Rocky's flashing teeth came closer to their target this time, but when his jaws snapped shut with an audible click, the bite managed only to clip a tuft of hair from Yukon's shoulder. This was because the challenger did not simply stand still and wait for the attack but, instead, even as Rocky was making his moves, Yukon made some of his own which were quicker and more deadly and had the advantage of height and reach.

To attempt to describe sequentially what took place during those brief seconds of savage turmoil is impossible. The eyes took in the whole scene and noted most of the movements, but the mind could not then, and cannot now, separate point by point all the actions of each antagonist. I had been so intent on watching Rocky that I was only generally aware of Yukon until he ducked under the other's jaw and reared upward suddenly, so that the back of his neck and part of his shoulders came into direct contact with the underside of Rocky's neck and jaw, throwing the smaller dog backward and off his feet.

The malamute was trying to regain his balance even while he was going down, but as he was doing so, the wolfdog moved with incredible swiftness, following through his attack so surely that by the time Rocky hit the floor Yukon was already on top of him, straddling him, reaching with those enormous and powerful jaws to once again to take hold of the neck in precisely the same place and in the same fashion as before. But now he held on, growling deeply, pinning Rocky down no matter how much he struggled to free himself.

I realized that Yukon did not intend to kill, and this was something that astounded me at the time, for I was not then aware of the built-in, inhibitory factors that prevent animals of the same species from destroying each other, natural safeguards programmed into every species with the notable exception of our own.

At first Rocky growled back at his enemy, but when he realized that he could not dislodge him and could not break the hold on his neck, his growls changed in pitch, got higher, then became interrupted by hysterical yelps. In the end the malamute admitted defeat. He ceased to struggle and became silent.

Yukon released his hold slowly and shifted his position, moving to the left, no longer astride his opponent. He, too, stopped growling, but he remained with his head down, jaws open, and eyed fixed on the other's face. At this, Rocky lifted his back leg in what behaviorists call the inguinal position, a stance with which all dog owners are well acquainted, for it is inevitably demonstrated by their pets when these are being caressed or when they are being "scolded." Whatever we humans call it, and whatever interpretations we choose to place upon the action, in the canine world it is one of many signs of surrender. Rocky capitulated by lifting his leg, but he made doubly sure that the new leader would understand this when he turned his head and neck, offering his throat as a target; the supreme and final gesture of surrender. Yukon was satisfied. Without more ado, he turned around, cast one long and challenging glance around the barn, and walked to Sooner, who was doing his best to hide between my legs.

The apprehensive husky took care to look away from his new leader, exhibiting one more of the many and complex patterns of behavior that are part of the social rituals of the pack. Avoidance of eye-to-eye contact expresses either neutrality or submission, depending on the status of each animal and on the other body gestures that accompany the turning away of the head. In Sooner's case, the gesture was submissive, and he reinforced its meaning by tucking his tail between his legs and lowering his head, ears pulled well back.

Yukon stepped up to his subordinate and grasped him at the back of the head with his teeth, delivering a ritualistic scruff bite, bloodless and painless, given in dominance and accepted in submission. When it was over, Sooner dropped to the floor, lifted his leg, and wagged his tail swiftly, puppy like, while Yukon sniffed him, paused, then turned to go and greet Sussie; the bitch came to meet him, and the two spent some moments licking each other and wagging their tails before the new leader walked casually toward Rocky.

This meeting was entirely peaceful, duplicating to some extent the rituals exchanged between Yukon and Sooner, except that Rocky was not such an abject subject. He kept his gaze averted, and he stood passively when Yukon, stiffly alert and seeming to be ready for trouble, delivered a perfunctory scruff bite, pushed him with his chest, sniffed him in several places, and then, evidently satisfied with the status quo, came to where I stood and nuzzled my hand. I spoke to him.

"OK, you've done it; you're the boss now. How about a *walk*?"

I stressed the last word, knowing that all the dogs recognized it and knew its meaning. Four heads snapped up attentively, four tails started to wag furiously. A second or two later I was surrounded by a press of dogs, and Yukon lost some of his dignity as he led the pack to the door.

For two hours they ran and rolled and yapped and staged mock combats in the clearing behind the farm buildings. It was marvelous to see how well integrated they had become, how gracefully Rocky accepted his defeat, and how well Yukon behaved in victory. There was no trace of antagonism between them when, motivated by some mysterious form of group communication, Sooner and Rocky and Sussie ganged up on Yukon in a game that was at first a sort of canine variation of hare and hounds, the three chasing their new leader while he dodged and jumped or stopped suddenly in his tracks to let the pack rush by while he reversed direction. After a time Yukon seemed to tire of this sport and initiated a new one; now his object was not so much to escape the others as to allow one dog to gain on him, then turn and bowl it over with a well-aimed chest blow, dodge the other two and repeat the procedure with the next dog.

During all this I was much ignored. Occasionally, when they got too close to the forest, with its irresistible hunting lures, I put fingers to mouth and called them back with a piercing command whistle, a signal well known to the three old hands who would immediately turn and run back; Yukon, perforce, followed. In this way, he, too, learned to respond to the signal.

After that day I started training them in team work, taking them for walks, two to a lead, and teaching them short commands, such as "stop," "left," "right," and "stay." "Go" was a word they all knew by heart! Never did they need to be urged to get going, but often, in their enthusiasm, they needed reminders of the other four.

This business of giving driving commands to dogs varies according to area and personal preferences. Some use the old horse commands: "Gee," for right, "haw," turn left, and "ho," for stop. In the far north the French *marche* has been turned into "mush"; hence, a "musher" is a dog driver, while words of Inuit (Eskimo) origin are used for the other commands: "ouk," go right; "rra," turn left; "hah" and in some cases "whoit" for start. In my own experience I found that single-word commands in the English language did just as well and had the advantage of familiarity— for me, not for the dogs! I came to this conclusion the first time I found myself trying to decide whether "gee" meant right or left and recalled an occasion when, as a youth receiving sailing instruction from a well-meaning, but irascible, uncle, I was given the tiller of the twenty-six-foot ketch "to get the feel of her." When about half an hour later I was suddenly ordered to go "hard aport," I swung the boat to the right instead of to the left; we grounded on the sandbar my uncle was trying to avoid and hung there for two hours until the tide was high enough to float us free. Twenty years later that story was still being told, and the tongue-lashing delivered with gusto by the old sea dog will never be forgotten.

I was in no mood now to begin to learn a whole new set of strange words while trying to gain experience as a dog driver. In any event, the dogs didn't mind the English one bit, and if some of the neighbors smiled superiorly at the tenderfoot's commands, I found this of little consequence.

Once, while quaffing ale in the town pub with a half dozen of my neighbors, I was asked why I used "them funny words" on the dogs. The speaker was good-naturedly trying to get a rise out of me, and wishing to give a noncommittal answer, I quoted Thoreau: "Well, I happen to like to march to the beat of a different drummer."

It didn't occur to me that these men were all born and brought up in the backwoods during a time when newspapers did not find their way into the hinterland, radios were few and far between, and libraries were nonexistent. None of my audience had ever heard of Thoreau, let alone read him. My reply mystified them, but they were too polite to ask for an explanation and instead turned the conversation to the subject of trapping. Much later I was to discover that they took my remark literally and spread the word that I was trying to train the dogs by beating on a drum! Of course, everybody loved this story, and behind my back they referred to the homestead as Drum-Heller, a pun on the name of a town in the province of Alberta.

After chores each day, the dogs were lead-trained for an hour, rewarded with a tidbit afterward, and allowed to frisk for fifteen or twenty minutes. When the play period ended, Sussie, Sooner, and Rocky were returned to the empty hay barn, a building forty by sixty feet where they could run, sit, or lie as they chose. Yukon was still receiving preferential treatment; indeed, he *always* received it, even against the well-meant advice of the local sages, who adhered to the philosophy that working dogs become spoiled if they are shown affection, as many dog handlers still believe to this day. I did not then, and do not now, share this view; but today I can be more positive when asserting that love, openly shown, produces far better results than relentless sternness, to say nothing about whip or club, and this, it seems to me, is as valid for dogs as it is for any other animal.

In any event, Yukon did not go into the barn. I was even then busy getting to know my trapline and some of the more distant country; it had been my habit, before Yukon's arrival, to spend a good part of each day walking the wilderness, clearing trails, marking with tall, peeled poles those locations where traps would be set later on, and carrying traps to leave tied to trees in strategic areas of the line. In addition to this, when there was time and the mood was with me, I would cut and peel spruce logs near the site selected for a small cabin, midway between the end of the trapline and the homestead, for those occasions in winter when I would have to spend the night in the wilderness.

Now I took Yukon with me on these journeys, keeping him on a lead for fear that he would scent some interesting thing and take off, but releasing him near home on the return journey so he could have a final run before nighttime.

Northern sled dogs are veritable "muscle machines," which for untold generations have been bred for their endurance and will to work. Typically, they have fairly short, erect ears, long, bushy tails, deep chests, big paws, and a double layer of warm fur composed of a fine, woolly undercoat and a coarse dressing of long guard hairs. Size and color of hair are widely variable, as are body markings.

Roughly speaking, there are three theoretically distinct breeds: the Alaskan malamute, the Eskimo husky (known as either *kiminik* or *kingmik*), and the Siberian husky. Malamutes and Eskimo dogs are big, weighing between eighty and ninety-five pounds as a rule, though some individuals scale over one hundred pounds. Siberian dogs are smaller, varying in weight between forty-five and sixty pounds, but here again, there are exceptions. Colors range from almost black to pure white, but the most predominant markings include a mixture of various shades of black, brown, and white. Pure white dogs are found most commonly in the far north, probably as a result of the long, snowy winters, which, during thousands of years of evolutionary selection, have influenced color for camouflage purposes—protective coloration. Thus, in the Arctic, many white animals are found, wolves, foxes, hares, ptarmigan, and snow owls, to name some of them

It might be argued that because the sled dog had been domesticated, there is no particular advantage to be derived from its color; this is true now, but it is almost certain that the camouflaged coat became the rule long before domestication, when the dog's ancestors were truly wild, were, in fact wolves, or a subspecies of wolf that evolved from a doglike creature called *Tomarctus.*

Trying to settle the question of canine ancestry is a bit like wondering whether the chicken or the egg came first.There are those who become almost violent at the suggestion that sled dogs, or any other dog, for that matter, are directly descended from wolves, while there are also those who contend just that; then there is a third group that clams the dog, and especially the sled dog, evolved at the same time, but separately from, the wolf. However this may be, I support the view of Colbert,* who, in 1939, proposed that the dog was a direct descendant of the Euro-Asiatic wolf, while pointing out that this ancestry was almost hopelessly complicated by domestication, crossbreeding, hybridization, and backcrossing once more with wolves. Colbert really goes back in time! He traces the ancestry of the canids to a small, catlike creature called *Miacis* who is said to have lived no less than forty million years ago, during the Eocene-Oligocene transition. During the latter epoch in North America, *Miacis* is thought to have given rise to two other types of neocanids, the big, long-tailed *Daphaenus* and its

* E. H. Colbert, "Origin of the Dog," *Natural History* 43, 1939, pp. 90–101.

smaller companion, *Cynodictis.* The former looked somewhat like today's wolverine and is thought to have given rise to the bears, while the latter is believed to be the ancestor of all dogs, wolves, foxes, and related animals. Tracing these ancient creatures backward, one eventually encountered *Tomarctus,* which doglike animal (or wolflike, as the case may be) gave rise to the modern canids.

None of this takes into account more recent (relatively speaking) crossbreeding between the sled dogs that accompanied early man to North America and the wolves of Eurasia and of the New World. Neither does it account for the fact that Yukon was fifty percent wolf and that practically all the sled dogs I have encountered during the last twenty-odd years have more in common with the timber wolf than with domestic breeds.

The fact of the matter remains that the sled dog has the stamina, keen intellect, and super senses of the wolf coupled with the deeper chest and generally more muscular body of the larger domestic dogs, features that were deliberately acquired through crossbreeding and that resulted in a remarkable species that will work itself to death for its master and survives, in most cases, on what a poodle consumes during an in-between-meals snack—only a *slight* exaggeration!

It is considered that a good sled dog can pull twice its own weight and can backpack half its own weight, depending on the fitness of the dog. Rocky, for instance, easily outpulled Sooner, while Yukon could pull me *and* an additional two hundred pounds and keep going for hours on a good trail.

Over the years, a variety of different harnessing methods has been devised, each dog driver preferring his own particular variation, from single file to tandem or fan hitches. My own method was simple, consisting of two traces long enough to accommodate the four dogs in single file. The ends of the traces were secured to the sled, and each trace was fitted at the correct distance with D rings into which the dog's harness was swivel-snapped; secured in this way to both traces, the team was hitched in the reverse order of its going. This meant that Yukon was invariably the last dog to be led forward to take his place, something that he disliked intensely and the only thing that could force him, however temporarily, to wait his turn. Inasmuch as it only took a minute or two to hitch the other three, he never had to wait long, and I could not be sympathetic about his tantrums, especially when he sought to nip one of the others as I was leading him to his place. In this sense he was a complete scoundrel and gave me the feeling that he would infinitely prefer to nip me, the cause of his ignominy, but refrained from doing so out of the pure goodness of his heart, preferring to take a swipe at one of the two males, usually poor old Sooner, who quickly learned to sidle out of harm's way whenever he saw me leading Yukon toward the traces.

In addition to being evilly disposed when he was made to wait like that, Yukon instantly developed another bad habit. The moment both his swivel snaps were clipped to the D rings, he would plunge away, as though seeking to make up in speed for the loss of face he felt he had endured. The first time this occurred I managed to grab the side of the sled and was thus taken for a wild ride through some dry and prickly brush—on my back, one-handed, being dragged more than a hundred yards in this ignoble fashion before my yells and the weight of my body through the snow and brush brought the great oaf to a halt. I wasn't pleased. To let him know how I felt, he was unhitched, tied to a tree, lectured gruffly, and left behind while I drove the others home, less than a mile away. A passerby would have thought he was being slowly killed by the way he howled and ki-yied. I almost relented.

He was most apologetic when I returned for him, fussing me, jumping up to lick my face and contorting himself like a puppy; but his remorse was purely momentary. The next morning he did it again, catching me totally unaware this time and leading the others across the clearing, down into a swale, and on into a frozen muskeg swamp where the sled hit a stump, up-set, cracked one of the runners and landed the dogs in a great yelping tangle.

That did it Quite obviously punishment was not the answer, but countermeasures could be taken. From that day forward the sled was tied to some immovable object while the dogs were harnessed, and because he was so quick to learn when it suited his convenience, he jerked away on only two occasions, each time being pulled up short and getting hit in the rump by Sussie, the only one who could do so with impunity. When *I* was good and ready, the sled would be unfastened, and if I was to ride the runners, we got off to a fast start on the command "go!" If I was to break trail, a ten-foot rope carried for the purpose was fastened to Yukon's collar and to my waist, while the hitching rope was left trailing behind the sled, just in case Yukon and I parted company and I was forced to make a grab for the speeding vehicle before it went too far. Eventually he managed to break himself of these bad habits, but it took quite a while!

On hearing about it later, Alfred expressed amazement that one should go to so much trouble to break a dog of his bad habits. The Indian had a simpler method.

"Anytime he take off on you, dat dog, give him heck with a two-by-four. He knows a club, dat dog. He sure does!"

He wasn't telling me anything I wasn't already aware of; there was no question that Yukon knew a club, just as there was no question that he would have killed Alfred given half a chance. The only time the Ojibway came to visit after he sold the dog, Yukon was in the house and began to bristle long before his former master arrived. Unaware of the identity of the caller, I opened the door without taking hold of the dog's collar, and if Alfred hadn't had the presence of mind to step out on the porch and slam the storm door, holding it shut against the dog's charging weight, I believe Yukon would have torn his throat out before I could intervene.

From the first day that he came with me on the trapline, Yukon made clear the enjoyment he felt during these wanderings through the bush, but he intimated by his manner that if he had a chance, he would become sidetracked by the first likely scent. I no longer feared that he would go and not return, but I didn't want him roaming alone, doing his own hunting, and picking up new parasites. Leading was a nuisance, because he would pull and tug when motivated by interesting sounds and scents, but it had to be endured by both of us.

Our encounter with the sick moose had occurred during the second of our trapline outings in an area of spruce forest on the eastern boundary of my line. Threading through the evergreens were a number of creeks that led to several good-size ponds interconnected by beaver-made spillways. From what I had seen of these ponds, the fur yield would be good this season, provided, of course, that I didn't continue to be interrupted by such things as recalcitrant dogs and charging moose. It was already late in the year, and there were still a number of traps to be hung outdoors to weather, so that the elements would remove the man scent from each new, factory-tainted trap before it was set in a beaver spillway or sunk through a hole in the ice.

In view of this, the wisdom of taking time to examine the tissue samples was debatable. Without electricity, the job could be undertaken only in daylight, outside, and would consume almost an entire day to do properly or, at least, as properly as was possible without use of a high-intensity microscope light and an adequate supply of stains. Nevertheless, I was intensely curious, and since I could not work indoors at night and had no means of freezing the samples to preserve them, I determined to study them the next day.

Microscopic examination of tissue is a fussy business the technique of which need not be described here; suffice it to say that by using some saffron from the food cupboard, I was able to distill a makeshift

stain that revealed a fair amount of detail, but it was
not until late afternoon that I found anything of significance.

There was no need of a microscope to see the flukes
that infested the animal's liver; these became visually
evident when the carcass was cut open. Neither was it
difficult to spot the roundworms in the gut samples,
like threadlike creatures tapered at both ends, the
sexes distinguishable because the male of the species
has a minute baglike appendage, or bursa, growing
at the end of its hind taper. Neither the gut worms
nor the liver flukes could have been responsible for
the crazed and sickly condition of the moose; both
these parasites are common in all wild animals, many
domestic animals, and even man. Some species of
gut roundworms are dangerous, of course, but the
symptoms displayed by animals suffering from a severe infestation of these nematodes are quite different
from those I witnessed in the moose. Even if I was
only able to identify the worms generally as belonging
to the subclass Phasmidia, this sufficed; I felt fairly
confident in dismissing them as relatively harmless.

The microscope revealed nothing abnormal in the
muscle tissue, but this did not mean there was nothing
there; what with the makeshift stain, the absence of
strong artificial light, and the limitations of the microscope's objectives, the chances of discovering anything beyond relatively large organisms were minimal.
Mostly because that kind of work fascinates me, I kept
looking, methodically scrutinizing one sample after another until only the spinal cord and brain tissues remained.

Without a microtome (an instrument designed for
cutting extremely thin sections of animal tissue), the
job of slicing the brain samples with a razor blade was
difficult, but I managed to obtain some more or less
adequate sections. Now I got a surprise. The first slice
of brain tissue revealed the unmistakable shapes of no
fewer than seven tiny roundworms! I could not believe the facts. I had been using a 10 x objective,
but now I rotated the turret to the most powerful lens.

There could be no doubt about the findings, the thready objects were, indeed, roundworms. But roundworms in the *brain* of an animal?

I had never heard of such a thing, yet I willingly conceded that I was not an expert in parasitology in general or nematology in particular, so after all brain and spinal cord sections were examined and found to contain varying numbers of worms, I burned the samples (I had no means of preserving them) and spent the rest of the afternoon and evening going over my fairly extensive biology literature. Not a single reference to brain worms could I find. The closest I was able to come to the organism resident in the moose brain was a nematode belonging to the family Strongylidae, a species of which, *Pneumostrongylus,* parasitizes the lungs of wild and domestic animals, but because all nematodes are known to be very host-specific—that is, they have become so specialized that they cannot normally survive anywhere but within the organs in which evolution designed them to exist—failed to establish a connection between the lung worm and brain worm, thereby passing up the chance of being the first to make a relatively important discovery. But I came close!

Evening after evening, sitting in the living room with Yukon, I pondered over the mysterious brain worm and continued to search the literature. Over the course of that winter I spent money I could ill afford buying more books by mail and reading them over and over until I felt that I knew Nematoda by heart. I got no closer to identifying the moose worm, as I christened it, but I did learn one interesting fact! Because roundworms are so specialized, they don't seem to know what to do if they get into the wrong host by accident as, for example, when dog and cat roundworms enter the human digestive tract. In such cases the larvae migrate aimlessly inside the "foreign" host and, failing to become established in their proper locale, may produce serious ailments, including blindness, when they inadvertently invade some other part of the body, such as the eyes.

Was it possible, I wondered, that *Pneumostrongylus* had in some way deviated from the lungs into the brain of the moose? If this was so, it would account for the animal's condition, its staggering gait and crazed behavior. That was as far as I got with the problem until the following spring, at which time, buying supplies in a distant city, I questioned a government biologist. He had never seen, heard, or thought about a brain worm, and he treated me as though he suspected that if there really *was* such an organism, I was surely its first victim. As for the blind staggers, he had seen a number of moose suffering from the condition, but this could be safely attributed to eating poison vetch. That seemed to end the matter. I put it out of my mind.

Ten years later I was to learn that my seemingly wild guess had been very close to the mark. Research in Ontario revealed that *Pneumostrongylus* was, indeed, responsible for the blind staggers! Poison vetch was not implicated at all, from which fact I derived the most satisfaction. I felt at the time that the poison plant theory was untenable because wild animals have the uncanny ability to distinguish between safe and harmful foods found in their natural habitat. Why, when there was plenty of its preferred food available, would an animal like the moose eat a plant that grows in relatively dry locations? In spring and early summer moose like to feed on plants found in shallow, marshy water, such as pond weeds and water lilies, but when these begin to decline, become tougher, in midsummer, the animals feed on herbs and the leaves of bushes and trees; in fall and winter they browse on the twigs of a wide variety of trees. It may be that poison vetch in some areas of North America grows in heavily wooded habitats, but I have never seen the plant inside the ddep forests which are the preferred range of moose during summer and autumn. For these reasons, and because of the animal's condition and behavior, I was inclined to dismiss the poison theory, which was why I took tissue samples.

The story of *Pneumostrongylus* as described by

Ontario government biologists in a report issued in 1964 is this: The parasite is commonly found in the white-tailed deer, to which host it appears to do little harm. The worms do enter the nervous system, but from there they migrate into the bloodstream of the deer and are carried to the lungs, where they remain until fully adult; now they migrate to the esophagus, are swallowed, and are carried into the stomach, where the eggs are laid and later deposited on the ground mixed with the feces of the deer. The larvae hatch from the eggs, live "free" for a time as they undergo several molts, and next invade small land snails of various species. It is at this stage that they are picked up by deer (or moose) feeding on the vegetation to which the snails are clinging, and the cycle begins anew inside the final host.

Nematologists believe that roundworms may well be the largest single class of all animals on earth, not only in actual numbers of individuals, but also in numbers of species. At this point in the history of their biology, no one really knows how many species are in existence, but because new worms are being discovered at an average rate of *one per day*, informed biologists estimate that some 500,000 different species may eventually be classified. As an example, at the time (1955) I examined the worms in the moose tissue, the latest literature on the subject I could obtain gave the number of species classified as being in excess of 8,000; by 1969 this figure had climbed to more than twelve thousand.

Large numbers of plants and almost all animals are parasitized by at least one, and often several species of the worms; a spadeful of earth from the garden submitted to microscopic examination will probably contain up to *one million* tiny wriggling worms. Fortunately the majority of these hard-shelled, itinerant "moochers" are harmless enough, yet among those that do inflict damage are found some pretty horrifying creatures, such as *Pneumostrongylus,* the trichina worm, hookworms, and stomach worms, all of them capable of killing their unwitting hosts.

It seems evident that during the course of its evolution the white-tailed deer developed immunity to the lung worm, but the moose, apparently exposed to the nematode only when the bigger browser finds itself sharing the deer's range, is far from immune and rarely survives an infestation of *Pneumostrongylus*.

Chapter 4

After the moose affair, Yukon and I spent several peaceful and uneventful days walking the trapline, carrying supplies and tools. The weather became colder, and the skies remained cloudy; but the snow held off, an unusual situation in a country where the first flakes not infrequently come by mid-September to dust the landscape. Yet there was a feeling of snow in the air; daily I expected to wake up to a whitened forest and found myself looking forward to what I call the clean and quiet time, when the dead leaves of aspen and birch and oak are decently buried and lie silent underfoot and the evergreens sport clean white mantles that sparkle in the sunshine as though they had been sprinkled with diamond dust. Before the snow, the land seems somber, even on the sunniest days, an illusion created by the fall of the deciduous leaves and by the starkly naked branches of birch and poplar, trees that not long before were covered by crowns of rich, green foliage. But all this changes when the snow arrives; the forest becomes a suddenly exciting milieu that invites attention.

As that particular autumn was about to disappear forever, I found myself at the crossroads of a friendship that was to become so deep and abiding that it had the power to change my life, though hitherto I would not have thought it possible that a ragged, seemingly vicious animal could exert such influence on a human. And yet, had I given it enough reflection, I suppose I mightt even then have recognized that the symbiosis of man and dog, ripening as it had done during unknown ages, does indeed have the power to affect the future of a man, especially under conditions such as Yukon and I were to share in the years to come. Together we traveled the wilderness, and we gave each other strength, and friendship, and a kind of love that really cannot be described: unromantic, yet deep. Perhaps it stemmed from a love of life or from the excitement we felt when we challenged the elemental forces and came through the worst they could offer, or maybe it was our understanding of each other or a combination of all these things, and more. I cannot say.

Yukon now carried his share of the load, for I had made him a backpack. Out of old horse harness straps scrounged from a neighbor and a supply of heavy canvas and thread, the twin pouches were laboriously fashioned during finger-pricking sittings beside the yellow light of kerosene, sessions enlivened by "fittings" during which Yukon behaved either with patient decorum or with hilarious obstreperousness. The finished product was hardly aesthetic: but it was practical and durable, and Yukon carried it over many miles of wilderness trails and more than halfway across the roof of North America.

After he had come to me, during the wine drinking that followed the exchange of money, Alfred said the dog was used to sled pulling but had not been trained to back-carry, so when harness and pouches were completed, I naturally wondered how he would react to his first load. But I needn't have worried. Perhaps because he was so intimately involved with its construction, Yukon took an immediate and proprietary interest in the backpack. Indeed, he accepted his burden eagerly.

The first load he carried for a short trial walk in the immediate area of the homestead was made up of twenty pounds of sand packed in two gunnysacks, one to each pouch. He bore this weight casually, turning his head to sniff at it for a second or two and then putting his mind to the more serious and pleasurable business of walking the woods. It was difficult to be sure initially, but after I watched him carefully for more than a mile, it became evident that he derived a sense of purpose from working in this fashion, as though he *knew* that what he was doing was useful and necessary. He carried himself differently, not because of the weight on his back, but more as if he were glad to be so employed; there was a new spring in his step, he was more erect and attentive; his bush was a tight spiral, its tip actually sliding from his back to rest lightly against his kidney area.

Back home, he refused to allow the pack to be taken off, avoiding my attempts playfully and seeking to promote a game. It would have been simple enough to ask him to "stay" while the harness was unstrapped, but I allowed him to keep it on and, on the spur of the moment, decided that he might enjoy showing off in front of the other dogs, thinking that his willingness to "tote a load" could even be a good example for Rocky and Sooner, neither of whom had backpacked to date. As it turned out, the example was neither good nor the one I had hoped for, and am sure that both Rocky and Sooner could have done without it altogether!

When we entered the barn, Sussie and Sooner were already on their feet and came galumphing toward us immediately, but Rocky, busy chewing at an evidently persistent itch on his hindquarters, was slow to get started. Sussie reached us first, welcomed Yukon in her usual way, showed little interest in his satchels, and came to me to be petted.

Sooner was always eager to investigate anything that might possibly contain food, and now he forgot pack ritual in his anxiety to be the first to sniff the bags. He was almost treading on Sussie's heels as he pushed forward and stretched his neck and head the better to nose the canvas and leather, but when Yukon snarled angrily, he quickly realized his error and tried frantically to back up. He was too late.

Using his by-now-familiar chest punch, Yukon knocked the luckless husky clean off his feet, thereafter ignoring him as he scrambled away, yelping disproportionately to his hurt, overreacting as usual. Now Rocky arrived. He was unaware of the reason for Sooner's punishment and was also intrigued by the newness strapped to Yukon's back. He too forgot his manners, though it is possible that he was not yet accustomed to occupying a subordinate role. In any event, he approached arrogantly, tail high, gaze fixed on his leader, to whom he extended none of the ritual courtesies, not so much as a casual wag of the tail. Most of Yukon's hackles were trapped under his harness, but his mane erected fully, and his growl was heavy with menace. Rocky ignored the warning signs.

Yukon's entire mien denoted his "Alpha," or dominant, status, a station which he now felt was being once again challenged by the smaller dog; according to his precepts, he could not afford to allow such cavalier behavior to go unpunished if he wished to continue to lead the pack. With the same sure swiftness that he displayed when he attacked the moose, he turned, surged forward, and fastened his teeth in Rocky's right shoulder, biting hard and shaking the other with such strength that the unfortunate malamute was thrown several yards across the barn floor, his shoulder becoming lacerated when the big fangs ripped through flesh and hide.

I was so taken aback by this turn of events that I stood undecided during the few seconds it took Rocky to pick himself up and shake his head once, as though to clear away the whiplash effects he must have experienced, immediately after which he launched himself at his attacker, emitting a series of loud and furious snarls. Yukon, meanwhile, was already moving to head off the charge. The two met and became united in a series of swift contortions accompanied by a paroxysm of deep-in-the-throat snarls that to my excited imagination sounded as though they ought to be coming from some dark, dense jungle instead of the almost empty interior of my own barn.

Yelling at the scrappers produced no results, but I found myself doing it anyway, the while casting about anxiously for a solid object with which to pry them apart. The only thing available was the cut-down five-gallon metal drum used to hold the team's drinking water, which was full to the brim. As I stooped to pick it up, intending to douse the contestants, the battle came to a sudden end.

Yukon seized Rocky by the muzzle, twisted viciously, and threw the malamute to the ground, pinning him there. The hold was different, but the events that followed were almost identical to those that had concluded their previous argument. Rocky capitulated, Yukon released him and walked away, still bristling slightly, but evidently satisfied that he had once again established his superiority.

The fight couldn't have lasted for more than ten seconds, but it was so utterly feral that at one point about midway through it I felt myself strangely impelled to dive into the melee and to rend and tear as the dogs were doing, as though some dormant, starkly primitive part of the brain had reacted to the bestial magnetism of the duel. I found myself unaccountably moved by the experience. Often since then I have tried to convince myself that it resulted from fancy, yet I can't rid myself of the feeling that for an infinitesimal fraction of time, emotions hidden beyond the reach of my understanding turned me into a prehistoric man.

As a result of the fight, Rocky was stiff and sore for several days. He received some bad gashes on his shoulder, one deep puncture on the back of his head, and a half inch slit in his left ear. Yukon came off lightly; he got a bloody nick on one paw and a small cut on his right foreleg. Both dogs were treated with permanganate of potash, after which nature and their own tough constitutions did the rest.

Responsibility for the fight was mine. I unwittingly contrived to create a situation of novelty, not realizing that dogs are inherently driven to investigate anything new in their domain. In addition to this, by allowing Yukon to spend so much time in the house, away from his teammates, the dogs were not given a chance to establish the routines of their pack. It was as important for Yukon to become accustomed to leading as it was for Rocky and the others to become used to being led. Henceforth, Yukon was to spend more time in the barn and less in the house, only occasionally being allowed to sleep indoors; this was a good thing in the long run because he disliked the warmth, and sleeping in the unheated barn, apart from being more comfortable for him, caused his fur to become thick and prime, making him impervious to even the coldest weather.

The next morning, after chores were completed, Yukon and I left early for the trapline, each of us carrying our own share of the load for the first time. The dog's pouches were stuffed full of traps, the last of these, a load that probably weighed about forty pounds; I carried tools, rolls of wire, food, and non-perishable supplies that were to be left by the cabin site. Mine was the lighter of the two loads, but Yukon carried his effortlessly, prancing along contentedly as far in front of me as the length of his lead would allow.

The previous night's frost was lying hoary in the shadow places, but the sun had come with the new day, and had stayed until the clouds came back a couple of hours later, melted the rime in exposed areas and left the ground vegetation limp and soggy. This made for quiet walking, allowing us both to listen to the sounds of the wilderness undisturbed by our own footsteps.

For me, the morning was replete with birdsongs orchestrated into a series of wild and tuneful sonatas.

Gray jays, chickadees, nuthatches, and woodpeckers rendered their autumnal solos, as though voicing their pleasure at being left behind by the flocks of less hardy species that had winged away from the approach of winter. Occasionally the hoarse cawing of some solitary raven added deep bass to the cheerful melodies of the other birds, and if I looked up on these occasions, it was to see an ebon bird floating above the trees with consummate ease while it scanned the ground with one sharp black eye.

In contrast, Yukon was interested only in the many small noises that issued from within the forest, those stealthy, rustling sounds that are made when mouse or shrew scuttles swiftly through the dead and dying grasses or when the red squirrel climbs gymnastically up the scaly trunk of a spruce, sometimes dislodging bits of red-brown bark that tumble down whispering as they journey through the stiffened green needles. Watching the dog, I discovered that he was always listening and sniffing, that he paid attention to every single sound that reached his sensitive ears; he was forever turning his head, flicking first one ear, then another, independently if the noise was small, in unison if it was louder and closer to hand. Already he had tried to dart away in pursuit when a louder-than-usual rustle came from nearby, and the way his nose twitched led me to conclude that it had picked up scents too faint for my own inadequate nostrils to detect.

It occurred to me presently that Yukon "telegraphed" the degree of interest with which he greeted each new sensory experience, and I began to pay close attention to him, realizing that if I could interpret his "body language," as I immediately thought of it, his keen senses would considerably extend the range of my own duller ones. It wasn't merely the way in which he sniffed or moved his ears and head, but rather the way in which his entire being reflected the degree of interest aroused in him by the messages that he picked up from the wilderness. It would be impossible for me to know exactly what it was that he was reacting to, but I felt that I could at least learn to distinguish between the significant and the unimportant. Checking, as he routinely did, every sound and scent and vision that presented themselves to him, he appeared to "sort" these according to priorities. An old spoor he investigated briefly, gave it a cursory sniff or two without tightening his tail or pricking up his ears, and continued walking; a small, but fairly distant, rustle was noted by the flick of an ear and a casual glance, while the same kind of sound coming from nearby was treated to more careful inspection from eyes, ears, and nose; his tail became tighter, and his walk changed from what I can only describe as a stroll to a sort of semistalk, rather like a person who wishes to tread quietly without actually going on tiptoe. These mannerisms appeared to be reserved for relatively unimportant things such as, perhaps, mouse, squirrel, or bird, and the degree of interest they aroused depended on their proximity.

In like manner he responded to influences beyond the range of my senses, though in these cases he seemed to rely more heavily on his olfactory and auditory faculties. Yet his reaction to these, to me undetectable, influences was always more pronounced. This was puzzling at first, until it dawned on me that a sound or a scent so distant from us that it would go completely unnoticed by human faculties must surely emanate from an organism larger than a mouse or a squirrel and therefore proportionately noisier or more odoriferous; perhaps the source of this sort of environmental disturbance was a hare, or a groundhog, or some other creature of similar size, something that would make a better meal for a hunter.

Not all these things occurred to me on the day I first became aware that Yukon was a sort of animate and eminently portable radar station, but as time passed and we drew closer and our understanding of each other became greater, I gradually compiled a sort of "Yukon Response Chart" that proved itself to be remarkably useful in the years ahead, and inasmuch as

canines are all almost equally able to offer a similar
service to their owners, I include it here.

The response chart had these gradations: Hot,
Warm, Lukewarm, Cold, and Very Cold, applied to
three general classifications—namely, Great Interest,
Medium Interest, and Little Interest. At first I added
a fourth class, No Interest, but I removed this when I
realized that there was nothing on earth in which Yukon was *not* interested to at least *some* degree.

To illustrate further, the old scent of a wolf always
merited Medium Interest, but the same scent recently
deposited invariably rated Great Interest. In like manner, a nearby mouse rated Medium, a distant mouse
Little, while a nearby hare rated Medium-Great and a
more distant one Medium. *Sight* of a wolf far away
rated Great-Great; so did a wolf howl from nearby,
except that in the latter case Yukon always replied.
Lastly, his reaction to something such as our encounter
with the moose rated Great-Great-Great, the ultimate
classification, invariably demonsrated by an outburst
of explosive activity. But in such cases one hardly
needs a graph, for the situation is abundantly clear,
even to human senses!

Despite my early recognition of the dog's super-
faculties, it was no until the following summer that an
incident occurred which made me realize just how
marvelously acute was his sense of smell. If he had not
already learned from his association with Alfred the
relationship between the discharge of a firearm and
the killing of game, he absorbed this immediately after
I shot the moose, even to the point of distinguishing
between a gun slung on the shoulder, which was only
of passing interest, and a gun in hand and ready for
action, which immediately caused him to become fully
alert. When, on occasion, he got away from me to
chase something in the forest, I learned that it was
easy to bring him back from anything but a hot and
close chase by shooting in the air, the crack of the gun
being an irresistable lure in most cases.

On one such escape I was carrying the .22 rifle. I
was about to shoot in the air when I spotted an old

rusted can left goodness knows when on a pile of small rocks that had been picked off the home clearing. On impulse I tested my marksmanship by shooting at the can, spinning it off the top of the rock pile. In seconds Yukon emerged from the forest running, at full stretch, slowed when he was twenty or thirty yards from me, and began questing the ground and the air with his nose. Intrigued because he was working a zigzag course toward the distant rocks, I watched him intently, never for one moment thinking that he could actually locate the tin can. *This is exactly what he did!*

Within seconds he had narrowed his field of search to the area around the stones, found the place where the can had been at the time of the bullet's impact, and moments later located the can and sniffed it carefully, devoting most of his attention to the bullet holes.

It was an almost incredible demonstration of his olfactory powers, but it held even more meaning than that: It told me that Yukon was able to classify and immediately to identify *kinds* of smells, that, in fact, he could make intelligent, reasoned choices based on experience and memory. In itself this did not surprise me unduly, because by then I was already aware that animals, even the most humble, are certainly not irrational, as they were so glibly labeled in the days of medieval ignorance. What did surprise me was that it took me so long to arrive at such a conclusion in the face of the many bits of evidence I had picked up during my association with Yukon and the other dogs and with the animals of the wilderness. Beyond the humbling reminder that we humans tend to overrate our own intellect while underrating the intelligence of the beings that share our world, the experience pointed out the folly of assuming that animals are mostly programmed by instinct and are therefore hardly able to make free and reasoned choices.

Not long after noticing how the dog reacted to the influences of his environment, perhaps an hour or so before reaching the cabin site, which was to be our first unloading stop, Yukon turned off the trail and pulled hard at the lead, standing still and refusing to continue. It was evident that whatever held his interest was of more significance than anything else heard or scented so far; because of my earlier realization, and probably more to test the theory than for any other reason, I gave him his head, holding him in check with the lead, but allowing him to advance toward a clump of leafless poplars, at which he looked intently. From our position about seventy-five yards away, I could not see anything out of the usual.

Guided by his line of travel, we approached the aspens slowly (if Yukon had got his own way, he would have dashed over there), but I could neither see nor hear the cause of his interest; I even tried to smell it, without success, needless to say. But by using my nose deliberately, I did manage to capture the collective odor of the forest, and I was even able to distinguish some of its components: the tangy fragrance of the evergreens; the rather acrid aroma of decaying vegetation; even the smell of the dog. I had discovered a new dimension in myself or, at least, had broadened an old one beyond the sniffing of some strong and obvious odor.

Yukon pulled harder and tightened the curl of his tail and sharpened the forward angle of his ears, telling me that we were getting closer to the quarry. We were twenty yards from the nearest poplar, a tall tree of thick girth that grew a little distance from the others on a small, comparatively open patch of ground covered, for the most part, with a mixture of sere blueberry bushes and clumps of frost-blackened grass. I still couldn't detect anything of significance, but Yukon was getting more excited with each step he took.

When the quarry finally revealed itself to me two or three strides later, I stopped, slid my hand down the lead, and held Yukon close, intrigued by the spectacle of two animals maneuvering over an area of grass which had been concealed by a cluster of dwarf juniper that grew on a slight rise of ground. Because they were so intent on each other, neither was aware of our

presence. One was a red fox; the other, a porcupine. I
had seen members of each of these species before,
but I didn't know that a fox would try to kill a porcupine, an animal almost as big and heavy as itself and
formidably armed. The fox was a large male, probably
weighing twelve or fifteen pounds; the porcupine must
have weighed no less than eight pounds.

Experienced predators are always cautious when
attacking their prey because even a comparatively
minor injury detracts from their efficiency by slowing
them down, causing them to fumble their strikes, and
reduces the frequency of kills. An injury that would
offer only slight inconvenience to a domestic dog, fed
regularly by its owners, can mean death from starvation to a predator living from feast to famine, as even
the healthiest and most powerful of them do.

This is why I was surprised that a comparatively
small hunter like the fox would dare attack an animal
that could inflict swift and terrible injury when there
was an abundance of smaller game in the region that
was easier to kill and presented hardly any risks. I
could conclude only that the fox preferred to eat porcupine meat and was prepared to take the risks at-
tendant upon securing the meal. In later years my own
experience and that of others have tended to confirm
this conclusion, adding one more predator to the list of
those that attack and kill the porcupine, popularly believed to be too prickly for the majority of predators.
In fact, the slow and docile "quill pig" has a long list
of enemies, including the wolf, coyote, cougar, wolverine, fisher, bear, lynx, bobcat, and fox.

Nevertheless, those hunters that would dine on porcupine must first surprise their quarry in the open and
then spend some time jousting with it until the animal
is tired enough to allow the attacker to secure a firm
hold on the only vulnerable part of the body, the quill-
free nose (the stomach is also free of quills, but it is
not readily accessible until after the animal has been
killed).

From a line roughly in front of the porcupine's
ears, on each cheek, down the back, on both flanks,

and on to the tip of its stubby tail, the porcupine bristles with some thirty thousand quills, each finely barbed, that it can erect instantly. These barbs are specially adapted hairs that, like the ordinary variety that furnished the animal with a thick cover of fur, are soon replaced if they are lost during an abortive attack or are molted normally. Rather like the shark with its layers of teeth ever ready to replace losses, the porcupine continuously sprouts short white quills beneath its underfur, and if these small needles are not as formidable as the fully developed quills that measure from three fourths of an inch to two and a half inches in length, they are yet sufficient to deter a predator that attempts to bite into an area where the old quills have been lost.

The porcupine's tail is its most effective weapon. It uses it as a club, lashing it from side to side and always seeking to smash it full force into the face and mouth of an attacker. The hunters know this, probably because when young and inexperienced, they have been pricked by a few barbs in nose or cheek and have never forgotten the burning agony, or perhaps they have been fortunate to learn by watching the caution employed by their parents when attacking such quarry. However this may be, the predators given to attacking the quill pig employ almost identical methods for killing the animal; the porcupine, perforce, has developed a remarkably good defense.

Watching the small drama that was developing in the backwoods that morning, I noted at first hand the techniques employed by each contestant during the short time I was able to observe the two unnoticed.

The porcupine was hunched up, its tail slightly raised, jerking spasmodically from side to side; its vulnerable nose was pulled down between the front legs, almost like a turtle about to hide its head within the shell. Every quill on its body was fully erect, yellow-white spikes with black tips clearly visible within the short mat of underfur. Using its stiffened front feet as an axis, the porcupine met each rush made by its attacker by kicking sideways with its back legs, always presenting its rear to the enemy, a defense unique in a world where all animals at bay invariably face an attacker, but one that is nonetheless effective in view of the powerful, well-armed tail.

The fox was intent on breaking through this defense, hoping to reach the unprotected nose, grasp it firmly, and shake vigorously, breaking the neck of its victim so that it could turn the body upside down and rip into the unprotected belly. Circling, feinting, actually jumping into the air on occasion, the fox tried time and again to get at the tempting nose, but the rodent blocked every attempt with a fast, jerky turn of its body that forced the fox to swerve aside or to back up hurriedly. There was no means of knowing how long the two had been maneuvering in this manner before our arrival, but it was clear that at this point the protagonists were at an impasse.

The fox had evidently surprised the porcupine while it was walking on open ground, too far from a tree to allow it to scrambe to safety, and because its best speed is only a little faster than the pace of a man walking briskly, the rodent had no choice but to meet its attacker. Normally the outcome of such a contest depends on which one of the two tires first. If it is the attacker, it simply walks away. If it is the porcupine, it becomes slow, makes mistakes, and dies.

Yukon caused the fight to end in a draw when he became impatient, lunged hard at the lead, and yelped excitedly. The startled fox didn't bother to glance our way as it wheeled about and streaked for the forest. The bewildered porcupine waddled as fast as it could go to the shelter of the tree, then climbed the poplar with more speed and agility than it had displayed on the ground.

I was tempted to shoot the animal out of its perch to give Yukon an opportunity to know that it was dangerous, even in death, by allowing him the sniff the carcass and most likely impale himself on a quill or two. But I relented, sorry for the creature, feeling it had earned itself a respite. And for all I knew, Yukon might well have already gained experience of the species, but I would have liked to be sure of this all the same.

At the end of that day, with all the traps distributed, hardware supplies ready near the site of the cabin, and a dozen more logs cut and peeled for the building's construction, Yukon and I set out for home, returning through a section of forest dominated by tall and closely packed cedars where the ground was for the most part covered by a thick carpet of bright green moss. It was about three in the afternoon when we entered this forest; the light was fading, the skies filled with a cover of sullen clouds that advertised snow.

I chose this route for two reasons. Although the going was less comfortable because of the labyrinthine quality of the forest, it was more direct and would shave a good half hour off our journey. In addition, my depleted meat supply had warned me that morning that I must soon devote time to hunting; the area of cedars ought to turn up a moose.

As we traveled, I kept a sharp lookout for sign, but it was Yukon who led me to several places where deer had bedded down the night before, leaving on the ground clusters of bean-sized droppings. I was not averse to venison meat, but it was moose that I *really* wanted, for one good-sized animal would keep the larder stocked for the winter.

Not a trace did we find during the two hours we walked the forest, and by the time we got home that evening I knew I must scout further afield, in among the spruces and beaver ponds, where the animals were sure to be, but from where the job of packing home between six hundred and eight hundred pounds of meat would be made harder because of distance. The reason I was looking forward to the snow was the opportunity to use sled and dogs to haul back meat.

By early December I was worried. The small line cabin was completed by then, half the traps were set, and I had sold the cow, realizing that with the work ahead of me there would be little time to spend on an animal that must be milked twice a day and that demanded a good deal of attention if it was to be properly cared for. But I had not yet managed to shoot a moose. The hunting season had closed a week earlier, yet this was not a matter of great concern; most of us in those days and in that region "bent" the law several times each fall and winter, harvesting "tamarack beef," as we referred to the moose, if not with the cooperation, at least with the tolerance, of the game wardens. In fact, hardly any of us hunted during the open season when trigger-happy fools were prowling the bush country shooting on sound, spraying indiscriminate bullets without regard for their own safety or the safety of others.

The country was big, and the invading nimrods were not nearly so numerous as they are today, yet the deep forest was dangerous in the legal hunting season, and it was shunned by all of us. Instead, we confined our activities to those parts of the wilderness that were close to home and, therefore, relatively safe.

We all purchased an annual license. This legally entitled us to one moose; but between September and January we usually counted on at least one extra animal, depending on our needs. I have always held the law in great respect, and still do, but in that particular regard I felt that the legalities of the hunting season were unjust. Those of us who lived in the backwoods had need of the meat, in some cases urgent need. Money was short, stores were few and far between, roads were bad all year around, but particularly treacherous in winter when the mercury dropped to between thirty-five and forty-five degrees below zero Celsius. Hardships were many, starvation for some was an ever-present threat, but these things were endured cheerfully and willingly by a people made hardy by their constant struggle with the land. Yet annually, this same land was invaded by those who hunted for sport, who could at any time buy fresh beef from the butcher at prices that none of us could afford, who often shot moose or deer and let the animal lie to rot because the antlers were not "trophy" size. Every time we found such evidence we became angrier and felt, rightly or wrongly, that our government was selling us out, that if the authorities could allow such indiscriminate butchery and lable it sport, we could take what meat we needed, license or no.

In any event, as the weather became colder and the snow refused to fall that winter, the moose retreated into their hiding places, there to shelter from the biting cold while leaving hardly any tracks on the frozen ground. Day after day I set out at first light carrying rifle, Thermos, and sandwiches, alone now because Yukon would have been too much of a hindrance— or so I thought then—only to return at dusk empty-handed and dispirited and to sit down to a dish of beans laced with a meager amount of bacon, for what was left of September's moose was needed for the dogs. It was not the lack of hunting success that bothered me; I knew that sooner or later I would line the rifles sights on a moose. It was a question of time. There was the trapline to run, and in August I had secured a contract to cut and deliver fifty cords of spruce pulpwood to a mill some seventy miles to the south; deadline for the total amount was set for January 31, less than two months away, and it was a company rule that deadlines must be met or future contracts would not be granted to the defaulter. Since this was the only source of "grocery money" during the winter, I wasn't anxious to fall down on the job. And still the snow kept away.

The calm before the storm is not a cliché in the north. Usually snow arrives in stealth and in the dead of night, bringing as a companion the big cold. At one moment it seems that the usual background sounds of the wilderness are present; at the next, the land becomes utterly still, yet the calm has not arrived suddenly. It is hindsight that creates the impression of sudden stillness, for the human mind has retained its primeval ability to tune out constant, familiar sounds and is more apt to notice their absence than their presence, though it takes an indeterminate amount of time before the total cessation of these accustomed noises registers on the conscious part of the brain.

Little by little the breeze loses momentum, and the cold increases its grip, and the animals, still magnificently primitive and sensitive, notice the change of tempo and respond to it, gradually quieting the slight noises that even they must make as they move. By the time that the full calm settles over the wilderness it is as though all life had vanished from the surface of the land, leaving only the silently moving aurora that reflects itself endlessly on each particle of frost and creates uncountable, tiny "frost stars" that would seem to duplicate in miniature the incessant glitter of the Milky Way. And the mercury keeps dropping.

The calm arrived sometime between the supper hour and bedtime at the end of that first week of abortive hunting. Just before sitting down to my dull supper, I went outside to bring in some logs for the fire. The night was as I had last seen it; the mercury reading was twenty degrees below zero Celsius. After supper I washed up and sat beside the heater with a book for a couple of hours, then got up to go out for more logs, first intending to have a visit with the dogs and settle them down for the night; this was expected of me, it had become routine.

The change of temperature struck me as soon as I opened the door. When I walked out on the porch, I felt the intense stillness and saw the blue-green lights creeping and pulsing and rippling in a firmament peppered with bright stars and backdropped by a blue-black veil. I watched the spectacle for some moments, never tiring of the display of the northern lights; then when Yukon howled and set the other dogs to singing, his way of letting me know that he knew I was out of the house and thus should be calling to pay my respects, I paused only long enough to look at the thermometer and to note that the mercury had now fallen to forty-six degrees below zero, which, for those still accustomed to Fahrenheit readings, is fifty-one degrees below zero.

I almost didn't believe the thermometer; it seemed

so *uncold* (one can never say "warm" when describing a night of northern winter), until the heat that I had brought with me from the house, which at first clung to my garments, became dissipated, causing the legs of my pants to feel like ice. I hurried to the barn, worrying about the dogs and the chickens, needlessly, as it turned out. The hen coop was small and well insulated with hay, the birds were huddled together on their roost, keeping each other warm. On the other side of the barn, despite the fact that I had forked in a number of big piles of hay for the dogs, only Sussie was curled up in one of these; the others were lying on the bare boards, except Yukon, of course. He was waiting for me at the door, and I had to restrain his enthusiasm until I hung the lantern on its accustomed nail, out of harm's way. Then I was mobbed and during the few minutes of canine affection, I was pleased to note that each animal felt warm. In a little while I untangled myself from the press, intending to go home, but instead, I decided to take them all for a good, brisk walk. It was not really a night for wandering the wildwoods, but leading the dogs, I returned to the house, dressed in my warmest clothes, and we all trooped out into the brilliant night.

At first only the cold made itself felt, nipping like some sharp-toothed microscopic animal at the exposed skin of forehead, nose, and cheeks, invading the nostrils with each inhalation and turning into ice the breath moisture that adhered to the nasal hairs, until warm air from the lungs was exhaled and thawed the ice, and things were normal until the next intake of air formed new crystals that were as quickly melted by the next exhaust. The mind noted automatically this freeze-thaw cycle, but mostly it became occupied with the flashing aurora and with the great noises that our feet were making on the frozen ground as we crushed the stiffened grasses and shrubs and caused them to squeak and groan under the impact of our feet. The outing was brief and contained within the boundaries of the clearing, but we all enjoyed it; the dogs played their usual games of tag amid much ritualistic wetting by the males, while I stood and took in the incredibly beautiful skies, becoming so mesmerized that for a while I felt as though I were standing in a colorful vacuum; it gave me a sense of disembodiment, as though the mind had somehow issued alone into the wilderness night.

The sharp, loud crack of a splitting branch, like a rifle shot repeating itself endlessly as it echoed over the wilderness, was so startling that I felt myself jump. The dogs, too, stopped in their tracks, ears pricked forward as they tried to determine the direction from which the noise came. We all had experienced this sound before, and I had actually been watching one branch of a deadfall tree when it split under the pressure of ice; but those outbursts had been like the popping of a cap pistol compared to the robust crack that rang over the forest that night. I stood unmoving for some minutes as the dogs resumed their play, but when the cold began to cut cruelly into my body, I called the dogs and led them back to the barn.

Keewatin came that night and brought rising temperatures and drove endless, fat snowflakes before him. *Keewatin,* the north wind of the Cree, spawns the blizzard and may blow for four or five days without cessation, piling snow on top of snow, packing it into every nook and cranny of the forest, even into its very heart, where the spruces and the cedars press close together and try with their branches to stop the whirling flakes from settling at their skirts, places reserved for the wild ones that must endure the storm curled up under the low-trailing boughs, there to stay until *Keewatin* loses his anger and retreats whence he has come.

When I got up next morning, the temperature was up to ten degrees below zero, but I had to go outside to look at it because the snow was compacted against the windows. As I stood in the doorway of the porch and looked across the clearing, my eyes could not penetrate the wall of moving white that lay between the house and the forest, a distance of three hundred paces. Never had I imagined such snow! The whole world seemed to be wrapped in white. After hurrying to the barn, I fed the chickens, then led the dogs out and took them to the house for breakfast, a treat for them that I was given slight cause to regret.

All was well while they were eating, but as soon as the last one had done, this being Yukon, of course, their energies uncoiled like the sudden release of a tight spring, and they dashed wildly through the entire house, upstairs as well as downstairs, now and then mobbing me and trying to initiate a game as I was attempting to cook some bacon and three eggs. In the end I had to return them to the barn before I could sit down to my own food.

The blizzard continued for two days with hardly a pause in the strength of the wind and no letup of snow. The flakes kept coming down at a slant, but were blown upward instantly, creating a storm within a storm, making dancing wind devils such as I had last seen during desert sandstorms. Twice I went outside after giving the dogs their morning feed, each time I returned before I had made it more than halfway across the clearing, fleeing to the shelter of the house almost blind and on the threshold of fear lest I became turned around and lost only yards from home, a very real possibility. After the second try, I gave up, there being no point in it anyway, and contented myself with watching through the window every now and then while lazing beside the cherry red stove, reading Thoreau's *Walden,* picking out particular passages to suit the mood of the day.

In late afternoon of the second day the force of *Keewatin* slackened; by evening the wind had blown itself out, leaving behind a snowy rear guard that continued to drape itself atop the fresh mounds until sometime after midnight, when it stopped snowing. I went to bed; but my sleep was restless, and I awoke at first light and got dressed and went outside without even bothering to make coffee. The snowshoes were hanging in the porch, where they had been since last March; I put them on.

Now the walking was silent, the webs sinking four

or five inches into snow that was two feet deep. But the forest was a place of sounds again. The nasal, shrill call of a pileated woodpecker issued from the mixed woods where I had set my first rabbit snares; presently I spotted the great cock of the north as it flew with its jerky wing-folding movement across the small clearing to disappear into the spruces. Chickadees were busy everywhere, twittering softly as they searched for dormant insects after spending two foodless days huddled on some sheltered perch.

A soft breeze tousled the tops of the trees, dislodging cascades of snow that came rattling and hissing down as each crystal encountered intervening branches. Soon the sun rose full over the trees, and the wilderness was bathed in golden light. Content, I retraced my route, spent some time tramping down a good trail between barn and house, my marching accompanied by the howls of the dogs, who wanted to be free to join me; then I got their breakfasts ready. While they were eating, the hens were fed, three eggs, frozen, alas, were collected, and I went back to the house to cook my own food. An hour later I was off, rifle hanging from the shoulder, in quest of moose and followed by a chorus of reproachful howls.

I do not enjoy killing, and today I don't hunt, haven't done so, in fact, for many years, not since I found myself able to afford to buy meat that was killed and butchered by someone else, by proxy, as it were. It isn't a question of morals so much as a question of distaste. Killing is such a barbarous, bloody business, an essentially ugly act now that man had learned to walk upright and has perfected the ability to appreciate beauty and to become aware that life is a precious thing. Yet man must eat, and he has never lost his appetite for meat, so the need results in killing and the argument against the taking of life breaks down, becomes sophistry, unless, of course, one is prepared to live on a purely vegetarian diet. So I am a contradiction, a being prepared to eat meat if it is decently slaughtered for me by someone else, prepared to go out and slaughter my own if I really must; but I don't like killing. I don't think it is a good sport. I don't even think it is sporting in any way, shape, or form, not while the quarry is unable to shoot back! Yet I recognize that there is the need in some men to go out and seek to kill an animal once a year, and I respect those who do so *well,* who take pride in exercising efficiently the oldest profession in the world.

For these reasons, when I hunted, I made myself become very single-minded. There was no room in my head then for the aesthetics of the wild; the mind was locked against the intrusion of beauty and forced to concentrate solely on the task at hand: the tracking; the stalking; the testing of wind; the detours needed to outflank the quarry; the wit to outthink an animal and beat it at its own game. None of these things are easy, and if the beginning hunter is not favored by luck, his chances of success are slim. I was not a beginner, having hunted long before I left Europe, though the quarry had been different; it could shoot back. So in the forests of Canada I made myself hunt again in cold blood, and I was usually successful, in time.

I was successful that day, but six hours were to pass between the sighting of fresh moose tracks and the final squeezing of the trigger. It took another hour before the animal was slit open and its entrails were removed, and more time was spent kindling a fire on top of the pile of steaming guts so they would not release their parasites into the systems of the scavengers. And when all things were done and the carcass had been hoisted off the ground with a light set of tackle brought for the purpose, so the blood could drain and the small hungry ones couldn't nibble at the meat, there followed a two-hour tramp home, a footrace against darkness, after which the dogs were hitched to the sled, with Yukon at the head of the team for the first time.

A wild and silent journey ensued. I stood on the ends of the runners, feeling the wind slice into my face, seeing the stream issuing from the mouths of the dogs, listening to the whisper of the runners as they slid over the compacted snow of my return trail. Can there be a more exhilarating experience?

It was full dark when we got home with more than six hundred pounds of meat, a big hide, and a grotesque head from which the antlers had been shed. Everything but the dangerous guts was carried back, feed in plenty for all of us.

We dined regally that night, the dogs and I. The got a great helping of cooked liver, lungs, and heart mixed with a double handful of chow; I sat down to a huge, tender steak of tamarack beef, fully at ease with my conscience.

Chapter 5

The western horizon was the dark purple of an old bruise. The forest below the tree line was an amorphous black mass overpainted by the white traceries of the snow that patterned the unseen trunks and branches; protruding above this somber bulk, the crowns of the spruces and poplars were visible as charcoal sketches executed on purpureal parchment, while in the east an aquamarine sky flushed gently, a peach bloom suffusing its landward edge. It was dawn, more or less, but the breaking day was struggling against an invisible cover of heavy cloud that forbade the morning star from welcoming the first faint streaks of crepuscular light.

It was the last day of the old year, and as I stood outside the doorway scanning the forest for the first time since the previous day, the depression I felt on rising in the cold darkness of the bedroom vanished almost at once, for no matter its mood, the wilderness is nearly always able to tranquilize my mind. Not far from the house a great horned owl hooted several times in quick succession, was silent, hooted again, and was heard no more. From the barn came the sounds of the dogs, movement, scratchings, some soft whining; they knew I was up and about. A few birds chirped softly from various points in the neighborhood, sleepy notes uttered halfheartedly, as if the early ones felt impelled to acknowledge the sluggish sunrise but would have preferred to ignore it. Mostly, though, the land was wrapped in the preday silence.

For several months now it had become my habit to spend a few minutes each morning in contemplation of the wilderness, a sort of pantheistic communion during which I tried to absorb the mood, the *feel,* of the land while noting its appearance. Everybody, it seems to me, begins each new day in some personally characteristic fashion; the devout may say their prayers on rising or attend early mass; some live inside their own heads for a while, morose and uncompanionable; others rise late and rush at today as if to beat it into submission. For myself, I need a little time for inner contemplation, a few moments of peace and quiet during which the chimeras that come with sleep are chased back into their subconscious hiding places. After this, I am ready to face the day.

On that December 31 I awoke to the ringing of the alarm at 4:45 in the morning to discover at once that the heater had gone out during the night. The outside temperature was twenty-five degrees below zero; the room temperature was ten degrees warmer. This is not a good way to wake up. Later, after the fire was going anew, I went out to get water from the well; the rope broke in the pulley, and the pail plunged into the cistern twenty feet below. It took fifteen minutes to fish it up again with a big three-gang hook, and during this time the cold crept through clothing and skin and flesh almost to the very bones. Depression set in, the temptation to return to bed and stay there was well-nigh irresistible. Hot coffee helped a little, at least it dispelled the sloth, and last night's decision to cut one more cord of pulpwood before the end of the year enlisted my sense of duty and kept me on my feet, albeit in a gloomy frame of mind. But now, as I took in the wild world that spread itself before me, the lure of the forest, the magic that filled the eastern sky, the promise of one more day of life surrounded by the things of nature crept into my consciousness and restored my equanimity.

Work had been divided between logging and trapping, both full-time occupations if done properly, but the night before, when I added up the result of my cutting operations, it became obvious that I was going to have to pull the traps and devote a month to logging if I was to meet the January deadline. So I decided that I would cut one more cord on December 31, spend New Year's Day pulling the traps, then concentrate on the pulpwood until my quota was reached.

The cutting site was four miles from the home clearing; I usually walked to it, not only because I enjoyed the hour's stroll through the forest, but, more particularly, because I felt it was unfair to hitch the team to the sled solely for the purpose of transporting me over such a short distance and then to keep the dogs tied up all day while I worked. If there was a load to be carried or if, as happened often enough, there was a stack of dry firewood to haul home, deadwood salvaged during my work, the dogs came along; otherwise, they were better off loose in the barn.

When my contemplative time was over that morning, I went indoors for breakfast, prepared midday sandwiches and coffee, and took a light morning meal to the dogs, a snack they soon disposed of. This was followed by ten minutes spent fondling and playing with the team, devoting special attention to Yukon in case he took it into his head that one of the other males was getting more than his share of my attention. I quickly learned that the big leader would not tolerate this, meeting swift punishment to those of his subordinates that dared abuse their privileges, but by now it was the *feelings* of Rocky and Sooner that were hurt, rather than their bodies. Yukon no longer needed to become savage with these two; a growl, a curling of the lips to reveal the gleaming predatory teeth, and a push or two with his great chest were sufficient to cow thoroughly his two underlings. Despite this, I felt guilty whenever one or the other of the males was disciplined because of my intrusion into the pack hierarchy, and at first I would become angry with Yukon, judging his behavior by human standards, thinking that he was wrong—greedy, if you will—in always seeking the most and the best for himself.

On reflection, however, I realized that the disciplines imposed by the pack leader, while nakedly feral, were as important to the well-being of the group as the disciplines imposed by our own species are important to societies.

Human leaders do not physically and personally enforce societal laws, but they do have the power to punish, using specially hired enforcers to uphold the rules of their "packs." This is leadership by proxy. In contrast, wolves and dogs must do their own dirty work.

From this perspective, it seemed to me that the canine way was fair, effective, and good for all, and that provided I learned the pack rules and did not interfere, peace would reign under Yukon's benevolent dictatorship.

The skies had lightened somewhat when I set out on snowshoes, pursued by the cacophonous howls of the dogs. I was dressed warmly, as usual, on my head a woolen toque and on my back the ubiquitous pack containing lunch and coffee. Visibility was reasonably good in the open, but once I was inside the forrest, the world was toned a somber gray in the shadow places and a glaring white wherever the snow lay.

It is not usually necessary to wear snowshoes when one walks an often-used wilderness trail because the compacted snow freezes hard and will take weight as easily as asphalt pavement, but the evening before a strong wind had risen in the west and the crystalline snow drifted before it, in some places leaving "dunes" several feet high. From past experience I knew the trail would be filled in again wherever it was exposed to the west and would have to be tramped anew so as to ensure good footing for the dogs as well as for me.

Snowshoes are excellent aids when one travels through deep snow, but they don't compare to well-maintained winter trail, especially when one drives dogs through the forest. Without firm footing most dogs will soon tire from the exertions of lunging out of chest-deep snow while pulling the sled; it is for this reason that the driver must trot ahead of the team to break trail with the snowshoes.

It wasn't long before I found myself silently cursing the trail *and* the snowshoes. The wind had driven the snow in a capricious manner, in places leaving the pathway clear, in others filling it completely, making the walking erratic and difficult. Tramping the soft snow, the webs behaved as they were supposed to do, but on the bare trail they acted like wooden boards, became encumbrances that slowed me down. Yet it was too much trouble to take them off between drifts and almost as bad to step out of the trail into the bush, where the snow was deep and soft and right for snowshoeing, but where brush and deadfalls impeded the way, forcing me to make detours around the obstacles.

I reached the logging site half an hour late, bathed in perspiration and already regretting the decision to work this day. It was now as light as it was going to get, the sun being totally concealed by the overcast, but I didn't think it was going to snow. There was no wind, the temperature was rising, and the clouds didn't carry the leaden look that usually forecasts a snowfall.

For two hours I worked methodically, getting nicely into stride and feeling pleased with my accomplishments, but "pride goeth before destruction and an haughty spirit before a fall!" I swung the ax to notch a spruce preparatory to cutting it down. The blade flicked against a nearby branch and deflected the stroke, and instead of biting into the wood with the steel, I hit the trunk with the handle, about four inches behind the axhead, snapping the hardwood as though it were a carrot. Not to worry, I soliloquized, it was for such unforeseen accidents that I always carried a spare, but then I remembered that the extra ax was not here, it was at home, taken there several days ago for sharpening and left behind, forgotten until now. I should have called it quits right then, but I'd become stubborn.

By alternately running and walking, I made it back to the homestead in three-quarters of an hour, lost little time in getting the spare ax, harnessing the team to the sled, and setting off anew.

The dogs were well rested, impatient to get going, and as mettlesome as thoroughbreds at the starting gate; even Sooner was eager to run, but whether this was because he felt personally good or because of Yukon's influence and discipline, I was not to know. Standing on the ends of the runners, I let Yukon set the pace, watching as the dogs got into stride, working up to that fluid, mile-consuming gallop that whisks the sled atop the hard snow and that is accompanied by the *shishing* of the runners, the scrunching sound of broad pads, and the breathing of each dog. I enjoyed the experience, as I always do, and my irritation vanished. When the journey ended fifteen minutes later at the logging site, I was disappointed that it was over so soon; so were the dogs. They hadn't really warmed up yet and were still raring to go.

Determined to make up for lost time, I drank a fast cup of coffee, skipped lunch, and attacked the job vigorously, hoping that I would manage to cut a full cord before dusk.

Now and then I looked at the dogs; patient as ever, they were curled up in the snow, their leads slack, their bushy tails arranged so that each black nose was covered. Soon I became engrossed with my work, and I lost track of time. I became almost an automaton, axing, sawing, limbing, and cutting up each tree, then piling the logs and beginning anew.

During late afternoon a brisk wind came up, knifing through the trees and driving a sleety snow before it; it drew itself to my attention, but I dismissed it in my eagerness to tackle a new stand of timber that was somewhat deeper in the bush, where the trees were tall and of good girth. There wasn't much cutting time left, I knew, but these spruces promised four logs per tree and would probably allow me to make up for lost time if I kept going for another hour, when it would be too dark to work but light enough for the return journey. Glancing once at the dogs, who were about seventy-five yards away and visible through the evergreens, and noting that they appeared as content as circumstances would allow them to be, I went back to work, once again becoming oblivious of all but the job at hand.

I don't know how long it was before Yukon drew my attention to the storm by yelping at me loudly, the kind of high-pitched intense cry he reserved for matters of note. Pausing in the act of limbing a newly felled spruce, I looked up to see him lunging at his lead and gazing my way with ears and tail at "half-mast," an attitude denoting distress. The other dogs were getting to their feet, watching their leader and signaling their own uneasiness in the same fashion. I took these things in at a glance; but before I had time to wonder about the cause of their restlessness, the driven snow struck my face with the sting of ground glass, and even as I swiveled my body to shield my cheeks and to wipe the moisture from my streaming eyes, I knew I was witnessing the birth of a blizzard. Yukon, more experienced in such matters, had become aware of the storm before I did, drawing my attention to it.

It didn't then occur to me that we were in danger. Even if conditions were such that they doubled our return time, we could still get back in about half an hour, I reasoned; besides, the snow was light, and the dogs would be more than eager to run at top speed, knowing that the sooner they returned, the quicker they would get their supper. In any event, I thought, as I started to get ready to leave, most of the way back was through thick evergreens that would shelter us even if the blizzard became intense.

As soon as I had turned the sled around, facing it

101

toward home, Yukon began to dance, anxious to get going. By the time that Sooner, Rocky, and Sussie were hitched, the big dog was almost frantic to take his place in lead. I paid little attention to his behavior because he was always anxious to travel, and I assumed that after lying curled up for so long, and being, as he always was, ravenously hungry, he simply wanted to get going.

On the afternoon of the storm, more for the sake of insurance than for reasons of apprehension, I decided to pack all my gear on the sled after the dogs were harnessed; ax and saw were lashed down, the packsack that contained my uneaten lunch was tied to one of the handle supports, and a square of canvas, used to cover the tools when they were left at the cutting site, was folded on the sled bottom. It didn't take long to do these things, but before I was ready to set out, the blizzard literally enveloped us.

The wind, which had been blowing strongly hitherto, increased suddenly, bringing great dancing flakes, driving them at an impossible angle through a forest that was now cloaked in a moving white shroud. It seemed unbelievable that wind and snow could combine so quickly to obliterate almost totally the outlines of the trees, even those that were only a few yards away. And the blizzard was getting steadily worse; before I managed to untie the rope that anchored the sled to a standing tree, I knew the trail would soon be filled in completely. Instead of riding the runners as first planned, I was going to have to go ahead of the dogs and break trail.

I hurried; as a result, I fumbled as I tied Yukon to my waist with the lead rope. No more than a few extra seconds could have been squandered in this way, but my anxiety over the delay rose out of all proportion to the loss of time. Preoccupied as I was, the sound of the wind as it passed through the crowns of the trees was yet able to attract attention, a sort of hollow moaning combined with an eerie screeching, a fugue, composed and rendered by the evergreens.

In the particular section of the forest in which I was

then logging, only one species of tree grew, typical northland black spruce (*Picea mariana*), miles of them, which topped a rugged muskeg bottom that was almost impassable during the wet season. Get in there after breakup, and one must tread with care to avoid plunging waist-deep, or deeper, into the soupy bottom. Muskeg is a sort of giant compost manufactured by nature during hundreds, even thousands, of years, an organic sponge that will support the trees only because their roots extend deeply into the muck and are spread over a wide area. It is treacherous underfoot unless man or animal knows the high places, such as rock ridges and pockets of clay soil that offer firm footing. Between the springtime and the autumnal freeze-up, a traveler moving through unfamiliar muskeg needs a long pole with which to test the bottom in doubtful places. I have done this many times, and it is no exaggeration to say that I have found areas where a ten-foot pole could be thrust down completely out of sight with hardly any effort. I know of one spot where a large bulldozer was forever buried in the muck of ages after it broke through the ice crust one January. The driver escaped, but the machine was sucked out of sight before a second crawler could be brought up to pull it out. By midsummer the sun has drawn off a fair amount of surface moisture, and though the bog is still treacherous in places, a damp, moss-topped, spongy mat six or eight inches thick will support a man's weight if he treads lightly.

In such forests the spruce trees range across the upper half of North America from coast to coast, following an irregular line that dips as far south as latitude 45 and as far north as the Arctic Circle, in some places even beyond it.

In the far north, especially in the barrens, this spruce is a runty, twisted tree no more than a few feet tall and perhaps several hundred years old. Even on the best of ranges the slow-growing *Picea mariana* does not often exceed fifty feet in height and an average diameter of ten inches, although on especially favored sites it grows to be one hundred feet tall and reaches three feet in diameter.

Black spruce habitat varies considerably. The tree is rugged, capable of growing in almost any kind of soil offered by its range. In the southeast it is found for the most part in muskeg bogs and on the margins of swamps, but in the northwest it more frequently grows on stony slopes, on the sides of hills, and up in the mountains as high as any tree can grow. Where it exists in pure stands, competition between each spruce is fierce. Such forests are labyrinthine. The trees stand close together, their tops, characteristically conical and green, peppered with verdant-brown clusters of cones. Each crown is dense and thick and presses against its neighbors, putting a roof over the land through which the sunlight cannot penetrate to the forest floor. As a result, the lower branches cannot synthesize sun energy and die off, leaving each straight scaly-barked trunk studded with dry, brittle branchlets. On the ground, or that which passes for it, luxuriant sphagnum moss forms a thick evergreen carpet littered with old spruce needles in various stages of decomposition, intermingling their tea brown color with the sparse, stunted shrubs such as cranberry viburnum and northern honeysuckle and with a wide variety of fungi that impart delicate hues to the penumbral landscape.

The winter snow smothers practically all of the ground cover, allowing only the leafless branches of the shrubs and creepers to poke out of the white, while the upper story is festooned with varying amounts of very dry snow that even during sunny days continues to cascade downward, hissing and pattering through the branches, now falling as fine, glittering mist, as suddenly dropping in miniature avalanches that encounter the bottomland with an audible thump.

It is never difficult for an inexperienced woodsman to get turned around in these forests on dull summer days, although in winter it is easy enough to return home following one's back trail. In some parts of the forest, well-defined game trails will guide the traveler, but these can't be relied on. Animals usually follow the easiest course, keeping to more or less regular pathways that generations of hooves and pads have fashioned along the ridges and over the firm ground, but all too often the bottom is so boggy over such a wide range that even the inhabitants of the forest must make long detours, picking their way as best they can and often covering a mile or more to reach a goal that may be only five hundred yards away in a straight line from the point of detour.

When the muskeg freezes, the entire forest floor offers good, firm footing, but in some years an early and heavy fall of snow insulates the understory before the frost has had a chance to penetrate the mulch. The frost came early in 1955, and by the time I started logging it was a simple matter to make a good, firm road into the cutting site, tramping the snow and cutting out any trees and shrubs that would have stood in the way of the sled.

Travel through the black spruces in winter is an aesthetic, exciting experience. The land is quietly majestic; its rhythms can be felt with every sense. The tangy perfume of the evergreens, the small sharp sounds, the crisp, tricolor beauty, and the intense cold —all are individually noted; each adds a quota of atmosphere to a world that is still primordial and undefiled. Any but the most insensitive must soon come to realize that this wilderness has existed thus since its rebirth after the last ice age, that it is vibrant and self-perpetuating.

Yet it must not be supposed that one goes marching over the frozen muskeg consciously formulating thoughts of this kind. Nevertheless, the part of the mind that is responsive to atmosphere retains the feel of these things and manages to pass them upward into the cortex at certain intervals, sometimes long after the experience.

I was definitely not thinking about the aesthetics of the wilderness on that afternoon of December 31. To the contrary! When I finally realized that missing the New Year's party was of no significance compared to the problems that could result if I missed my way, I began to worry.

Dusk was descending quickly, the blanketing snow adding to the murk; by the time we left the small clearing I had chopped out of the forest, the pathway home was already indistinct. If this was not enough, Yukon was acting up, pulling away to the left, jerking the line around my waist, and throwing me off stride. I thought he was being willful because he had been made to wait his turn during the hitching of the dogs, and I was losing patience with him; I had enough to worry about already without his nonsense.

Like the animals of the forest, I had followed the easiest course when I made the trail from home to logging strip; the result was that it traveled in a south-westerly direction for about a mile before it veered due south on a line with the homestead. Now I was to pay for my sloth; we had to move directly into the teeth of the blizzard, and the trail was already full of new snow that was piled in undulating mounds, like the sands of the Sahara.

Traveling head-on into a howling gale, pelted by excoriating snow, and moving over scalloped drifts within a forest suddenly become tenebrous, make heavy demands upon the body and the mind of a man; it is an experience that must be actually endured before it can be fully understood; the writing of it can explain events only in separate order and not in simultaneous multiples as they actually occurred.

The snow rasps the exposed parts of the face and bruises the eyes, making the tears flow, blowing them sideways and downward, congealing them. The wind finds its way into the parka hood, ballooning it, exposing the ears and other features to the knifing cold, pushing the breath back down the throat. The feet and legs are continuously jolted by the uneven snow surface, and these jerks are transmitted to the rest of the body.

While part of the mind tries to deal with the physical, another part dwells on fear, fanning the imagination until the bowels churn and the mouth becomes dry and sour; and while these things are going on simultaneously, the eolian scream of the storm inflames all the senses, turning sound into a force capable of assaulting every nerve in the body.

Within minutes of starting I had to stop to rip my handkerchief into three strips that, knotted together, were fastened around the parka hood, under the chin, to protect myself from the wind. As I tied this improvised bandanna, my back was turned to the storm. I looked at the dogs. They were burred white, crusted by snow that had been melted by their body heat and then covered by new particles that turned to ice, giving them a pebbled look. After the sled stopped, they had lain down, averting their faces from the blizzard's punch, but they were quick to jump up again when it was time to go on.

A while later I found myself sobbing for breath; my body was clammy-cold in places and uncomfortably hot in others. The last of the light had vanished.

I had made up my mind to stop for a rest, but at that moment we came to a bend in the trail that I could not recall; negotiating this, we were brought to an abrupt halt by a tangle of deadfall timber that arose out of the gloom like some monstrous, long-legged spider. Even in the darkness it was impossible not to see that this untidy barrier had been there a long time. I was lost. Somehow we had passed the proper trail, turning, instead, onto a wide game track that now ended, broken up into several thin pathways that sidestepped the deadfall. My stomach turned spastic; my heart beat alarmingly. How had I missed the way so soon? Where? It was impossible to think clearly. Then I had this great urge to rush blindly ahead, to beat the bushes in frenzy until I found the lost pathway.

Time becomes meaningless when panic inflames the mind and befuddles reason. I remember getting the irrational feeling that I had always stood in that cold, shrieking vortex, that everything else in my life had been a dream. Warmth, comfort, security— I had never really experienced any of these things; they were figments. The storm and the darkness and the phantom trees and the cold and the fear were the ghastly realities.

Panic is difficult to subdue; it washes over the brain like some great cold wave. I stood there witless and fearful for an indeterminate time. Then Yukon was beside me, his big head was pressed against my thigh, and he nudged me several times in quick succession. How can I explain the sudden surge of relief, of gratitude, that filled me when that wonderful dog came to tell me that I was not alone? All I can say is that he gave me heart, that in some mysterious fashion he was able to instill in me a bit of his own courage. I know that he sensed my fear; he was always able to read my emotions. Now, in his way, but most clearly, he was offering his companionship. I went down on my haunches and put my arms around him and hugged him, resting my head on his ice-filled shoulder. Who knows how long we remained there? Not I! But I do know that Yukon helped me regain my reason.

There are some who may say that I am being anthropomorphic, that I am "humanizing" the dog. I submit that I am doing the absolute reverse. I am "animalizing" myself. I was, indeed, a pack animal at that moment, a primitive creature with a mind tortured by adversity; according to his own lights, Yukon saw himself as my near equal. I was the Alpha male of the pack, he was the Beta, my good right hand. Now that his leader was in trouble, he just naturally came to help, for that is the way of the wolf.

In any event, with reason returned as an ally, I felt reassurance. The biggest danger was the cold; I *could* freeze to death if I wasn't careful, but if I stayed calm, and with Yukon's help, things would turn out all right. I was warmly dressed, had plenty of matches, and there was an abundance of firewood all around me. The dogs and I might have to spend a restless and uncomfortable night huddled together in front of a fire, then, in daylight, we would find our way back home. "But what if the blizzard lasts for days?" whispered a small mind voice.

This last thought put a timely end to the melodrama I had been consciously rehearsing. I'd had a big fright, and I still had to keep the lid on my emotions, but I couldn't expect to improve matters by indulging in dime-novel sensation. I was worried, of course, and my heart pounded more vigorously than normal, but thanks to Yukon, the grip of panic was broken and confidence returned.

We had to go back; our only hope of getting out of the mess was to retrace our route and return to the logging site, from where I could start over. But first the sled had to be turned in the narrow trail. I unhitched the dogs as a team, unfastening the traces at the sled, then tying the two loose ends to a tree. Working as quickly as possible, but severely hindered by the storm, I manhandled the sled around and over obstructions until it faced in the direction we had come from. As soon as the dogs were hitched again, we set off. Now, however, I didn't trot; even if I had wanted to run, it would have been unsafe to do so because it was too dark to see properly; but more important, by going slowly ahead of the team, I would stand a better chance of picking up our old trail.

About an hour later I was still hopelessly lost. At first I had been able to discern our old tracks, but as it became darker and darker, my only guides were the vague outlines of the trees, which seemed to be pressing closer together, and the pallid snow cover that not even the pitch dark could entirely conceal. I stopped often, sometimes tying Yukon to a tree while I went ahead to reconnoiter, but if there were any tracks along the way, the snow had hidden them. When we resumed our journey, it was necessary to go even more slowly and to peer intently at the whitened ground, continuing to halt often. And I would bend down and feel with unmittened hand, trying to detect the hard ridges left by the sled runners under the newly drifted snow.

There was one small blessing. Because we were no longer traveling on a westward course, the snow and wind were at our backs; on the other hand, this meant that we were moving in the wrong direction.

The blizzard continued unabated as we slogged onward in the darkness, while I did my best to pick a route through the more open places, which showed as white slashes against the indistinct outlines of the trees.

Yukon continued to be balky, pulling periodically in an unsettling way. He was probably as upset by the storm as I was, I thought, no longer annoyed with him and trying to make the best of his behavior. I was hungry and cold; undoubtedly so were the dogs. Maybe this was Yukon's problem.

The instant relief felt when I turned my back on the storm soon faded before another kind of discomfort. Viewed from the opposite direction, the blizzard was composed of thick streamers of snow that danced before the eyes instead of against them as before, and the wind whipped the old stuff off the trees and up from the ground to form a whirling white curtain that was forever changing quarter. This was hard on the eyes; it had an almost hypnotic effect that made me shake my head repeatedly to clear my vision. I had hoped that I might by able roughly to orient myself by the direction of the blow, but I now realized that Favonius had turned itself into a round wind: it had no beginning and no end, swirling around and around through the forest.

When the trail became so narrow that there was hardly room for the sled to pass, I knew I had missed the way back to the logging strip, but because there was no place to shelter, I kept on going, searching for a recent deadfall that would give us some protection. Presently the game track, if that was what it was, turned to the right and led us into a more open section where the trees were larger; it seemed that we had emerged into a new kind of forest, an area of mixed growth. To make sure, I stopped and felt one of the trunks with a bare hand; it had a girth of about three feet and smooth, papery bark: a birch. A few feet away the dark bulk of another tree suggested a big balsam.

I had no idea where we were, but this place was even more open than the spruce forest; the round wind gyrated through here violently, piling the snow in great drifts, from the tops of which loose particles erupted like foam spewed from the crest of a Pacific wave. I was exhausted, my legs felt like rubber; my heart was beating at an alarming rate. I knew that if I didn't rest soon, I would collapse.

I couldn't turn back for the simple reason that I didn't know rear from front; there was no point in leading the team to nowhere. What I needed was a big deadfall, preferably one of those blowdown situations where a large old birch had collapsed and in falling had brought down one or two spruces or balsams, making a tangled mass that would trap snow and provide us with a decent shelter where I could light a fire that would not be extinguished by the blizzard.

Strangely enough, now that we were squarely up against it, my mind was calm. I could think clearly and objectively, unburdened by worry. As I reasoned in this manner, it became clear that my physical condition was of paramount importance; I couldn't afford to collapse. At the same time the dogs appeared to be in good condition, especially Yukon. Indeed, watching him for the few moments that we stood beside the birch identified by touch, I could tell that he was full of energy, actually eager to get going. I decided to ride the runners, to let the dogs go ahead through this more open country, knowing that their natural instincts would make them avoid collisions with the trees. I urged them on, leaving them to do the running, concentrating my own energies on the search for shelter.

That's when Yukon took over. He suddenly charged left, ignoring the drag exerted by the foot brake I automatically pressed down into the snow. Admittedly, it wasn't much of a brake, just a piece of sheet iron eight inches wide by six inches deep, toothed on the bottom, which could be pushed down to bite into the snow. In hard pack it worked fairly well, but in soft snow, such as we were traveling over, it had little ef-

fect. I pressed unthinkingly, because Yukon had
veered so sharply off the course I thought we should
follow and seemed to be aiming away from the mixed
forest in which we found ourselves.

There was no stopping the big dog once he took
control, and on the theory that he couldn't do any
worse than I had done, I let him go. Besides, there
seemed to be so much purpose in his actions, so much
confidence in the way that he was moving that I began to hope.

Did he know the way back? What mysterious senses
did he have that would enable him to find the way
home through this stormy darkness across totally
strange country? Or *coul*d he do it? Was I just hoping
that he might, while in reality he was choosing the
easiest ground over which to run?

Because we couldn't become any more lost than we
were already, I put my trust in him. I thought I might
as well make myself as comfortable as possible and
husband my energies for whatever might yet lie ahead.
I put both feet on the left runner, balanced, swung one
leg over the sloping side of the sled, and scrambled
onto the platform.

Wrapped under the canvas tarpaulin, I waited that
outcome of Yukon's leadership, not entirely believing
that he would be able to guide us home that night,
but praying that he would.

Now that I had nothing to do, my imagination
started to get active again. I had experienced fear in
the past often enough to know how easily it can return
to create havoc in a mind dwelling on danger, particularly when its owner is physically inactive. But
constructive thought will maintain reason; this was
one of the few beneficial lessons learned during six
years of war in Europe. To be alive and bodily unscathed is not enough if the imagination is allowed to
turn the brain into mush, I had concluded during a
particularly nasty time in the summer of 1940. So I
trained myself to think positively whenever I was idle
while perched on the edge of oblivion.

That night in the Ontario backwoods I kept steady at first by trying to find a pattern in the storm, then by willing my eyes to see through the darkness and the swirling snow, seeking to identify the trees and to pick out landmarks. I was surprised to discover that the snow, for all its mobile qualities, lifted slightly the veil of night. Before this experience I would have said that the forest was pitch black; in fact, it was more of a deep, opaque blue. Light was filtering down out of the concealed heavens, even through the snow and the canopy of the trees, faint light, but definitely there if one forced the eyes to function fully. I have never again thought of night as being totally dark, even when there is no snow to reflect the stellar seepage.

Peering into the forest with head turned away from the worst of the blow, I began to feel exhilarated. I chuckled to myself at one point when I remembered how desirable adventure seems to be to those who are comfortably bored within a civilized, sophisticated environment.

The fact of the matter is that adventure is something nasty happening *to somebody else*. If a drama ends well and we read about it afterward, we think of it as adventure; if it ends fatally, it then becomes tragedy. Yet there I was, definitely having an adventure in the former sense and actually *enjoying* it.

After that I watched the dogs, whose whitened outlines were easy to detect. Yukon, naturally, was taking the brunt of the pull, breaking trail for the others, often physically turning the whole team when he lunged to left or right in order to dodge past a tree. He was magnificent. In those few places where the snow hadn't drifted deeply, he trotted, lifting his long legs high and digging powerfully with his big feet; when he was faced by a heavy drift, he charged into it, pushing with his hind legs, lunging upward, bounding into the deep snow, and tearing it aside. The others followed in his wake, but Sussie, immediately behind the leader, was taking the brunt of the next assault on the snow; she was the smallest and most slender of the dogs. I had put her behind Yukon because I feared that if Rocky was placed in that position, he and Yukon might fight. Now I realized that this was a mistake. Sussie henceforth would be the last in line, preceded by Sooner, Rocky, and Yukon. Yet the bitch was aided by her leader; if she had to struggle, his forward momentum pulled her through. She seemed to be still in good shape.

Man places great stock in objective reasoning, and so he should, for it works well as often as not, but there are occasions when he should pay more attention to these unexplainable, hidden senses that our species has somehow retained. That night, against all logic, I suddenly became quite convinced that Yukon knew exactly where he was going, that he was taking us home. *I* was lost, but that half-wild dog was not. His fine homing equipment was serving him as smoothly and efficiently as it served his wolf kin. Tail up and head held high, he churned through the snow tirelessly. I marveled at his stamina.

Yukon guided us back as surely as if he had been tied to the homestead by some invisible thread. When we came out of the forest into our own clearing, I jumped off the sled, stumbled in the deep snow, recovered and ran awkwardly behind the team, floundering occasionally, but so elated and relieved that I felt impelled to give physical vent to my pent-up emotions.

Crossing the opening took only minutes, yet it was here that the fullness of the blizzard hit us, made me realize just how stiff and cold I really was. The wind buffeted us with seemingly demoniac intent. Within the confines of the trees the swirling snow posed some real problems, but these were minor compared to the fury of the storm that battered us from the right quarter. The wind was like ice; the thick snow struck my exposed face like chips of splintered quartz. It was as well that the distance across the clearing was short, else I don't believe I would have made it.

By the time I unhitched the dogs and led them into the shelter of the barn and returned to the house to cut up a liberal amount of frozen meat for their suppers, I was near the end of endurance. I warmed up a little after the fire got going and while I was heating gravy to mix with the dog food, but the return journey to the barn, a matter of 150 yards, seemed endless. The big food pot in one hand and the kerosene lantern in the other, I stumbled my way through the drifts, for the first time realizing that this unwelcome storm had made a new job for me. When the blow ended, there would be an awful lot of shoveling to do.

Inside the barn the dogs were clustered expectantly near the doorway, noses wrinkling as they sniffed the aroma of the food, tails wagging furiously. Already they had shaken off most of the snow that had caked their bodies, and they didn't seem to have been unduly affected by their experience. Sussie looked a bit droopy, but there was an eager gleam in her brown eyes; the others were in fine fettle, especially Yukon.

Feeding the team was by now a ritual; every dog knew the routine. First the lantern was hung on its nail; next the big pot was placed on a shelf nailed to one wall for this express purpose, then, hands free, the food dishes were picked up from wherever they had been scattered across the barn, and carried back to the food shelf. Yukon would move forward and watch as his portion was ladled into the dish; when this was full, it was placed about ten feet away and immediately received its owner's attention; Sussie was next, followed by Rocky and, lastly, Sooner. Usually I lingered until each dog was finished, and we would socialize for a while; but tonight I was too cold, hungry, and tired. I took the lantern and again crossed the shrieking space between house and barn, entered, and slammed the door.

Because I was at last able to relax, my body immediately reacted. I started to shiver violently, my teeth chattered like castanets, and I felt sick to my stomach. For some strange reason I was colder than ever, especially in hands and feet.

Only the lantern was lighted when I first got home. The storm blew it out as I stumbled back from the barn. I tried to strike a match, managing only to break the wooden stem. One after another I broke matchsticks, so stupefied by the cold that it didn't occur to me to use the hot stove to ignite the phosphorus. In the end I put a matchhead between my front teeth and pulled; it lit all right, but it also burned my upper lip and singed my mustache.

I fumbled in a cupboard and found the bottle of scotch whiskey I had planned to take to the New Year's Eve party. The cap spun off and fell to the floor as I put the neck to my lips and guzzled until my eyes watered and I was forced to stop and catch my breath. The raw spirit put heat in the belly, but it stayed there when I wanted it in hands and feet. I put the bottle down and made myself dance, capering around the living room, flapping my arms like some grotesque bird, already slightly inebriated by the alcohol and bumping into things, giggling foolishly and without amusement.

When new blood started to move through toes and fingers I stopped. I lit two more lamps, this time striking the match across the top of the heater. In this light I examined my face; the tip of my nose was ivory yellow: first-degree frostbite. I rubbed it until it hurt. The fingers were next examined; they were also tusk white, especially the right index. Somebody had told me that coal oil was good for frostbite. I got a glassful and began to rub it in vigorously. It worked, or maybe it was the rubbing. By the time I was done fingers and nose felt as though they were on fire. Sitting in a chair as close to the stove as I dared get, I removed boots and socks, and the dead-looking toes were rubbed back to life, presently to join the other painful parts of my body. It was like a toothache, a fine, throbbing pain through which I imagined I could actually hear the new, hot blood pulsing out of the arteries into the veins. I poured another stiff drink and sipped it, forcing myself to back away from the stove, because I thought the circulation should be restored gradually rather than in a rush.*

Presently the pain subsided and was replaced by a feeling of pins and needles I felt better, but my index finger looked as though it had been burned; it was actually blistered. This was because frostbite damage is similar to the lesions produced by burns, progressing in three stages. The first of these produces inflammation, the second blisters, and the third results in permanent destruction of the tissues in the affected parts. I was lucky. Except for second degree blisters on one finger, the rest of my fingers and toes suffered only first-degree frostbite.

The heat from the kitchen range and the living-room stove brought the inside temperature to ten degrees above zero Celsius, no mean achievement when the outside temperature was twenty-three degrees below and the tireless wind was seeking out every tiny crack in walls and ceilings. Too lazy to lift the trap-door that covered the root cellar under the kitchen floor and to crawl down there to get potatoes, I opted to have boiled rice with the grouse I had that morning planned for supper.

I dined late that night. The grouse was frozen when put into the oven and was not ready until ten o'clock. But I sat down to a feast all the same: roasted

---

* At that time it was erroneously believed that slow thawing of the affected parts by rubbing was the most effective treatment of frostbite. In fact, quick thawing, preferably in warm water (102 degrees Fahrenheit, or 38.8 degrees Celsius), is now the recommended and most effective treatment. Rubbing with snow is not recommended at all, especially in severe cases of frostbite (deep freezing). Thawing of severely frostbitten areas should not be attempted on the trail because the affected parts are quite likely to become frozen again before shelter and warmth are reached; if this happens, gangrene will almost certainly occur four to seven days later. Physicians now say that a deep-frozen part of the body can wait for between four and eight hours before being thawed without experiencing ill effects, whereas a thawed and then refrozen part can create serious problems, including infection. The medics also say that alcohol should be avoided!

grouse, rice mixed with dried apricots, leftover carrots boiled lightly to be thawed, then fried in bacon fat and soaked in corn syrup, the whole topped off with bannock and marmalade, and washed down with strong tea toned up with whiskey. The eructation that escaped me as I got up from the table would have won acclaim at the festive board of an eastern potentate.

By now the last thing I wanted to do was go to a party. Replete to the point of discomfort, I went into the living room, pushed an old armchair near the heater, found my copy of Gordon MacCreagh's *White Waters and Black,* and settled down to read, sip hot whiskey sweetened with honey, and await the coming of the new year.

At midnight I raised my glass and drank a toast to the future. What would it bring? I wondered. I got up, went to the window and peered outside. The storm was still raging; the temperature was down to thirty-four degrees below zero. I went to bed.

Chapter 6

All the trees were dressed. Crowning the poplars and the birches, the new leaves, each still wrinkled and tender, glowed in the sunlight and mixed their lemon yellow and saffron hues with the fresh green of the conifers. The forest was a sleek, well-tended wild garden relaxing in the sun after a long, hard winter.

Wherever we walked, Yukon and I, the trees seemed to be competing with one another as though each was striving for first prize in this pageant of natural beauty. And the birds, with their songs and their flashes of quick color, added to the illusion. But there was nothing illusory about the perfume of the wilderness, the aroma of the balsams, the sweet scent of honeysuckle, and the more robust, medicinal tang of the balm poplars.

These were the sights and the sounds and the fragrances of spring that the dog and I were privileged to experience that morning. Color and song and soft, clean air; flower and leaf and straight new shoots; small eggs in artfully woven cups in bush and branch or hidden in grasses apple green.

Although it was early in the day, the sun was well up. As we walked the new land that was all agleam with shimmering dew, my eyes feasted upon those places where the sun danced and glided and arranged in layers the colors that formed a glorious rainbow over the northeastern part of the forest, the Arch of Iris produced by last night's rain and this morning's sun, as though the goddess herself had come to lead her favorite peacock over the tops of the evergreens.

I stopped to admire a spider's web while Yukon tested the breeze. Threads of gossamer had that mite woven in a symmetrical net of perfect lines that was now embellished by droplets of dew, each globule a minute mirror that returned images of the sky and the grasses and the trees, tiny cameos enameled in color against a background of burnished silver. In the heart of the masterpiece was the builder, a small, crouched being all furry and gray and black, whose shining legs gripped the silks they had so carefully arranged.

I have lived through more vernal seasons that I care to think about, but I did not really appreciate, or even properly note, the engrossing and rejuvenating properties of spring until I went to live in the north woods and had weathered my first winter there. Since then I have seen twenty-three springs. Each has been as new and fresh and exciting as the last.

On that particular morning in early May, Yukon and I were enjoying the new season to the full, taking our individual pleasures rather like hungry diners faced by a mouth-watering buffet who pick the delicacies they each crave.

I stopped to watch a ragged wedge of Canada geese, laggard flock, evidently, for most of the waterfowl were already arrived. The high-pitched voices of the flock aroused my wanderlust. Yukon, running free now that I understood his body language and could thus more or less anticipate his moves, was busy with one of those fascinating smells that dogs so delight in, sniffing intently while pushing down with his nose in excited little jerks.

On we went, wandering aimlessly through the cloisters of forest until we emerged into a small natural meadow bedecked with scarlet columbines, snow-white baneberries, and green-yellow clintonias, or corn lilies. After traversing the open, we entered the forest again, but this time aromatic cedars closed their striated ranks about us, darker green trees with brown, ragged bark beneath the shelter of which scampered snowshoe hares already slightly demented by the breeding lust. Seeing that Yukon was ready to hunt, I slipped the lead on him; there was too much temptation here for wolf-dog.

Three grouse hens suddenly burst out of cover like feathered projectiles, their stubby, fast-whirring wings creating explosive sound as they took to air in erratic flight that was yet purposeful, intended to confuse a hunter during those few vital seconds while the escaping birds gained height.

A little while later we heard the drumming of a cock bird. *Bup . . . bup . . . bup . . . bup-bup-bup-bup-up-urrrrr . . .* a slow-starting, rapidly increasing tatoo announcing that the spring drummer had staked his claim to a piece of forest and was even now standing on a fallen log beating his powerful wings.

The sound, so similar to the noise made by a distant two-stroke gasoline motor, is caused by air that rushes into a vacuum created by the extremely fast beating of the grouse cock's wings not, as many people still believe, by wings themselves hitting a hollow log. The bird prefers a downed tree on which to strut and drum, hollow or solid, but if there are no suitable logs around, he will make do with a stump or a rock, provided these are above ground level and clear of obstructions that might interfere with his strokes.

As though to challenge the grouse, a pileated woodpecker produced his own drum roll, an arpeggio of sharp, individual beats. Unlike his rival, this bird uses a hollow standing tree to beat out his message; his rhythm is faster, louder, and clearly more percussive. Whereas the grouse produces his booming notes by breaking the sound barrier, the woodpecker uses a tree as his tabor, beating it powerfully with his beak. In this way the cock of the north, his vivid crest and mustache turned a deeper scarlet by the chemistry of the mating urge, rattle-bangs his love calls.

It occurred to me that a clever musician might produce a spectacular wild concerto could he but orchestrate the many calls voiced by the birds of spring during a morning such as the one that Yukon and I were sharing. I tried to get a mind picture of the songs. The first to register were by a flock of marauding blue jays whose comedic screams, akin to the crashing of cymbals, could not yet subdue the delicate, tintillating tunes made by chickadees. Nearby, several whisky jacks rendered solos, composed on the spur of the moment, in which they incorporated many of the notes of other songsters with variations of rhythm and tone, while the basso profundo of an occasional raven came to remind one that not even vocalists had been omitted from this performance.

We moved on, and presently the cedars began to thin their ranks and the noise of rushing water told us we were about to reach a beaver dam. I slipped Yukon's lead, letting him run ahead because I knew that the odoriferous weir attracted him greatly. He loved the scents it offered; swamp mud full of methane gas, the boiled-cabbage smell of rotting vegetation, and the spicy tang of beaver musk. These essences drew him as surely as free samples draw a coquette to a perfume counter.

The water spilled over the dam into a meandering creek that eventually led to a small pond. The beaver had erected their barrier at a place where a fairly large lake once leaked its surplus waters into the creek, which was faster and wider before it was obstructed. At this time of the year the twisting, liquid ribbon almost attained the proportions it had maintained before the big rodents erected their barricade; later, in summer, the waterway would become narrower. As the dry season depleted the lake and the beaver built up the dam to husband their reserves, the creek would be reduced to a trickle coursing slowly over a bed of washed pebbles.

Beyond the dam, visible as soon as we emerged from the cedars, was the open space I had been aiming for, an area of pre-Cambrian granite that arched like a hog's back above the lowlands. Only an occasional evergreen could find enough soil in which to anchor itself here, so that for the most part the wide and shallow ridge was covered with blueberry bushes, pale-green lichens, thick mosses, and tan-barked, stunted pin cherry trees. In a variety of places no soil had formed to cover the layered rocks, and these, mixtures of pink feldspar and gray granite crisscrossed by dead-straight ribbons of whitish quartz, attracted the sun and offered warm resting places in a land that was for the most part chilly-damp on contact, despite the mild weather.

The sun, a huge, glaring orange suspended directly overhead, made the small shadows of noon. It was time to eat. I sat down on a warm bare patch, stretched my legs straight out, and slipped the packsack off my back. Yukon wagged his tail, waiting expectantly for the bone he always received before I found my sandwiches.

As I munched contentedly, I scanned the countryside, listening to its sounds. From within the shelter of a dense patch of rushes that were dry and brown at the top but already greening at the bottom a number of newly arrived ducks were gossiping. Nearby, a redwing blackbird cock was balancing precariously on the very tip of a dead willow stick that jutted out of the water: he was flashing his scarlet and yellow epaulets and singing his flutelike melody.

Without conscious volition, I began to examine the recent past, becoming aware that I had fallen into the habit of reviewing events according to season and not according to the calendar. Despite paying lip service to December 31 and socially celebrating January 1, I was now taking the measure of a year from spring to spring, marking its middle, as did the plants and animals of the wilderness, in autumn rather than in June.

Viewed from this standpoint, the old year had been a good one. It had, of course, brought a variety of uncertainties, a number of hardships, self-doubts, and a quota of fear. But it had also brought Yukon to me, along with newness and self-reliance; it had taught me much and made me realize that I knew so very little. By now many of my old, urban values had tumbled. Things that had always been taken for granted because they were so readily available had either become luxuries to be used sparingly and appreciated fully or discarded altogether.

Goods and services furnished by others for a nominal fee vanished the moment I took up residence in the backwoods; electricity, water on tap, plumbing, heating fuels derived from seemingly inexhaustible sources that kept the house warm with no greater effort than the writing of a check; theaters, libraries, public transportation, the telephone—the list was long, yet about the only things I missed were libraries, theaters, and, most of all, a good, hot, easily procured bath before going to bed.

On the other hand, the pleasure and the sense of self-worth derived from making do, from creating out of available materials useful and needed items, from improvising and from literally becoming one's own "butcher, baker, and candlestick maker," made life an exciting and stimulating challenge. Satisfaction such as never before experienced followed the accomplishment of relatively simple, but important, tasks. Even the most rudimentary things were appreciated to the full. A week-old newspaper was read slowly from first page to last, then saved to be recycled in some other way if it was not cut into neat squares and hung on a nail in the outhouse. A visit to some "rich" man's home twenty or more miles away, which had electricity and, best of all, a radio, was an event to be appreciated and never abused. A trip to the nearest town was a highlight of each month, a one-day gala affair when seldom-seen friends were greeted over a glass of beer and when the purchase of a few staples, followed by a bowl of chili con carne in the local eatery, produced ineffable contentment. And later, driving the aging car over the rutted road, going slowly so as to conserve as much precious gasoline as possible, one sighed with pleasure and felt that life was *good*. All these things combined to make memorable each and every day, and when night arrived and a satisfyingly tired body trudged off to bed, there was the thrill of expectancy just before sleep, when one wondered what tomorrow would bring.

Then came Yukon. He changed my life by giving me love and companionship and knowledge that I could not have gained without him. He had the courage to charge the moose when I stood inactive, he brought us all home out of the maw of the blizzard, he carried me and my loads through the wilderness, and he was always ready to offer himself unstintingly. I looked at him now. He had finished his bone, and he lay, head on front paws, watching me. When our eyes met, he wagged his tail and smiled; then he yawned. He was at peace. But, suddenly, I found that I was not. Despite the good year, despite my general contentment and stimulation, there remained one concern, a latent thing not yet inwardly resolved that had begun to nag during autumn and had persisted no matter how I tried to put it aside. It now surfaced with a rush. I could put it off no longer.

It was thinking about the fur that did it. I had worked hard tending the trapline, visiting each set daily and removing promptly the unfortunates who had stepped into the steel jaws. Each animal had been pelted, its body gutted and quartered and eaten. Soon the fur sale would start, and the bundles of hides would go under the hammer so that buyers from "the outside" could compete for them.

Thinking about the killing I had done, I realized that this was the hub of my concern. Whenever it had surfaced to my consciousness before, it had puzzled me because I viewed myself as a person who was selfishly unsentimental. I was equally puzzled now, and for the same reason, yet I was forced to admit that trapping was an ugly business. It appeared that I was not as ruthless as I had thought I was. I was too weak-willed to kill for profit! I became angry at this concept; it was as though I had suddenly discovered a serious flaw in my makeup. But I was forced to admit that each day it had become harder to set the traps, to slit into belly and guts, to scrape fat and flesh from the pelts and to dismember and carve the bleeding meat. At the same time I had become more and more intrigued with the study of life, though I was not sure why this should conflict with trapping, a pursuit that, after all, taught me much about the workings of the animals I was killing. Sitting on that sunny rock with Yukon at my feet, I became confused. My anger subsided, but I could not understand myself. The fact remained, however, that I was clearly aware of my distaste for trapping; indeed, it was more than distaste, I realized: the job had become abhorrent.

I tried to argue against myself. I needed money, more than I could earn logging. Trapping seemed to be the only other way of earning a living out here in the backwoods. I had to live, didn't I? There were lots of animals in this wilderness, and I wasn't taking *that* many. In any case, what difference would it make if *I* quit when there were so many other trappers at work throughout the north?

Such logic couldn't change the feeling that trapping was morally wrong, at least as far as I was concerned. I was unable to understand why this should be so, but I knew that I couldn't continue to destroy life simply for the sake of its garments, even though much of the meat under the coat was put to useful purpose.

Having made this decision, I felt better, but I remained confused. It was not until sometime later that I would come to understand my emotions.

That afternoon, with Yukon at my side, I started pulling traps, a job that continued all the next day. At the end of it, I did what I then considered a foolish and most irrational thing; instead of carting the traps back to the homestead so that I could sell them and in this way recover some of their cost, I dumped them into the lake. On the way home, thinking about this final act, I became confused all over again, and rather than soliloquize anew over the issue, I put my mind to work on other matters.

Of late I had been too busy and too tired at the end of the day to do any writing; I would now devote a part of each day to my chosen profession, but because I'd lost the habit of working on the typewriter, I made a big notice to hang in the living room, a bit of Latin learned at school that has served me as a reminder ever since: *Nulla dies sine linea*, "Never a day without a line."

That was long-term. More immediately I proposed to buy a horse with the money from the furs to help me expand the logging operations. I would also buy a hundred chicks and "grow" eggs and half a dozen piglets and "grow" pork.

A week later an order went off to the hatchery, and from a neighbor six hoglets were purchased. The horse arrived, a dappled-gray gelding who was five years old.

Not long after this, I got a summer contract from the pulp mill to cut and peel twenty-five cords of balsam, a better-paying proposition than logs with the bark on, but a dirty job, for the balsam is heavy with pitch that oozes out of the bark.

For a month I kept busy and remained content, refusing to debate the matter of the trapline any further. In between chores I continued to take Yukon for a daily walk and exercised all the dogs morning and evening, in this way occupying myself ten hours a day outside and putting in a couple of hours at the typewriter at night.

Then, in the second week of June, Yukon had a fight with a bear. It happened at twilight.

I was sitting at the typewriter. Yukon was lying on his back against the kitchen door, his legs sticking out at odd angles. Suddenly he sprang to his feet, thumped the door with one paw, whined, and looked at me. Because I knew him so well by now, I understood from his behavior that something unusual was going on out-side, an event that he felt must be investigated. It wasn't a visitor, for he faced differently in such cases; it was not the need to void bladder or bowels, for he asked for this by standing near me and whoofing softly. No, this, he was telling me, was something of importance.

I rose, walked over to him, and took hold of his collar, and opened the door, whereupon he immediately dragged me outside, leading the way toward the pigpen I had built near the barn. Within an enclosure made of two-inch spruce saplings I had constructed a small, low house of logs roofed with rough lumber and made waterproof with tar paper.

On top of the lean-to roof stood a large bear. It was tearing off the tar paper, obviously trying to get at the hoglets that had been locked in for the night. The neighbors had warned about this predilection that bears have for tender pork.

Without stopping to think, I released the eager dog and urged him to "go get it!"

The bear heard us. It stood upright, the way bears do when they want to check a doubtful situation, then it whirled around and scrambled off the roof almost at the same time that the streaking dog reached the rail fence.

Yukon swerved away from the pigpen, caught up to the bar, and charged into it. That's all I had time to observe because I realized belatedly that the dog was in danger and I turned and ran back into the house to get the rifle.

By the time I had taken the rifle down from its rack, inserted the loaded magazine, and worked a shell into the breech as I ran outside again, the two had disappeared. The crashing sounds of their going were audible, coming from the northwest.

No dog is a match for an adult bear. Even timber wolves avoid the large and powerful animal unless it is threatening their young, when, by combined attack, they usually manage to drive it away, although one or more of their number may be killed or injured during the battle, while the bear, made almost bite-proof by its thick coat and tough hide, usually escapes unscathed.

As I ran toward the fast-fading sounds of the chase, I hoped that Yukon would either make the bear take to a tree or break off the encounter quickly; otherwise, he could be seriously injured, perhaps killed. But I tried not to think of this as I entered the darkening forest.

The idea of Yukon lying somewhere out there bleeding was unthinkable. He *had* to be all right. I willed him to turn away, to come home, all the time knowing that he would not, that he would chase the marauding bear until it either treed or turned at bay, knowing also that I stood little chance of finding the two animals unless the bear stopped quickly.

I was too worried about Yukon to consider what my own danger might be if I did catch up with him and the bear. In daylight a Lee-Enfield bullet will stop a bear clean in its tracks if the rifleman knows how to handle the gun. But inside a nearly darkened wilderness the rifle sights are invisible. One must shoot almost by instinct then, either by using the dark outline of the barrel and swinging it more or less on target, when the equally dark shape of the quarry blots out the vague silhouette of the gun, or by shooting from the hip, John Wayne stuff, keeping the body lined up on the animal.

I preferred the latter method, but in either case, accuracy is lost. A miss at short range will almost certainly make a bear run; a lucky shot may kill it. But a wounding shot might make it charge, maddened by pain, seeking to claw and bite; then only some fast, chancy shooting and plenty of luck can settle matters finally. But I wasn't debating these things as I stumbled through the gloomy forest, calling Yukon's name and whistling intermittently.

When it was too dark to search without light, I returned home, planning my next moves. I didn't intend to give up the search.

At home I exchanged the rifle for the 12-gauge shotgun, loaded this with 00 buckshot, and fastened the flashlight clamp on top of the barrel just forward of the trigger. I had made a holder for the light to fit either rifle or shotgun after I had experienced some difficulties tracking, and eventually killing a deer wounded by a snap shot in early evening. The animal staggered into the heavy bush, and when I put the gun up the second time, it was too dark to see the sights. At some fifty paces I missed clean with the first five shots, finishing the deer off with the sixth by pure luck. Because the thought of an animal wandering wounded through the wilderness, dying miserably perhaps days later, was abhorrent, I determined that I would not hunt after sundown again, but to be on the safe side, in case an animal wounded in daylight eluded me until it was dark, I made the flashlight holder. Now I put the five-cell light into it, got a lead for Rocky, and set out anew, taking the malamute with me in the hope that he would be able to pick up Yukon's trail and feeling personally more secure with the shotgun instead of the rifle. Loaded with heavy buckshot, a 12-gauge at short range is a devastating weapon capable of stopping the heaviest game. With 00 shot, at eight lead balls .33 of an inch in diameter in each shell, it is just about impossible to miss; and even if the gun is a somewhat cumbersome bolt-action three-shot weapon, as mine was, it is yet able to outclass a rifle during close shooting at night.

I didn't really believe I would have a confrontation with the bear at this late stage, but by then I had learned that caution equates with survival in the wilderness; taking the gun was instinctive. I didn't give the matter much thought. My one and only concern was for Yukon's safety.

As Rocky and I moved through the darkened forest, I kept repeating Yukon's name aloud, coaxing the malamute to "seek." As a result, though I could not know whether he understood or even if he was, indeed, following his leader's spoor, I was forced to give the dog his head, hoping he was on track.

As may be imagined, when a chase takes place in

heavily timbered country, the escaping animal does not stick to well-defined pathways but charges pell-mell into brush, jumps deadfalls, and squeezes under obstructions that are almost impassable to an upright human. Through such obstacles did Rocky lead me, pulling eagerly.

It was a grim course over which I was dragged that night, a black marathon during the running of which I was scratched and buffeted by branches and shrubs, my clothes were torn, and my right eye was almost put out by a needle-sharp spruce twig. But it was not the physical discomfort that caused my mood to match the darkness; only later did I notice the cuts and scratches. I cannot fully express the state of my emotions during that seemingly endless night except to say that I alternated between hope and despair, that I blamed myself for allowing Yukon to race after the bear, and that my love for that dog can really be understood only by those who have had the good fortune to love a dog of their own.

Adrenaline kept me going long past the point of exhaustion, but there were times when I was forced to stop, to pull Rocky close to my side, while tortured lungs gasped air. During the first two or three hours I whistled almost continuously; then my lips couldn't obey anymore, and I called until my voice gave out; periodically I fired the shotgun, hoping that the irresistible sound would bring Yukon back if he was able to travel. And then it was dawn.

Orienting ourselves by the sun, I realized we had traveled a circular course; we were now moving toward the glowing east.

After such a wild journey I should have been hopelessly lost, but the forest in which we now found ourselves was familiar; a number of its trees carried blaze marks I had made more than a year earlier, when I was exploring the wilderness adjacent to the farm. We were about two miles from home.

I didn't want to, but it was necessary to go back. In my haste and anxiety last night I had neglected to feed the dogs; worry killed my own appetite, but Rocky and the others would by now be starving. In any event, I needed a rest.

I started to pull Rocky off the trail, but he fought the lead anxiously, wanting to continue in an easterly direction. My hope was forlorn, but I decided to let him go on for another half hour.

A few minutes later we emerged into a fairly open grassy area. At one end of this Rocky found the place where Yukon and the bear had fought. A section possibly ten yards square had been beaten down by the action; there were tufts of shaggy black fur scattered around, bear fur. And there was blood; in some places just a few drops, in others big smears, as if a wounded body had rolled, rubbing its gore on the grasses. After fastening Rocky to a tree, I search for tracks on my hands and knees and in this way learned that the fight had broken off and that the bear had run again, pursued by Yukon. Who had lost the blood? Once more Rocky was put on the tracks.

The trail led to a small beaver pond. In the mud at the edge of the dam there were footprints, Yukon's and the bear's. The right-front-paw impressions left by the bear were bloody.

There were spots of dark blood on some bushes, but it was impossible to determine which animal had left these. The trail ended, and Rocky, despite frantic casting about could not pick it up again. It seemed that the bear had taken to the water and Yukon had followed.

The bent grasses at the scene of the scuffle were beginning to straighten and the blood was coagulated, the lighter spills a rusty brown color. These things told me that the fight must have taken place during the night, probably not long after the chase began. Where was Yukon now?

For three days Rocky and I searched the forests. On the evening of the third day I gave up; either Yukon had been killed by the bear, or he had followed it so far into the wilderness that he would not now return. Yukon was gone.

THE NORTH RUNNER

At fourteen, when the civil war in Spain came to ‹ set the tenor of my youth, I somehow learned to cope with the emotions engendered by the loss of relatives and friends. In my late teens and twenties, during World War II, this emotional shield was made stronger, perfected to a point where, by my early thirties, I rather boasted that death could not affect me; I was no longer vulnerable because I thought I knew how to live within myself. Friends were enjoyed in the present and dismissed in the past; romance was an interesting exercise of the moment, real enough while it lasted, quickly disposed of when it ended. In a vague sort of way I knew I had become incapable of really caring for others; it didn't bother me. Indeed, I preferred it that way.

More recently, living in the northern wilderness, subtle, disturbing changes in my emotions made me occasionally uneasy, but except for some momentary spells when I silently wondered about the cause of this new concern I was beginning to feel, I devoted little time to the matter, putting it down to the circumstances of my present life and believing that as usual, it would leave me unscathed in the end. When the morality of trapping became a question, I realized that here was something different, but I concluded vaguely that what upset me was the carnage that went with the job, the blood and the smell of death that were too vivid reminders of the old days.

Sitting in the living room thinking about Yukon, I became fully aware that a great change had come over me. I discovered to my dismay that I had become deeply and emotionally involved for the first time in my adult life—with a dog! I immediately rejected the concept. It was nonsense. I was tired from the days of frantic search, out of sorts; I'd feel differently tomorrow. I got up and found the remains of the New Year's bottle of whiskey; there was about a third left. I drank. Two hours later the bottle was empty and I was angry, terribly angry. I wanted to do violence, to smash things. I paced about the house, kicking at anything that got in the way. As I was passing the kitchen

133

door, I punched the unyielding wood, hurting my knuckles and enjoying the pain because it gave me something tangible upon which to vent my temper. I knew I was drunk, yet I was sober. My body was drunk, my mind clear. I stopped, rubbed the swollen knuckles, heard the dogs howling in the barn, and rushed outside to stand spread-legged and to yell, telling them to shut up. I had not done that before. The dogs were silent.

Back in the house I stumbled upstairs and went to bed fully clothed. Without knowing why, feeling utterly unmanned and ashamed, I cried.

When I woke up next morning nursing a deserved headache, I realized almost immediately that I could not escape reality. Yukon was gone, but I could not dismiss the hurt of his going. I cared. And somehow this made me feel better. It did not minumize the grief, but it allowed me to accept it.

The dogs greeted me effusively when I took them their breakfast, but although I patted each for a moment or two, I could not stay to play with them; I was too depressed.

Thinking to take my mind off my problems, I made a shopping list and drove to town, changed my mind about shopping in Ontario, and drove across to Minnesota to visit Old Alec,* as he was universally called, an octogenarian whom I had accidentally met after arriving in the backwoods and who had become a good friend. Sitting in his small, neat log cabin, playing chess, and drinking the aquavit his Swedish palate was so fond of, we talked between moves, and I told him about Yukon, and about my grief. In the end, looking at me intently with his rheumy blue eyes, he summed up my problem.

"You are in love, Ron. Not yust wit' a dog, wit' life. Yesuss Christ, tho'! You sure did take a long time to love! Yah, Yesuss Christ, you shore took a long

---

* See *Paddy, A Naturalist's Story of an Orphan Beaver Rescued, Adopted and Observed by R. D. Lawrence* (New York: Alfred A. Knopf, 1977).

time. . . . You're lucky, tho'. Yust so you love some-
thin' beside yourself, that's good, ver' good. Yah. . . ."

He poured me another measure of aquavit, filled
his own glass, and started to set up the chess pieces.

"Now ve play. Yust one more, yah?"

Old Alec lived eighty miles south of the homestead.
I spent the two-hour return drive examining the state
of my emotions. When I got home at dusk, I knew
that the wilderness and especially Yukon had combined to make a considerable breach in my old de-
fenses. I wasn't sure whether I liked this greatly, but
there seemed to be nothing that could be done about
it. I had become emotionally involved with a life other
than my own in a lasting manner for the first time
since infantile dependency had bound me to my parents. Recognizing these things, I knew I would never
forget Yukon, but I hoped that the sadness, the depression, generated by his disappearance would not
take too long to become dulled and bearable.

After the other dogs had finished their suppers that
night, I led them all to the house, feeling somewhat
guilty that I had neglected them. During the play that
followed I discovered that I cared for all of them to
a degree greater than I would have admitted to myself a few days before, but not in the same way that
I cared for Yukon. No other dog would ever replace
him in my affections.

Afterward, the dogs back in the barn, I stood outside for a while and watched the moon come up. Inside, I found my copy of Steinbeck's *Sweet Thursday*
and began to read it once more, knowing it almost by
heart, but never tiring of it, and finding that, as
always, Steinbeck's sensitive feelings for his subject
and his marvelous storytelling abilities were able to
assuage my troubles.

When something scratched against the south window
of the living room, I was so engrossed that I almost
didn't bother to glance up, but when I saw what was
out there, the sudden rush of gladness that filled me
was beyond description.

Standing with both front paws on the windowsill, his face blurred in the yellow light of the kerosene lantern, was Yukon. But even as I jumped to my feet and started moving toward the doorway, the gladness changed to deep concern as I saw the bloody look of him.

His entire face and head seemed to be plastered in old gore and one corner of his mouth sagged dreadfully; his lips, on the left side, were slit beyond his jawbone, their edges tinged the dirty white that is characteristic of an unhealed wound.

It didn't take but a second or two to reach the door and open it, but he was already there. He rushed at me, whining his gladness, pushing against me, his matted tail wagging furiously. I wanted desperately to examine his wounds, but I couldn't help hugging him, and it seemed that he was just as determined to make a fuss over me.

He was filthy and bedraggled, his coat was filled with wood ticks; they were big on his skin. He was thin and starved. But he was back!

I knew that his stamina and my care would return him to health; nothing else mattered. As we were telling each other how glad we were to be reunited, the other dogs greeted their returned leader in their own characteristic way; they howled as I had never heard them howl before. A pack of wolves baying at the moon, the primordial song of the ageless wild.

What actually happened between Yukon and the bear remains a mystery to this day. At best I could only make a guess as to the cause of his injury, a single wound that began at the very corner of his mouth and continued for three inches, slitting open the side of his face so that his left cheek gaped and exposed all his molars.

It seemed that the wound had been made by something sharp and pointed, almost as though the tip of a knife had slashed through about a quarter of an inch of skin and flesh.

The injury could not have been caused by a bite;

it *could* have been made by a claw. I was able to picture the scene: the bear, turning at bay, trying to close with its pursuer; Yukon, swift and agile, dancing around it, rushing in, biting, darting away again. Then (who knows by what mischance?) he got too close to one of the bear's great, swinging paws, and a single claw caught the corner of his mouth, ripping through it.

Perhaps the fight continued; perhaps Yukon broke off the engagement. Bleeding, in great pain, the dog may have gone to hide somewhere to lick his wound as best he could, hurting too much to come home or perhaps too weak for a time, seized by shock.

The condition of the wound suggested that it had been inflicted the evening of the encounter. The edges were partially healed, showing dead tissue wherever they were not inflamed by infection.

The nearest veterinarian was more than seventy miles away, but I would have driven ten times that distance if need be. I knew full well that it was now too late to stitch the edges of the wound together. If anything could be done, Yukon would have to be anesthetized and the dead tissue snipped off down to new flesh that could be drawn together and stitched.

The vet confirmed this, adding that if the wound was clipped and sutured together, it would probably distort Yukon's mouth and cause more discomfort than if it was left to heal by itself. He would always have a lopsided face, of course, but this would be better than mouth distortion.

This diagnosis was not arrived at without difficulty. Yukon let me see to his injury, but as soon as the unsuspecting vet came near him, he growled deep in his throat, baring his dangerous fangs. I couldn't blame the man when he suggested that since the dog could not be muzzled because of the wound, he would check it from a safe distance while I did the actual work. Thus Yukon was examined, diagnosed, and treated with supplies passed to me by the veterinarian.

Finally, the animal doctor prepared a syringe with some sort of antibotic solution, and I administered it, jabbing Yukon in the bum, whereupon he reacted to the prick of the needle by lunging for the vet. But the latter had wisely retreated to the far end of his dispensary, and I was able to restrain the dog in time. The animal doctor was very glad to be rid of us.

The wound healed well enough, but it left Yukon with a definitely sinister appearance, as though he were grinning at some macabre joke that only he could appreciate. Henceforth he salivated continuously from the left side of his mouth, a habit that was disconcerting when he would come and drop his big head on my lap and cover me with his rather slimy discharge. Yet I was thankful that his injury caused him no other problems. In a month he was his old self.

Chapter 7

She knew that I was going to kill her. Her eyes said so for those few seconds during which I sighted down the barrel, aiming directly at her forehead. Came the sharp crack of the gun and the recoil that took my eye off Sussie's head. And she was dead.

My eyes were closed when I lowered the gun, but I had to open them to make absolutely sure that she was past feeling the agonies of the bear trap that had crushed her pelvis, mangled both her legs, and ripped open her stomach, near the groin, where the full milk dugs were. I looked. Her accusing eyes were closed, the small, purplish, lymph-filled bullet hole made a third orb, between the other two; at the back of her head was a great red hole in which were mixed lighter pieces of brain and chips of bone.

The powerful trap, anchored by a long chain to a twenty-foot poplar pole intended to act as a drag in the event that a bear stepped into the deadly gape, lay a few feet away from the dog's mutilated body, its big steel fangs bloody; the gore also smeared the jaws and dripped onto the grass, forming a carmine pool that was even now coagulating. Sussie had been in the trap a long time.

The September sun was not yet above the trees when I turned my back on Sussie and set out for the homestead that lay about a mile south of the abandoned farm where the bear trap had been set by an unknown. But even across that distance, I could still hear the dogs howling in the barn.

It was their howling that had wakened me before daylight that morning, a continuous farrago of distress that caused me to jump out of bed, dress in haste, and go out to see what the trouble was. As I walked toward the outbuilding, I heard the distant, agonized yelping, coming from due north. It was faint, almost drowned by the voices of the other dogs, but I knew at once that Sussie was in some kind of trouble.

Four weeks earlier the bitch had given birth to pups, Yukon's children. In her desire for privacy, she had crawled under the barn floor from the outside, finding for herself a good and secure den in which to nurse her little ones. Because of this, I allowed her to run free, but she showed no desire to leave the area of the farmyard, at first being too busy feeding her pups, of late too jealous of them to go farther than the house. I didn't know how many young ones she had delivered; the only way to get at them would have entailed cutting through a couple of the hewn logs that floored the barn, which I was loath to do and didn't consider necessary in any event, supposing that when the pups were ready, Sussie would lead them out. I often listened to their mewling voices while squatting over them on the barn floor, interested and amused by Yukon, who stood guard over that particular place, not allowing Rocky or Sooner to come near it. The big dog spent practically all his time sitting over his offspring, listening to them, his ears moving stiffly at every sound they made; now and then he would whine softly, as though talking to them.

His anxiety over his children was touching, but the location of the den selected by their mother created a problem for him; he would have preferred to be in two places at the same time. If all the dogs were out of the barn, he immediately went to lie down beside the hole that Sussie had dug, her tunnel into the den, but if Rocky and Sooner remained in the barn, Yukon wouldn't leave it either, not trusting them inside on their own, though, of course, there was no possible way in which to reach the pups from above.

Once, a week or so after Sussie gave birth, Yukon tried to crawl into the den, whereupon his once loving mate growled so furiously, crawling toward the entrance, that the impatient father backed out, getting the message. Nevertheless, like all wolves, he was a concerned and solicitous father, so much so that despite the fact that Sussie was fed regularly and given extra rations, Yukon would no longer eat the bones that I gave him but would take them over to the den entrance and leave them there for Sussie, a bit of self-sacrifice that I found touching; he wasn't to know that his mate didn't need the food he left for her, of course. And Sussie, perhaps because she took them to her pups or perhaps because she chewed them for extra calcium, collected Yukon's offerings every day.

As nearly as I could judge, the bitch became pregnant soon after Yukon's recovery from his face wound, sometime in June, but my first awareness of her condition came when I noticed that Yukon was becoming exceedingly jealous of the other males, warning them away every time one or the other went near her and staying by her side when the dogs were taken outside for exercise. One day I noticed that Sussie was decidedly heavier around the belly. I called her to me to feel her bulge and Yukon came too, pushing my hand away with a rough cast of his nose, not growling or showing his teeth, but telling me quite clearly to keep my hands to myself. I respected him for it and obeyed, and thereafter I made sure that Sussie got extra rations.

By mid-July, when the bitch was obviously heavy with her young, disaster struck the homestead in late afternoon. The weather had been stiflingly hot all day; there was no wind, the sky was overcast, the humidity uncomfortably high. By noon the thermometer registered thirty-six degrees Celsius.

The morning was spent in the bush, about a quarter of a mile from the homestead, where I was cutting cedar fence posts for sale to a buyer from Minnesota. The flies were vicious. Big inch-long horseflies ganged up on the horse, despite the insecticide I sprayed on his coat; and wherever the horseflies didn't settle, the deerflies feasted, and the mosquitoes. The horse kept twitching and stamping and shaking his head, his tail swishing constantly. My own person was a little better off than his, but the discomforts associated with protection against the flies were almost as great as the pests themselves. Fly repellents were not as sophisticated then as they are now; most were downright useless, others kept the pests away for only a short time. Oil of citronella helped, but it was too volatile.

After making these discoveries during my first summer in the backwoods, I adopted the method used by my neighbors, a most uncomfortable, messy business that nevertheless was effective against the flies. It consisted of a mixture of about equal parts of lard and roofing tar which was smeared over the exposed parts of the body: face and neck and the backs of the hands, unless one was wearing gloves. As a result, it was necessary to reserve a set of bush clothes exclusively for the job and wear them until they literally disintegrated. To a stranger coming upon me unawares, the scarecrow figure I presented would have given cause for concern!

By noon the horse and I both had had enough. I finished loading the cut poles onto the flatbed wagon, and we returned home. Later, after I wiped myself clean and had a tub bath, I rubbed down the horse and led him to the water trough. As we were on the way back to the barn one of my neighbors arrived, driving his team and wagon; the gelding became immediately excited.

The man had come to inquire about a heifer of his that had strayed the day before. He was making the rounds of all the homesteads, looking for her. Because my gray was acting up in the presence of the strange team, I tied him to a tree while I talked to the neighbor.

A little while later, when the man was driving off, I remembered the stew I had put on the stove, and I hurried back to take it off the heat before it burned.

Never dreaming that the gelding would come to harm during the few extra minutes it would remain tied to the tree, I stopped to fill and light my pipe. That was when I heard the noise. It was like the rumble of an express train, a roaring sound that seemed to be approaching from the west. Curious, I went to a window.

A purple-black curtain filled the western sky. The trees were leaning toward me, as though some giant invisible force were attempting to knock them all down. At first I couldn't understand what was happening, but when I actually saw a number of treetops snapped off and flung upward and carried away as the great roaring got louder, I knew it had to be a tornado. And it was coming fast. Mesmerized, I watched for a few minutes before I remembered the horse.

I ran to the door, opened it, and dashed outside. It was as though a huge and powerful hand had hit me. One second I was running on the ground, the next I was swept off my feet and slammed against the well. I tried to get up, felt a stabbing pain in my side, and knew I had broken a rib.

I couldn't get up; the great roaring vortex was trying to sweep me away just as it was snapping trees and carrying them before it. Lying against the wooden well housing, I clung to the boards, making myself as small as possible, feeling the monster wind suck at me, trying to pluck me from my meager shelter. What a noise! A madness of sound, a fulminating and savage descant made more frightful because it came alone, without thunder or lightning or rain. Across an open plain it would have moaned; coming through the forest, it plucked demented chords from the trees and drew harpy screams from the branches, an indescribably primordial cacophony that had the power to invade every corner of the mind.

The bulk of the house interposed itself between me and the direct path of the freak wind, screening me from most of the flying debris, but even so, I was hit several times by broken branches, and my right hand was cut by a cedar shingle, ripped off the roof, that came spinning down like a well-aimed frisbee. The top sixteen-foot section of a poplar landed near the well with enough force to shake the ground under me, but I didn't hear it land, so great was the noise of the wind. That must have happened when the eye of the tornado passed directly over the homestead, for soon after the poplar hit the ground, the worst of the storm was over.

In the wake of the twister came the rain, big, warm, heavy drops that pommeled the ground and rattled like machine-gun fire on the roofs of the buildings. The afternoon was dark, like late evening; there was no wind now, but the departing roar of the racing tornado continued to dominate all other sounds.

I made to get up and fell down again, unable to stifle a cry of pain. Gingerly feeling my right side, midway between hip and armpit, I discovered I had been wrong in my earlier diagnosis; three ribs were broken, not one. Holding my right arm tight against my body and moving slowly, I managed to gain my feet. Feeling my ribs again, I took several cautious, shallow breaths. They hurt, but the pain was more superficial than internal. This suggested that my right lung was not in danger from a sharp, inward-stabbing rib end. After a couple more, deeper breaths, I was sure of this; my side hurt like hell, but it seemed that the bones were cracked rather than completely broken.

The homestead was suddenly a place of quiet except for the rapid drumming of the rain. It amazed me that such an intense and violent storm could come and go so quickly; it had lasted not much more than ten minutes. It had killed my horse.

The gelding, crazy with fear, had wound himself

around and around the tamarack to which he had been tied. He had strangled himself. His eyes protruded so frightfully they almost seemed to be set on stalks; his tongue, swollen and purple, hung out of the corner of his horribly grinning mouth; his head, held by the rope, was twisted upward at an impossible angle. The unfortunate beast had emptied his bowels; it seemed ironic that whereas life had gone out of the horse, his dung was yet steaming. I stared at him until my stomach churned, and I vomited painfully on the leaf-strewn ground, clutching my side.

Afterward, when the pain from the broken bones became bearable, I drew my belt knife and bent to cut the throttling noose. The rope was so tight that it was impossible to slip the knife between it and the neck, and it was necessary to saw at the knot. The head fell to the ground.

My mind was a little less foggy now, but I was still in shock, not knowing what to do and unable to think about anything but the fury of the storm and the tragedy of the horse. In a vague sort of way the barking of the dogs penetrated my consciousness, yet I stood there, trying to decide on the next move.

I couldn't seem to help staring at the dead horse; I began to feel sick again. When I turned away, it was to see for the first time the debris that littered the yard, the downed trees, the profusion of scattered branches. I blamed myself for the horse as I played that most pointless of all games: what if . . . if my neighbor hadn't arrived when he did, if I hadn't put the stew on the fire, if I hadn't stopped to watch the storm, if I hadn't tied the horse to the tree. That was the biggest "what if" of them all.

The dogs continued to howl. I went to them, petted them, each movement producing a stab of pain in my side. When the three males were settled, I went outside and called Sussie, but she wouldn't come out, and I went back to the house.

Using a wide elastic bandage, working slowly and painfully in front of a mirror, I strapped up the ribs. They felt better at once. When I was dressed again,

I walked to my nearest neighbor's place, about a mile away, to find that he had come off lucky during the storm and was already clearing up the mess of branches in his yard. He loaned me his team of horses and a towing chain with which to drag the gray into the forest. I almost asked him to do the job for me but refrained from doing so; he was busy enough with his own affairs, and in any event, I felt it was up to me to do the job.

It was night by the time I returned home after taking back the neighbor's horses, a starry, moonless night. The dogs were now fed. I went to bed.

I could not, of course, be aware of it then, but the unusual tornado marked the beginning of a bad time, a period of depression, poverty, and mental anguish that came close to bringing to an end my life in the wilderness.

A week after the storm I was able to drive to town to see a doctor, who confirmed what I already knew, told me to take it easy, bound me up with heavy adhesive that pulled like hell and itched like the mange, and charged me fifteen dollars. Counting the cost of the gasoline used to drive in and out of town, the wasted time, and the doctor's fee, getting medical advice didn't turn out to be such a great idea, especially in view of the fact that two days later I peeled off the adhesive when I couldn't stand it any longer. I replaced the sticky stuff with the elastic bandage and left the rest to nature. Two weeks passed before I was able to clean up the damage left by the storm; even then the ribs were still tender.

By the end of the first week of August the bones were fully mended, and I resumed work in the cedar forest, cutting and trimming fence posts and carrying out small loads with the help of the three male dogs hitched to a light four-wheeled wagon I had made, a contraption not much bigger than a sled and slung low on the ground. The dogs pulled; I pushed from behind. Between us we managed to fill the first order of posts before the end of the month.

Things seemed to be going better for me now, and

despite the serious and grievous loss of the horse, I thought that I might yet be able to establish myself in the backwoods on a more secure footing.

The morning after I formulated these thoughts, disaster struck again. This time it hit the chickens, which had appeared to be doing well and were already of respectable size.

Going to feed them, I found twenty-three of them dead and a large number of the others squatting listlessly, very sick birds. Later I learned that chicken cholera was the villain, but by then it was too late. Every one of the hundred pullets died of the virulent sickness.

Not long after this second blow, Sussie gave birth to her pups and had to be allowed to run free. Perhaps if my economic position had not been so bleak, I might have paused long enough to get the pups out from under the barn and settle them and their mother in a more suitable place in the stable. As it was, the loss of the poultry coming so soon on top of the death of the horse kept me fully occupied with the problem of financial survival.

I had completed and sold two free-lance articles, but the rates of payment were ridiculously low, and the periodical market was not greatly interested in pieces dealing with the problems of a tenderfoot homesteading in the backwoods, about the only subject I could then write about because I was too isolated to develop articles that would have wider appeal. The money was useful, of course, but it could not solve my difficulties.

Food was no problem. The garden yielded more vegetables than I could eat, and there were plenty of groundhogs and hares to put meat on my table and in the dishes of the dogs. Occasionally I would use the .22 rifle to hunt these animals, but most often it was Yukon who brought home the metaphorical bacon. He was a master hunter, and he had an uncanny ability to assess instantly the moves of the quarry and to work out a hunting technique for each.

If I took him after groundhogs, he would quarter

the more open habitat of these rodents, holding his head high until he got a good scent, whereupon, if the 'chuck was out in the open and feeding some distance from its burrow, Yukon would streak away and grab it in a trice, sometimes just as the fleeing victim was about to dive down a hole. One shake of his head, and the groundhog's neck snapped, and that was that; but since he was not a retriever, I always had some difficulty persuading him to bring the prey to me before it was totally mangled.

If a groundhog was sunning itself outside its burrow, Yukon would stalk it, creeping up on it against the wind until he was close enough for the swift lunge that almost always ended in a kill.

His technique for hunting hares was more direct. He soon learned that these animals rely heartily on camouflage and stillness to avoid a predator and that they almost invariably travel in a semicircle when chased.

With his keen nose and ears, he could put up a hare within moments of being released, then he would chase it until the fleet-footed snowshoe outdistanced him, at which point he would cut across and intercept it. His success rates were not as high with hares as with groundhogs, but he got enough of both to ensure a continuing meat supply for all of us. When, as happened on occasion, he had a bad day, I would set out along with the .22 during early evening, spending a few precious bullets in order to make up for the dog's lack of success.

Autumn, of course, was the time for bigger game, moose preferably, deer if no moose were available. All in all, the problems of keeping myself and the dogs fed were relatively minor. I had no debts, I paid no rent, and because the homestead was located in an unorganized region—that is to say, it belonged to no municipality and was technically administered by the Ontario government—taxes for the two hundred acres amounted to six dollars a year.

Nevertheless, despite having enough cash money —as everyone around there called currency—to take care of immediate needs, the future financial picture didn't look rosy.

One of my maternal ancestors, a fellow called Sebastian Rodriguez, was with Cortés in Mexico. Pondering the problems of economic survival in the wilderness, I knew how my distant kinsman and his comrades must have felt when their leader burned the boats. That was what I had done, in a manner of speaking, when I sank the traps in the lake. It may be that I unconsciously disposed of the traps in this way so that there could be no turning back, but whether or not that was my design, the fact was that now, faced by economic failure and unable to afford new traps, I could no longer turn to the trapline for relief.

Three or four days before Sussie got caught in the trap I was awarded a new pulpwood contract, for fifty cords of spruce at $23 a cord, for a gross of $1,150. From this, $300 haulage fees had to be deducted, leaving a net of $850. I had earned $80 for the freelance work and slightly more than $300 cutting posts, and I expected to realize between $300 and $400 when the pigs were sold. Thus, between August and January my income would total about $1,500. Not a bad sum for that time but well earned inasmuch as I averaged twelve hours a day seven days a week, which brought my hourly earnings down to $0.65 an hour at a time when the minimum wage in the country was set at $1.05.

Nevertheless, the immediate present was assured, and if I could get another pulpwood contract in February and I continued writing, perhaps developing some particular theme into a regular monthly contribution, I might expect to go on living on the homestead indefinitely.

On the last day of August Yukon and I went to the cutting site to start geting things ready. A trail had to be blazed, brush cleared, and a 200-yard truck road needed to be brushed out. This was necessary because the old logging road over which the truck had traveled to load my previous pulpwood stopped short of the place where I was now going to work. Without the horse to skid out the logs, the truck was going to have to be driven right up to the cutting site once the new, somewhat crude road had become frozen solidly enough to take the weight of a four-ton vehicle.

Returning home that evening, Yukon got away from me. I was thinking about the work ahead and not watching him closely enough when he suddenly dashed into a thick clump of cedars. The next minute out came a large black bear; behind it was Yukon.

I had the Lee-Enfield with me because by then, although not yet the legal hunting season, the bull moose were in fine shape and I hoped to get my meat supply early this year.

One would have thought that Yukon would now stay clear of bears, remembering his previous painful encounter, but the opposite was the case. He had developed a consuming hatred for the animals and had chased three of them already, treeing them by staying on their rumps, no matter how the big animals dodged, and snapping furiously and continuously. But now he seemed intent on driving bruin right into my arms, as though he expected me to take part in the case. I yelled and waved the rifle, and the bear turned away, reached a tall poplar, and climbed up with amazing agility, its big claws leaving a set of tracks on the light-green bark. Bear meat is good eating; I needed meat. Besides, the government paid a ten dollar bounty for each animal shot or trapped by a homesteader, and the hide, properly fleshed, sold for another ten dollars. Since this animal had come to me almost gratuitously, I shot it through the head, but first I leashed Yukon and tied him to a tree, out of harm's way, knowing that he would stay at the foot of the poplar and that the dead animal could well land on top of him.

It was a big bear, a four-hundred pounder, I judged. It was a job to butcher it, quarter the meat, and haul it and the hide back to the homestead, using the small dog wagon.

It was not long after this incident that Sussie stepped into the trap. I had no idea why she wandered away from her young, and I never did find out who had set the trap and abandoned it. Later that day, after Sussie had been buried in the forest, I picked up the trap and took it to the lake and dropped it into the water. By its condition I judged it had been set for a long time, at least a year. Some irresponsible bastard had put it out and either forgot about it or was too damned idle to return to retrieve it after the carrion with which it must have been baited was eaten, not by a bear, but by the small predators of the forest.

In the evening I cut through the barn floor and got the pups. There were three of them, but one, the runt of the litter, was dead, had been for at least twenty-four hours. This may have been the reason why the bitch wandered away. The two survivors were in good shape and looked just like their father, without a trace of the collie line. They were roly-poly, fluffy wolf pups with perky ears and great big paws, dark gray in color.

I tried to raise them on canned milk and Pablum. But they died. First one, then the other, at two-day intervals. Today, after having raised literally hundreds of young animals orphaned for one reason or another, I know what went wrong: The formula was too rich; it gave them dysentery.

There followed a time of bitter depression during which the dogs were fed daily but neglected emotionally and left locked in the barn while I tried to get rid of my black mood by working furiously and for long hours. The dogs, especially Yukon, could not, of course, understand my change of attitude and invariably tried to get close to me and to initiate a game.

In any event, it was Yukon who returned me to my senses and made me aware that I was being foolish and grossly unfair to him and to Rocky and Sooner.

It was about a month after the pups died; the land was snow-covered, and the cold was starting to bear down hard at night. I was late returning from the logging so that it was already nine o'clock when I prepared supper for the dogs. On the way to the barn with the food pot and lantern, I paused a moment to look at the sky. There was an early moon, the stars were out in their millions, and the aurora was shifting luminously, creating plume-like patterns that held their shape for some moments before breaking up into spears of greenish light. I noticed all this, but I wasn't gladdened by the spectacle.

When I put the dishes in front of the dogs, Yukon wouldn't eat; it was the first time since he had come to the homestead that he refused food, and when Rocky, already finished, edged toward his leader's dish and began to eat its contents, the big dog took no notice. I chased Rocky away, picked up the dish, and put it under Yukon's nose. He didn't glance down. Instead, he whined loudly, pranced once, rose on his hind legs, and licked my face. My mood of maudlin self-pity could not continue in the face of the dog's distress and affection. All at once I was filled with contrition. I squatted and opened wide my arms; Yukon came into them and Rocky and Sooner rushed up also. The three dogs mobbed me as of old, whining and licking and pushing against me with the unabashed honesty of the breed.

I took them outside, and we ran over the snowy clearing and played our games, and I became angry with myself and felt very, very guilty for having neglected my friends. During this moonlit romp it occurred to me that Yukon must have gone through a bad time because of Sussie's death, a bewildering time, wondering what had become of his mate. Wolves' emotions may differ from those of humans, but there is no doubt that they have the capacity for love and for sorrow. I now felt guiltier than ever; I had withdrawn from Yukon when he needed me, whereas he, as always, was prepared to offer himself as unstintingly as ever.

The next day, there being enough snow on the ground, I hitched the three dogs to the sled, and we went for a fast, long run through the wilderness, leaving at dawn and not returning until dusk It did us all good. The dogs were stale from inactivity and were tired when we got home, but they really enjoyed the workout and devoured the extra big meal that I gave them.

While I was eating my supper that evening, Yukon lay sprawled under the table, his big head resting on my feet, drooling as usual. He slept beside my bed that night.

Chapter 8

Against the indigo of the big sky, individual white clouds scudded slowly toward the northeast like the sails of an armada of galleons moving in formation over a placid ocean. The rolling prairie, a gigantic greening field, spread itself under the golden sun until it became smudged at the circular horizon, where heaven met earth indistinctly. It was midafternoon, a warm May day on the Saskatchewan plains.

Yukon stood for a moment at my side, then moved across the gravel road to relieve himself over a small, dry bundle of tumbleweed. I stood, leaning against the car, and scanned our immediate vicinity. Although no flowers were readily apparent, bumblebees in plenty filled the air with their husky droning; when I looked more closely, following a furry gold-and-black queen, she led my gaze to a cluster of blue-violet alfalfa blossoms almost hidden beneath the coarse grasses that carpeted the roadside. Farther away a worker of the species drew attention to a tall-ish bladder companion, its white blossoms emerging from inflated green calyx sacs that looked like minia-

154

ture melons. The rich, bubbly song of a meadowlark drew my eyes down the road. The bird was perched on a swaying stalk of last year's chicory, but as I lifted the field glasses to watch it more closely, movement in the sky made me look up. A hawk that was new to me hovered with fast-beating wings some distance to the south.

I went to get Peterson's *Field Guide to Western Birds,* anxious to identify the buteo. That was when Yukon found the hole at the bottom of the tall chain-link fence that was strung parallel to the road on the east side. The dog crawled through quickly and dashed away to disappear over the brow of one of those undulating rises so typical of the southern plains.

I called him, of course, telling him to come back; when he didn't respond, I whistled, waited, whistled again, eventually deciding to go after him, sure that he was trespassing on private land.

The fence was strong, six feet high, and anchored in the soil by thick metal posts. Because it was un-like any cattle fence that I had ever seen, I deduced, incorrectly, that it was designed to keep things *out,* rather than *in.* Driving south from Moose Jaw, we had passed an air force base not many miles back; now I wondered if this section of prairie was also part of the military establishment and thus definitely out of bounds. I scaled the wire, jumped down on the other side, and went to find Yukon.

When I was fifty or sixty paces from the fence and in the act of puckering up to whistle again, Yukon appeared suddenly on top of the hillock over which he had disappeared. He was running fast, a good deal faster than he had gone. In another moment the reason for his hurry became awesomely evident.

Spread out in ragged formation, looking as mean and formidable as any group of animals I have ever seen, seven buffalo cows charged over the rise in pursuit of Yukon, who, when he saw me standing open-mouthed, changed direction slightly and aimed himself at me. The seven enraged cows also altered course.

That was my first experience of the North American bison outside a zoo. It was not to be my last, by any means, and I was to learn a great deal about them in time, but that initial and inopportune meeting stands out above all others. Later I was to establish that Yukon had scented the bison and had gone to investigate the new and pungent aroma, unwittingly invading a buffalo nursery. Protective of their calves, the cows turned on the intruder, who wisely beat a hasty retreat. That I happened to be in the way of the stampede was incidental to the issue!

Yukon reached me, passed me at full speed, and darted through the hole in the fence, which was large enough to accommodate him with ease, but much too small for me.

I became the sole target of the angry bison. Never has a fence seemed to be so unattainable as during those moments when I ran at top speed, very conscious of the huffing thunder-hoofed beasts that pursued me. It is a curious fact that of all the animals that inhabit our planet, only men and apes waste time and energy looking back when they are escaping danger. Perhaps it is because the hearing and olfactory powers of the primates are not nearly as efficient as those of other animals, which seem better able to use sound and scent in order to compute distance, or it may be that primates, having binocular vision, rely on it more than on their other faculties.

Whatever the reason, I felt impelled to take a quick look over my shoulder.

Perhaps that look saved me from being run down. Before turning my head, I thought I was running flat out, but when I saw, ten yards at my heels, that cluster of big heads with their black, stubby, curved horns, I discovered that I was able to increase my speed considerably.

Preoccupied though I was, some part of my faculties were able to note that Yukon, very brave now that he was on the safe side of the fence, was pacing up and down outside, whoofing and yelping, showing a *machismo* that had been quite absent when the cows were on *his* heels.

I like to think that he would have come to my rescue had the buffalo caught up with me, but I shall never know, because I reached the fence, clutched wildly at the links, and skinned up it like a monkey, dropping onto the roadside and not stopping to look around again until I was inside the car with the doors closed.

The big cows stood beside the fence, puffing a little, ears flicking back and forth, but otherwise appearing no more dangerous than domestic Herefords gazing at accustomed traffic. I stepped out of the car, and Yukon came to me. He looked into my face with those almond-shaped eyes and gave me the impression that he was mocking me for being a coward.

I was reminded of my favorite hunting joke. Three friends go off into the wilderness; two quickly shoot their quarry, the third, a tyro, has no luck. On the penultimate day of the hunt, he sets out early in the morning, accompanied by derisive remarks from his companions, who are playing cards and drinking in the cabin. The man is gone several hours. Suddenly his friends hear him call. Moments later he bursts into the cabin, closely pursued by a grizzly bear; as he is diving out of a window, the bear already inside the cabin, he calls out to his terrified companions, "Skin that one. I'm going to get another!"

Grinning at Yukon, I rebuked him mildly, "Next time you rustle up stuff like that, don't bring it to me. Kill it yourself, you big oaf!"

Yukon wagged his tail, looked at the bison momentarily, then sauntered to the car, there to stand and wait for me to open the back door for him, as though the entire episode was really quite beneath his dignity. But he wasn't fooling me! He had met his match at last! Admittedly that was the first and the last time that I saw him run away from anything, but run he definitely did.

I did not think the less of the dog because of his retreat, especially when I took into account that this wide and open prairie was an environment as alien to him as it was to me. He was a creature of the forest;

he knew its ways and the ways of its denizens as well as a man knows the neighborhood in which he was born and brought up. Here on the plains he was an intruder encountering for the first time a country where there were no trees or bushes through which to maneuver, or in which to hide, and where, instead, he had encountered strange huge animals that combined in order to drive him away. He was entitled to feel insecure and apprehensive.

Early yesterday morning he had lifted his leg for this last bit of ritual. We had become outcasts because near the house on the homestead. We left right after this last bit of ritual. We had become outcasts because of my refusal to earn a living as a trapper.

Following the disasters already narrated, a combination of events during autumn and winter made it impossible for me to continue living in the backwoods. Not long after the tragedy of Sussie I shipped the pigs to the stockyards in Winnipeg at the coincidental time when the bottom dropped out of the hog market. Then, after filling the pulpwood contract, I discovered that the mill had cut back production and was not issuing any more orders for logs from independent cutters such as me. I tried to find buyers for cedar fence posts, but had no luck there either.

With less than six hundred dollars in cash and no prospects for future work, the outlook was bleak, I would be broke by summer, fall at the latest.

There is no point in dwelling on the depressing time that followed. After weeks of pondering and soul-searching, I knew I could no longer remain on the homestead, though I delayed making a final decision until March, hoping in the meantime that something would turn up.

One morning, after returning from town, where I had bought a copy of a daily newspaper, I saw an advertisement for the job of city editor on a newspaper in a small British Columbia community. On the spur of the moment I replied, and got the job. The starting date was for mid-June.

I was going to have to dispose of the dogs.

Seeking a good home for them, I visited Old Alec, and he told me of a friend of his in Ontario who, in today's parlance, was a dog "freak" who ran a sort of dog haven on his one hundred acre smallholding. I drove over to see this man and found that what Old Alec said was true. Here was an excellent home for Rocky and Sooner. But not for Yukon; nothing would have then induced me to part with the wolf-dog.

Soon afterward the two dogs went to live with a man I'll call Bill and Yukon and I were left alone on the homestead. Since there was now nothing to do, we spent weeks roaming the wilderness, exploring the country for miles around, hunting a little for food, living the sort of nomadic existence that was to become a way of life with us for almost three years. It was during this time that I became deeply interested in wolves. With Yukon to lead me, I was able to log many sightings during which a number of packs and individual wolves were observed for hours: in one fascinating ten-day period Yukon led me to a den containing pups located barely a mile from the homestead.

Not wishing to disturb the bitch and her young, I left Yukon at home for a time—much to his disgust—and spent the daylight hours watching the wolves from the vantage of a tall, branchy cedar tree some two hundred yards away.

Despite uncertainties and concerns for the future, these were idyllic times, and I was loath to give them up when April approached an end.

Now the house was cleaned, a few things were sold: tools and personal possessions were packed in the car. Finally, my red Chestnut canoe was hoisted onto the roof rack and tied down. At last, and with a heavy heart, yet with a feeling of excitement, we set off, Yukon sitting tall beside me on the front seat. Dawn was breaking as the car nosed out of the yard gate.

The distance from the homestead to the boundary of the province of Manitoba was about 180 miles, but before we left Ontario, Yukon cost me fifteen dollars. It happened when we stopped to eat and gas up the car in a small town 150 miles along the road, soon after I let Yukon out so he could relieve himself against a wheel while I held onto his lead. Almost at once three local dogs dashed up, vociferous and snarling. Yukon was prepared to parley, but the foolish locals attacked immediately: I let go of the lead, not wanting my dog hampered under the circumstances.

Quickly I opened the back door of the car to get a stick I had brought with me, a stout, bone-dry length of tamarack sapling I had cut as a walking stick soon after I arrived at the homestead, now kept as a memento. That would soon end the fight. But I was mistaken: Yukon ended the fight before my hand closed on the cudgel. He killed the biggest dog, a brown mongrel, which now lay at the edge of the road, neck broken. The other two ran, but one traveled on three legs; both howled and ki-yied loudly as they made for home.

Retrieving Yukon's lead preparatory to putting him back in the car, my back turned to the restaurant opposite which we had stopped, I became aware of angry voices behind me. Turning, I was confronted by a number of locals who had evidently come out of the café. Among them was the owner of the limping dog. An altercation ensued during which it was established that the mongrel was a stray, but that the injured dog was considered very valuable by its owner: he crossed the street to his house, returned quickly, and told me that the dog had a broken leg and a number of deep slashes on its body. Then he became loud in demanding Yukon's destruction. At this I replied quietly, but with no less determination, that if the three dogs of doubtful ancestry had not been so stupid and vicious, nothing would have occurred beyond a few sniffs and growls and ritualistic wetting. Yukon, ever quick to sense my moods, offered to get into the argument by growling malevolently, raising his hackles, and baring every one of his fighting fangs. The crowd backed up, then thinned miraculously, and to end the matter, I offered the man ten dollars to pay for his dog's treatment. He demanded thirty dollars but settled for fifteen dollars.

We lost little time in getting out of there. Of course I was sorry that Yukon killed one dog and seriously injured another, but the affair was definitely not of his making. When attacked, he defended himself, and because he was fast, big, and powerful, he defeated his opponents. Nevertheless, I realized that we were likely to run into the same problem in other towns and that unless I took precautions, Yukon was liable to spill a trail of blood across four Canadian provinces. In order to avoid this, I adopted the practice of stopping between towns to let him out for his runs, tarrying in built-up centers only long enough to refuel the car and to buy food we could eat on the road.

Even so, Yukon did battle with quite a number of country dogs before we arrived at our destination six weeks after setting out. Fortunately these were all one-to-one encounters, and because he didn't feel himself seriously threatened, the wolf-dog ended the contests quickly and bloodlessly, once more making use of his chest punch if his adversary was a large dog. If, as happened, small pooches with more guts than brains attacked him, Yukon behaved rather strangely, seeming to look upon such antagonists as beneath his dignity. Instead of fighting them, he would pin them to the ground with one big paw and hold them there until they screamed. When he lifted his paw, the foolhardy curs would streak for home. During such comical altercations, Yukon would collect a nip or two on his right ankle, but these didn't seem to bother him.

When we entered Manitoba it was to find that the highway leading west was liberally sprinkled with towns and villages and for this reason I kept driving, halting only for gasoline, food, and wet-stops. As a result, I drove all night and reached Moose Jaw, in the province of Saskatchewan, at daybreak. Here the car was gassed-up again and I bought enough food to last for several days, for, having studied the area of the prairie Badlands, I knew there were many wild places where we could camp while we explored a region rich in history, wildlife, and scenery.

The incident with the bison cows occurred about an hour after we stopped for lunch and a short catnap. I had no idea that there was a herd of buffalo in the area and only later learned that they had been here for some time and were the responsibility of the Saskatchewan government wildlife department. It is quite likely that I would have driven past the buffalo pound if Yukon hadn't gone to investigate them, so I was grateful to him, even if the discovery gave me a good fright.

The cows soon tired of standing beside the fence, though perhaps it was anxiety for their young that caused them to turn around and to walk almost sedately away to disappear over the hillock. Curious now, and very much interested in these strange bovines, I left Yukon in the car and walked some distance north along the road before stopping, looking around to make sure that I was unobserved, and climbed the fence again.

Field glasses around my neck, I walked slowly and cautiously over the prairie, the hill that had obstructed our view of the bison from the highway now lying in front of me and to one side. In a little while, ascending slightly higher land, I saw the calves, six of them, most of which were playing friskily in a slight depression. The cows were there also; one was feeding her calf, which was bunting lustily at her udders while it sucked so avidly that a froth of milk decorated its lips and dripped off its hairy chin.

Two other cows were lying down; the rest were standing, gazing into space in that wool-gathering way characteristic of the bison.

Two bulls stood solitarily some distance away, evidently unperturbed by the recent excitement, standing as though asleep, heads down and bodies immobile except for the constant swishing of their ridiculous tails. One of them was not much bigger than the cows, the other was a huge beast with a great shaggy head and a long beard. In contrast with the untidy, still-molting cows, the bulls looked sleek and glossy, having changed their heavy winter coats while the females were busy birthing the young.

Flies clustered thickly around the bison, all manner of flies, including the tiny, vicious blackflies, or buffalo gnats, as they are also called. Some of the latter soon discovered me, but I was too interested to pay them heed.

The big bull looked up once, sniffed in my direction, and moved his ears from side to side; otherwise, I was ignored. Emboldened, recalling some of the things I had read about these animals, I dared to go closer, moving naturally but slowly, quite ready to bolt for the fence at the first hostile move from any of the big beasts.

When about fifty paces from the nearest cow, I stopped. She fixed her eyes on me but remained unperturbed, chewing the cud with a slow sideways motion of her jaws. It was difficult to reconcile this now peaceful scene with the angry and determined charge that had taken place ten minutes earlier.

Squatting in the thick grass, focusing the glasses on first one, then another huge animal, I marveled at their grotesque, but efficient, architecture, so well designed to withstand the fierce winds during winters when the mercury dropped to thirty and forty degrees below zero. Slim in the hips and heavy and well furred on head and shoulders, they were like wedges that forever presented their thick ends to the wind, even now, on this benign spring afternoon.

Looking at the little herd, I felt a sense of nostalgia tinged with regret that I had come to North America too late to see the bison as they once were. Audubon estimated that one billion bison roamed the plains of North America before the coming of Western man; this was perhaps an exaggeration, but there is no gainsaying the fact that millions of buffalo wandered over the Great Plains before civilization destroyed them. Seton estimated sixty million; most naturalists agree with him.

Early American explorers found buffalo widely distributed in North America, from western Pennsylvania on to southern Idaho, from New Mexico northward to Great Slave Lake and to Lake Athabasca in northwest Canada. They were even found in the southeast, in the area of the Potomac River in Maryland, in central Georgia, and in Florida. Yet by 1889 that great American naturalist William T. Hornaday could account for only 541 bison in the United States; a few years later only one wild band of bison survived, about twenty animals. In Canada the situation was about the same; a handful of plains bison roamed the prairies, while fewer than three hundred woods bison lived farther north. Belatedly, in 1902, the governments of the United States and Canada began a conservation project. Fortunately it worked, and it seems that today the buffalo are safe from extinction—at least until human greed caused the violation of their preserves.

These things were much in my mind as I watched the fifteen bison in Saskatchewan, and whether it was because of this line of thought or for some other, unfathomable reason, I suddenly felt a powerful sense of purpose, a calling, if you will. On the instant I knew that I was now committed to the study of nature, to the observation of the thousands of life-forms to be found in the wilderness regions of North America. And I knew that the years on the homestead had been but an apprenticeship, a time of learning and of trial and of self-doubts; it was as though I had put together enough pieces of a very beautiful jigsaw puzzle to allow me to gain an impression of the picture it represented, but not enough of them to see the fullness of the completed panorama.

Hunkering there on the plains, I was filled with a sense of wonderment, of unreality, at the manner in which my life had been influenced. It seemed hardly believable that the experiences of my past could have somehow prepared me for the sort of life I led on arrival in Canada, no less so for the kind of life I was now certain that I was going to follow. Even now, so many years later, I cannot quite understand how it all came about; but whereas today I can look back and know that I have only deviated circumstantially and for relatively short periods from the resolution that I made that spring day in Saskatchewan, I had no means then of knowing that I would indeed keep my hastily made resolve. Yet deep down, I was positive that I would.

As I rose to go back to the car, automatically noting the ripple of interest that passed through the small buffalo herd, I realized with uncanny perception that Yukon and I were destined to be wilderness wanderers. I know some who would be shocked by such a prospect and who would sincerely believe that a man should settle down somewhere. Indeed, as recently as this year, just before my wife, Sharon, and I set out to live in the Yukon Territory, an old and valued friend, on hearing our news, broached this very question.

"Don't you think its about time that you put down roots?" he asked almost diffidently for a man who is normally very direct, feeling he had to voice the question, yet not wishing to intrude.

I made some noncommittal answer then, but now I know the reply that I should have made:

"I have put down roots, they are big and deep and most tenacious in their hold. My roots are set in the vast, magnificent wilderness areas of North America."

Chapter 9

Majestic and beautiful, the Rockies pressed closely on either side of the narrow highway that threaded its way up the eastern flanks of the mountains, leveled off briefly as it slid through the pass, then plunged downward and westward to become lost within the labyrinthine forests that covered a distant valley.

Beyond the lush green lowlands, the serried peaks of the Purcell Mountains posed against the blue sky as though offering themselves to the canvas of an artist. Some of the distant tops were verdant; some were barren and scree-covered; a few were capped by snow or concealed by glaciers that glistened blue-white under the influence of the low sun.

From the vantage of the Crowsnest Pass, the world that spread itself before us dwarfed anything yet encountered during our wandering. The plains impressed with their big skies and the feeling of openness they generated; the foothills country of southwestern Alberta offered pastoral serenity mixed with glimpses of rugged wilderness. But this rather awesome, infinite land we were now viewing was capable of evoking hylopathic sentiments, managing in some way to impart a sense of life even to the most somber scarps.

Because the Rocky Mountains are so well known, one might think their name is generic for all the ranges that are to be found in the northwest; it comes as something of a shock to realize that beyond the nearest range there lies another line of mountains, and yet another: Rockies, Purcells, Selkirks, Monashees, Cascades . . . and so on to the Coast Range in the extreme west and to the Brooks Range in Alaska, whose northern flanks look down on the Beaufort Sea.

Journeying up toward the Crowsnest Pass from Alberta, I had been impressed with the scenery, but because the climb was steep and tortuous and I was unaccustomed to mountain driving, I was unable to devote proper attention to the country. As a result, when we reached the summit, the sudden, bursting panorama was astonishing. Seeing a small lay-by off the highway, I drove onto it and parked tight against a massive outcrop of granite that had been blasted sheer to make way for the road.

When Yukon and I got out of the car, we were rather like children given the freedom of a candy store. We didn't know what to sample first.

The dog ran a little way up a more gentle slope on the opposite side of the pavement, clearly full of excitement as he went from tree to tree, frantic to leave his mark on every larch, spruce, and fir, in between times sniffing with wild urgency at the rocks and bushes and grasses.

As for me, I couldn't concentrate on any one feature of this giant country for more than a few seconds at a time. My eyes slid from place to place, and my brain seethed like an overburdened computer.

The Crowsnest Pass was Canada's first overland doorway to the west. The boundary line between Alberta and British Columbia runs through it longitudinally. The Rocky Mountains at this point are almost ready to cross the border into Montana, there to arrange themselves so as to form the splendor of Glacier National Park.

I went after Yukon, who seemed fascinated with an upthrust of rock too steep to climb. As I reached him, a piercing whistle rang out, coming from almost immediately above our heads. I moved back, trying to find the whistler; moments later movement atop the columnlike rock attracted attention. It was a hoary marmot. Evidently the animal had been sunning itself at the entrance to its burrow, and we had disturbed it, whereupon it had whistled as it dived into its shelter. Because these animals are intensely curious, and no doubt because this one knew itself to be safe perched there above us, the marmot came out to get another look at the cause of its disturbance, initially showing only its head, presently revealing the beautiful silver-white mantle that draped its shoulders.

Yukon soon realized that he couldn't get at this roly-poly quarry. He gave up trying to scale the natural fortress and lost all interest in the marmot, which continued to insult the two of us for interrupting its siesta. Just then a different sort of call echoed through the pass. At the sound the marmot disappeared again, this time to stay hidden.

The falsetto cry was made by a bald eagle, a hunter far more dangerous to the whistler than dog or wolf. The big raptor with the pure white tail and head came sailing down from some invisible scarp, but when its intended victim ducked to safety, the eagle planed, braked with its spread tail, and raised itself once more by slightly altering the angle of incidence of its primaries. Performing this magnificent feat with ridiculous ease, it spiraled gracefully upward and eventually disappeared behind the bulk of a dogtooth mountain.

After climbing a little higher and standing on a block of granite, I had an almost undisturbed view of the land below. About a mile away and some thousand feet lower down was a smallish lake, its waters aquamarine, sparkling, a section of shoreline coming close to the highway. This would be a good place in which to spend at least one night. I lifted the glasses and scanned the area.

On the far shore, nicely sheltered by some stately

larches, was a flat piece of land big enough for the tent; dimpling the surface of the placid water, feeding trout brought the slaver to my mouth. Even before I lowered the glasses, I was visualizing our trip across the lake in the canoe, followed by the making of a fast camp; then, back into the canoe with the fly rod and fresh trout for supper roasted over a bed of slow coals!

I called Yukon. When he stood beside me on the flat rock, I patted his head and pointed downward, indicating the lake.

"See that water? We're going to spend the night there. Maybe even a few days. And we're going out in the canoe, and we're going to get some nice, fat trout!"

Yukon wagged his tail, bowed by bending his front legs and leaving his hind end in the air, straightened again, and yawned; this was one of the ways in which he showed his pleasure. He couldn't understand my words, but he could tell from my tone of voice and from the accompanying gestures that something of interest was afoot.

By now I had got into the habit of talking to him as freely as if he were a human companion, partly because I am somewhat garrulous and conversations with those of my own kind were few and far between and partly because I didn't think of Yukon as a dog; he was a friend, a being who shared my life as I shared this. It surprised me to discover, about a month after leaving the homestead, that we had drawn even closer and that we understood and respected each other in a way that we had not done before. It may be inconceivable to some, but we were now almost as one entity living in two different bodies, responding instantly to each other's needs even to the point of personal sacrifice.

I have met a few men, no more than a handful, with whom I could relate in this fashion while wandering through the wilderness. They were the rare ones who were not disposed to cabin fever or to develop a deep, burning anger toward a partner, a ran-

cor so strong that it could lead to lasting hatred—
usually because of some trivial happening or event.

Yukon and I never suffered from cabin fever for
the simple reason that were were rarely lonely inside
ourselves; that loneliness is the real cause of the syn-
drome, which affects people wherever they may live.
One might as well call the condition apartment fever
or city fever, for it is possible to be every bit as lonely
in New York, London, or Montreal as in the wildest
part of the northland.

In our case, and quite uncannily, when one of us
was on the brink of feeling lonely inside our heads,
the other would immediately detect it, respond to it,
and cure it.

If I happened to be the one, Yukon would come to
me, lean against me, and voice a sort of half howl,
half bark that ended with a long-drawn *a-woooo . . .
oooh . . . oooh . . . ah.* That done, he would raise
himself and put one paw on each of my shoulders and
lick my face. No mood, however gloomy, was proof
against such sensitive love.

If *he* was down-in-the-mouth, as did happen on occasion, I would hug him and speak to him gently, or
else I would lie down beside him and hold him. In
either event, his tail would start wagging, and he
would nuzzle into me. Moments later, restored to his
usual happy-go-lucky frame of mind, he'd jump up
and initiate a romp.

We were still living on the homestead when I discovered that Yukon was a prankster with a well-
developed sense of humor that he exhibited in many
ways, perhaps the most notable of which was a habit
of nipping me on the rump when I wasn't paying attention to him—hard enough at times to cause a small
blood blister! When the sudden and intense pain
caused me to jump and yell, he would bound away,
a big grin on his face, torn between the desire to
wrestle and the fear of the consequences of his action,
for I used to retaliate whenever I could by biting his
ear hard enough to cause *him* to yelp, after which we
would stage mock combat.

Yukon demonstrated his sense of humor a couple of times in as many weeks soon after we left the homestead. The first incident occurred while we were camped in the Cypress Hills of Saskatchewan,* when an overeager park warden interrupted our breakfast. The area in which we were camped was part of a provincial park and dogs were not allowed to run free within its boundaries, as posted notices proclaimed. We obeyed the signs, but it so happened that Yukon and I always had our meals together, so that he was not tied up during these occasions.

When the young official arrived, we were still eating, Yukon lying at my feet, completing the destruction of a large beef bone I had bought for him the previous day.

As the stranger approached, the dog rose to his feet but remained near me, and I put a hand on his head and asked him to sit; this he promptly did. At the same time I greeted the warden and offered him a cup of coffee.

Instead of acknowledging my greeting, and ignoring my offer, the man snapped a question and an order at one and the same time.

"Don't you know dogs aren't allowed to run free in the park? Get him tied up. *Like right now!*"

Even though I tried to allow for the fact that he was a very young official, and bearing in mind that we were technically guilty of an offense, I found his manner irritating. Nevertheless, I forced myself to see his point of view as I tried to explain that Yukon was not, in fact, running free and wouldn't go anywhere during the brief spell that he was off his lead within the park boundaries.

"Just get him tied up an' never mind the arguing.

---

* The Cypress Hills, a freak formation of treed highlands somehow left untouched when mile-deep glaciers bulldozed across the North American Middle West and formed the Great Plains, straddle the boundary between Saskatchewan and Alberta. Both provinces operate parks in their own sections of these rather beautiful, if humble, mountains.

Else get out of the park," interrupted the young man pompously.

I was about to tell him to go climb a tree (we were going to pack up and leave, in any event, right after breakfast) when Yukon got up and moved forward, looking intently into the man's face. The dog stopped beside the warden, sniffed inquisitively at one of the man's pant legs, lifted his own back leg, and peed on the neatly creased uniform without ever taking his eyes off the other's face, grinning all the time. This exposed every one of his very large fangs. It was a rout!

The green uniform turned dark as Yukon's urine soaked into the cloth, and the surplus that was not absorbed dribbled on the highly polished boot. But not a muscle did the bug-eyed young man move as the arrogance in his mien was replaced by a look of fear.

I grabbed for Yukon; he dodged me and wouldn't come back when I called him. Instead, he stood a couple of yards away, stock-still, opened his mouth wide and gave the man a good talking-to, *wooo . . . wooing* lustily. *I* knew he was bluffing, that this was his idea of a good joke, but the unfortunate park warden didn't. But I also knew that Yukon could well decide to stop fooling and bite the man in good and earnest if the latter continued to show fear, in which case no sound would precede the attack and no move of mine could forestall it.

Prevention was the cure. The only way to alter the circumstances was to get the man to sit down and join me in a cup of coffee, at least in semblance of friendship, for Yukon would not tolerate anybody who showed anger toward me.

Trying hard to control the levity that I felt, I explained the situation to our poor visitor, who was now looking very apprehensive.

"I'm really sorry, and I'll pay to have your pants cleaned, but you'd better sit down and have some coffee just now. If you do, the dog will come and sit beside me, and I'll put him on the lead."

The young man did as I suggested, albeit with very

little grace. Yukon immediately walked over and lay down at my feet, but kept his eyes fixed on our visitor's face. I put the lead on him.

As it turned out, he wasn't such a bad young fellow, that park warden, just overly keen. After he got over his fright and his sense of outrage was appeased, we actually became friends during the brief time that we were together, and Yukon partly made up for his shocking behavior by stretching against the lead and slurping his tongue against the man's face, though I'm not sure that this was greatly appreciated by our visitor. (If G.L.H. should read this today, I would like him to accept our handsomest apologies with the hope that now that he is twenty years older, he will have it in him to understand that Yukon was only kidding.)

Some days later another comical (to us, at any rate) situation developed, but this time I was as responsible for it as was Yukon.

Stopping by a roadside restaurant where the spoons were greasy and the decor ailing-Victorian, I saw a man emerge from the building leading a dog. Rolling down the window of the car, I asked him if I could take Yukon in with me. Yes, he replied, provided he was kept on the lead. My interlocutor, who was a local, said the owner "don't give a darn one way or t'other, so long's you leave a tip."

We went in. Yukon was a model of canine behavior. The flaxen-haired waitress who looked like the before photograph of one those advertisements that also show the after picture, glanced at us as we walked to a booth, but she didn't speak, being exceptionally preoccupied with one fingernail, at which she nibbled gently.

I sat down. Yukon backed under the table so that he could lie facing the traffic lane. The girl, spitting out a shard of nail, sauntered over with that meant-to-be-sexual hip waggle that unkempt women evidently believe can take the place of soap and water and a decent waistline. She didn't bring a menu.

Disposing of a wad of gum by the simple process of

spitting it on the floor, she asked, "What'll youse have?"

I gave her my order and asked for two uncooked hamburgers for Yukon. The food arrived surprisingly quickly. Mine was as cold as Yukon's, but since we were hungry and not fussy, we began to eat.

Halfway through my meal (Yukon didn't take long to consume the wafer-thin burgers) a man came out of the kitchen, saw the dog, and walked flat-footed to our booth. He was short and built like a pear, an excellent match for the waitress.

"Youse ain't supposed to bring a dog in here, ya know?"

He spoke tough, croaking the words from the corner of his mouth, both hands stuffed behind a dirty apron. Once more it was the tone of voice, the ungraciousness of attitude, that rankled. If I hadn't seen a dog come out of this very place, I might have answered differently.

"Gee! *I'm* sorry. Throw him out!" I invited sweetly and reasonably.

As though on cue, Yukon came out from under the table, hitting it with his back, since he was in more of a hurry to exit than he had been to enter, and lifted the board several inches off the floor, the while baring his teeth and producing a growl which I knew was uttered only in pretense because it lacked the deep-in-the-throat malevolence of the real thing. But like the park warden, the man didn't know this.

Our inquisitor's bluster vanished on the instant. He stared wide-eyed at the dog for no more than a couple of seconds, turned quickly, and scuttled back to his kitchen without uttering another word.

The waitress walked over to our table and gave me our bill, strangely enough not a bit afraid of Yukon, who actually wagged his tail at her when she patted him briefly on the head.

"Youse don't want to take no notice of *him*. He's like that sometimes; figures he'll get a bit extry so's he'll let youse keep the dog in here," she said in a low voice.

I left the "bit extry" in any event.

Scrambling down from the Crowsnest Pass viewpoint, leading Yukon to the car, I calculated that to date we had covered a distance in excess of two thousand miles. It was the middle of the first week of June; soon I would find myself anchored to a news desk again. I tried not to think of this as we drove down the western flanks of the Rockies heading for our last carefree campground, occupying myself instead by remembering some of the small adventures we had experienced, the country we had seen, and the positive plethora of wild animals encountered.

Driving down from the Crowsnest Pass toward the lake I had seen from our rocky viewpoint, I found myself wishing that I could stay a good long while in this part of the country, at least long enough to allow us to explore in detail its valleys and mountains and waterways. Alas, it was not to be! All we managed to settle for were three days beside the small lake—I have never explored that particular area, despite promising myself that I would do so one day.

But our stay by the water was memorable, nevertheless. The lake turned out to be all that I had hoped for; it was clear and cold, the trout were hungry, and the eagles came to call and to do a little fishing of their own.

A narrow gravel lane led us off the highway almost to the edge of the water, and here I took down the canoe, packed in it the tent and other supplies, pushed it into the water, and waited until Yukon was sitting bolt upright in the bow, like an overlarge, misplaced figurehead. It took half an hour to cross the lake, fifteen minutes to set up camp, and about three more minutes to relaunch the canoe and paddle out again, fly rod ready, Yukon once more in his place by the bow.

Four beautiful rainbow trout quickly accepted the dry mosquito fly that is my favorite and most successful artificial insect. Here was supper in plenty for both of us, so the rod was dismantled and put away, and as the sun disappeared behind one of the western peaks with the characteristic speed it displays in the mountains, I paddled gently around our half of the lake, indulging myself, for I dearly love an early-evening jaunt over dead-still silvery water when the stately quiet of what I think of as the in-between time of life allows me to dream my dreams uninterrupted.

The trout was delicious! Split and gutted and fastened with snare wire to a green willow branch, I roasted mine slowly. Yukon ate his raw and *in toto*.

That night, lying in the sleeping bag with Yukon stretched full length beside me, I was soon asleep. But not for very long! I don't know what time it was because I didn't bother to check, but I awoke to the howling of a wolf right beside my left ear. It was Yukon. When I managed to shut him up, I heard the reason for his call. Distant, but carrying clearly through the crisp night air, a pack of timber wolves were singing their ageless songs. My companion just naturally answered them. It was wonderful.

Two mornings later, just as dawn was breaking, the car was packed. Leaving Yukon in the front seat, I returned to the shore to get the canoe, whereupon the wilderness treated me to one more thrill. As I was about to pull the canoe all the way out of the water, the noise of snapping brush drew my attention to a place about forty yards away. Looking up, I saw a cow elk step out of the forest and walk sedately to the shoreline.

Behind her came her calf, a little, spindly-legged thing spotted white on back and flanks, the rest of its coat biscuit-colored. I remained perfectly still. The cow dipped her shiny black muzzle into the water and sucked audibly; the calf stood a few paces behind her, twitching its big ears. When the mother was finished, she turned around gracefully, refusing to let the questing calf suck, and she marched back into the forest, followed by the little one.

Minutes later we were again riding down the western slope of the Rockies. Late that afternoon, after descending to the valley first seen from the Crowsnest Pass, then ascending one side of the Purcell Range and dropping down the other, we arrived at Kootenay Bay, where, in due time, a ferry conducted us across Kootenay Lake to Balfour, a long detour today, but made necessary then because the southern route from Creston to Salmo (the Kootenay Skyway) was not yet built.

By now we had passed through so much breathtaking scenery that I had become almost blasé. After we left Balfour, we stopped only once, and that was by necessity. We were rounding a sharp curve in the highway when a mule deer bounded out of the brush and landed right in front of the car.

I was driving slowly, so I was able to pull up sharply; even so, the deer was knocked down. It rolled to the side of the road, there to lie still. With difficulty preventing Yukon from following, I got out of the car to examine the animal, greatly regretting the accident and fearing that the deer had been killed or seriously injured.

It was breathing when I reached it; there was no blood. I picked up one of the back legs, let it fall again, then squatted beside the head and grasped each of the velvety, not yet fully formed antlers, lifting the head. The buck awoke to sudden and agitated life, scrambled to its feet, and knocked me backward. Before I really knew what had happened, it bounded away, a trifle unsteady of gait, but otherwise seemingly unharmed.

We spent that night in a small provincial campsite, rose at first light, breakfasted hurriedly, and set off anew. We reached our destination just before noon, five days before I was due to start work.

By now funds were down to fifty-seven dollars; payday was nineteen days away. In the meantime, we had to find somewhere to live, preferably with room enough for Yukon to run in without getting into trouble, and cheap. Of more immediacy was the need to locate a campsite out of town, for we could not afford to spend money on motels.

Fortunately the community was surrounded by wilderness. I found what I wanted seven miles east of town, a flat space some ten acres in area that nestled between two gently sloping mountains, accessible by a narrow and overgrown track. Examining the place, I discovered the remains of an old log cabin; a couple of hundred yards up the side of one of the mountains was an abandoned mine shaft, a not unusual sight in a country that had at one time been overrun with prospectors trying to strike it rich in the most improbable places.

Here camp was set up, but on this occasion the task took a couple of hours, for this was to be a semipermanent campsite with a rock fireplace, a twenty-foot by fourteen-foot canvas fly projecting from the tent doorway, and a rack between two trees for the canoe to rest upside down. In addition, because Yukon was going to have to remain tied up while I was working, I pounded a heavy steel anchor pin into the ground in such a position that it would allow him to reach the canvas shelter while he was confined by a twenty-foot chain secured to the ground rod by a swivel ring. When brush and small trees were cleared from the area of his run, he could travel a complete forty-foot-wide circle without getting tangled up.

Even so, I knew he wasn't going to be happy confined daily in this way; but it was the best I could do for him under the circumstances, and he was going to have to endure it just as I had to suffer the tedium of editing a small, banal newspaper.

In a different way, but no less so, I too was going to be a captive, bound to a desk, if not to a stake in the ground, when I longed to be free to roam the wilderness with Yukon. But his plight was worse than mine. He was in ignorance of the causes of his captivity, and he didn't know that he was going to serve a relatively short sentence.

When I accepted the job, I did so with every intention of holding it for an indeterminate amount of time. During our wanderings through the prairies, I had not spent much time considering the matter of our long-term future. But now, confronted by the daily routines of an office job, an *inside* job, to be more precise, I realized that I had no stomach for that kind of thing. I had always avoided desk work like the plague, preferring to work as a reporter and even accepting lower pay because of it. The attraction was that reporting allowed me to write—my only love —kept me on the street for most of the working day, and led to frequent out-of-town, often out-of-country assignments. Now I was in no position to be choosy, so here I was, desk-bound.

By the end of my second week of work I was bored to distraction and frustrated beyond concept. Feeling somewhat guilty, but not guilty enough to abandon the decision, I determined to stay only long enough to accumulate a grubstake sufficient to take care of our financial needs for at least one year of wilderness wandering, during which time I would concentrate on what I now wanted to do most of all: study nature in the field as a free agent, unhampered by governmental or institutional loyalties, the two most powerful forces in the lives of biologists.

I did think at one point about seeking work in this discipline, but when I realized that there are only three major employers of biologists—government, industry, and universities—each of which poses its own kinds of restrictions, I put the notion aside.

I was now committed to making as much money as possible in as short a time as possible, with a minimum target figure of three thousand dollars. Finding that my employer was perennially short-handed and that paid overtime was almost always available, I volunteered for as much of this work as I could get. And I free-lanced, covering for several wire services and writing for a variety of general interest and business publications. So as to save as much money as possible, I delibereately avoided socializing with other people, causing my newspaper colleagues to believe that I was some sort of rabid misanthrope, not without reason, I suppose.

By the third week of July I was lucky enough to rent an abandoned cabin several miles out of town. The place was rundown, but cheap at thirty dollars a month, located beside a lake, and offered ten acres of property. Its owner, an elderly lady, wanted to sell it to me, but apart from the fact that I couldn't afford it, property ownership did not fit into my plans just then.

There was no electricity, of course, and no plumbing, but there was a good well, the logs were reasonably chinked, and adding to the sylvan setting were several cherry trees that had gone wild(but that yet were to produce more cherries than I could eat and preserve) and no fewer than nine aging apple trees, also rather overgrown. Within thirty or forty yards from our own little beach, rainbow trout and *kokanee*, a species of small landlocked salmon *(Oncorhynchus nerka)* that is delicious, were always eager to take my flies or small spoons, assuring us of a constant supply of excellent protein, free.

It took me a week to clean the place up during my spare time. There were several sections of logs where the old clay-and-straw chinking had fallen out, two places on the roof that needed patching, some rusted stovepipe to replace, and a whole lot of grass and brush to cut.

Near the back of the cabin was an old shed crammed with all manner of junk among which I found three big rolls of page-wire fencing. It was old, but still serviceable, and seventy-two inches high. Using this and some cedar posts cut on the property, I made a run for Yukon that was thirty-six feet long by twelve feet wide, incorporating the shed at one end so that he could have shelter from sun and rain whenever he wanted it. When all was ready, we moved in.

On the whole, we were both pleased with our little temporary estate. The cabin was twelve feet wide by twenty-four feet long, built of good cedar logs. The interior was divided into living quarters and kitchen. There was an old heavy-iron wood heater in the living room that was in excellent condition, even though it had been made before the turn of the century, and a wood-burning cookstove occupied pride of place in the kitchen.

Besides these things, there were two rather rickety tables, three aging straight-back chairs, and a broken rocker; meager enough furnishings, admittedly, but by the time I had made a bunk bed out of peeled spruce poles and canvas strips and a definitely rustic sofa padded with sacks filled with good, clean hay, I considered our nest more than comfortable. It wasn't exactly the Waldorf, but Yukon and I were happy to call it home.

There was one minor disadvantage. The property was located off the highway at the foot of a steep slope inaccessible to wheeled vehicles. All supplies had to be carried down a narrow trail that was a good three hundred yards long or else ferried over water in the canoe from a beach area three-quarters of a mile away. While this represented no great inconvenience as a general rule, there were times when I regretted the need to scramble down the pathway at night, carrying groceries home after completing a late shift at the newspaper. But when I considered the many advantages of the property, this one snag was of little consequence. Except perhaps for one notable experience that took place in early autumn.

Preceding this incident, while I was walking with Yukon one morning before going to work, I noticed grizzly bear tracks on the sandy beach. Coincidental with this discovery, Yukon darted toward one of the apple trees that grew fairly close to the house. He became preoccupied with something that was concealed from me by the long grass. I found that his excitement was occasioned by a great pile of bear manure. Fallen apples littered the ground around the tree, as they did around all the other trees, so it was not difficult to understand the reason for the bear's visit.

The discovery pleased and interested me, for I hoped that I might be afforded the opportunity to see the bear at close quarters; on the other hand, I determined to leave Yukon in the house on those occasions when I worked an overtime late shift, just in case he started an argument with the grizzly. I was regularly employed on days, starting at seven in the morning and finishing at three in the afternoon; the late shift began at four o'clock and ended at midnight; this gave me an hour for supper, when I would drive home, eat quickly, have a little time with Yukon, and leave again. Now, until our big visitor finished eating all the deadfall apples, I would leave Yukon in the house after supper, for safety's sake.

Two days went by. Each morning we would find fresh evidence that the bear had come visiting during the night; there were now fewer apples on the ground. On the third day I was invited to a double shift. That night there was to be a full moon.

I returned home from the office at 3:10 p.m., had a light meal, gave Yukon his supper, made a sandwich and a Thermos of coffee, and left again at 3:50, Yukon remaining indoors.

Shortly after midnight I was back again. As I parked the car on the shoulder of the highway, near the entrance to the trail, I naturally wondered whether I would catch a glimpse of the grizzly, feeling a slight tingle of apprehension. For this reason I walked softly, stopping often to listen. When halfway down, about to emerge into the more open section of the pathway, where the moonlight allowed for better visibility, I heard the crash of breaking glass, immediately followed by a great deal of commotion that appeared to be headed directly toward me.

I stopped, but before I was able to deduce anything from the noise, I saw the grizzly coming at full gallop up the pathway; a few yards behind it and going just as fast was Yukon.

I yelled, waved my arms, ordered Yukon to stop; neither animal took the slightest bit of notice. For a futile instant I clutched the empty Thermos bottle like a club and started to raise it above my head, but realizing the insanity of my action, I did the only other thing possible: There being no room on that trail for more than one creature at a time, I gave the grizzly the right-of-way by diving headfirst into what I had thought to be an impassable tangle of trees, saplings, and thick clumps of blackberry bushes.

Crawling as rapidly as possible through what felt like a giant tangle of barbed wire, I made so much noise that I was unable to hear what was going on behind me, but when I broke out of the clutching blackberry jungle and stood up among some crowded second-growth poplars, there to pause for a fraction of time while getting ready to climb the eight-inch trunk of the nearest aspen, all was quiet.

It is a marvelous fact of life that during moments of extreme personal crisis the flow of adrenaline allows a human being to move with remarkable speed and amazing insensitivity to pain. I have no idea how long it took me to wriggle like a snake through about ten feet of blackberry thorn, but I am positive that I felt not the slightest bit of pain while I was doing so. Once in the clear, however, and knowing that the danger was passed, I became immediately conscious of the many cuts and scratches acquired during my journey through the thorns. Probably because it was aimed at the ground, my face escaped relatively unscathed, but my head was considerably lacerated; so were my hands and arms and legs and backside. I picked thorns out of myself until dawn, and several days were to pass before the last festering spike worked its way to the surface and was dug out.

Yukon didn't return until half an hour before I was due to go to work again. I wasn't pleased with him.

"You *look* like a dog, but that's only an illusion. Without a doubt, you're the world's *biggest* donkey! You've broken a window, got me all scratched up, scared the hell out of me, and made me go without sleep. That's got to be a record, even for you!"

I spoke as sternly as I could manage. He looked so ridiculously crestfallen, as though he had expected praise for chasing the bear away instead of being scolded, that I once again fell for his wiles, knowing, as I bent to give him a big hug, that he was not really contrite and that he would do the same again given similar opportunity. He was grinning hugely as he followed me to his enclosure, entered it, and found himself a nice, comfortable spot in the shade where he could sleep through the day while I slaved, bleary-eyed and hurting, over a whole lot of badly written copy.

In retrospect, I have to admit that Yukon's actions, if drastic, were effective. The bear didn't return, though it may be that the imminent arrival of winter was in part responsible for his continued absence.

We met a new kind of cold that year, less severe, tempered by frequent periods of thaw that made the snow heavy and sticky during the hours of sunlight and crusted it hard at night. We enjoyed the newness of that winter, but neither of us was entirely content, being too greatly restricted by the daily routines of our existence.

The weeks passed too slowly; we became more restless; we didn't seem to get the same enjoyment from our occasional weekend outings, which, by the end of January, were severely restricted by the deep and mushy snow, the short days, and the steepness of the mountains.

By the end of February, having saved $3,213.55, I gave notice to the newspaper. We would leave in two weeks' time, weather or no weather.

Those last days were the hardest to endure! Every morning I ticked off another day on the calendar; every evening I did a little more packing. . . .

Then, at last, it was time to go.

Chapter 10

Beside me, Yukon was curled up on the seat, licking his wounded toe and paying no attention to the scenery picked out by the full moon. It was about an hour before dawn. The road was empty of other traffic; the moonlight cast arborescent shadows on the snow on the east side of the highway and caused the distant mountain peaks to glow as though they had been coated with a mixture of calcimine and phosphorus.

We didn't know where we were going, and we didn't care. It was enough that we were headed north; beyond this we were uncommitted, content to follow the road, to stop when and where we wanted to, and to leave when we felt inclined to do so. Time didn't matter; neither did the season. There were no deadlines of any kind to meet and no specific goals to reach—unless one can consider the unknown a goal.

The previous morning all our possessions were packed in the car, and the canoe was secured on the roof rack before the key to the cabin was returned to the lady who owned it. By noon we were back at our first campsite, there to spend the remainder of that day and most of the night relaxing and preparing ourselves for the start of our journey in quest of the wilderness. There was no particular reason for our return to the old campsite; we could have set out immediately after returning the key. But neither was there any reason why we should not do so. It was a capricious decision probably motivated by the fact that for the first time in my life I was able to heed the dictates of fancy unfettered by responsibility, as free as it is possible for mortal creature to be. When it occurred to me that it would be nice to end our stay in southeastern British Columbia where we began it, as a sort of appetizer preceding the feast of wilderness that was to come, we did so, making a fast and simple camp that was followed by a light lunch.

While I munched on a mixture of dry rolled oats, raisins, and nuts, Yukon sprawled nearby, chomping noisily on the entire thighbone of a cow given to him by our friend Jorge Jorgenson, who ran a small, busy country store a few miles from our previous home. Our friendship with Jorge was one of those brief, but memorable, affairs that so often develop between people in hinterland areas. We were never to meet again; but we enjoyed each other's company, and he was a good friend to us. As may be supposed from his name, he was of Swedish descent, though born in British Columbia. He had been miner, stockman, logger, real estate salesman, and, at sixty-eight, storekeeper. He liked dogs, probably the reason for our friendship in the first place.

After our first visit to his store, when Yukon quickly won him over, Jorge always had a big bone ready for his canine friend whenever we dropped in to buy groceries and to spend an hour or so chatting about inconsequential affairs, which was something that was very good for me in view of my elective withdrawal from social contact.

When we entered the store, Yukon would march in as though he personally owned it, ignoring any other customers that might be shopping at the time and threading his way between sacks of potatoes and crates containing ironmongery until he was behind the counter and speaking to Jorge, *wooo . . . woooing* until his friend turned around, opened the meat freezer that stood nearby, and produced the special bone he had been saving. Yukon would accept his gift courteously, bowing, somehow managing to voice his pleasure with the prize clamped between his jaws, and then would turn around to go and sit beside the exit door, clamping down tightly on the bone until it was time to leave.

It didn't matter whether our stay in the store was long or short; Yukon sat quietly with the bone in his mouth, drooling a lot, ignoring strangers and wagging his tail when either Jorge or I spoke to him, always patient and relaxed.

The bone he was now chewing with such relish was Jorge's farewell gift, and the dog took his time eating it. When he was at last finished and had licked his lips and paws clean, I put away our gear and zippered up the tent; then we went upmountain to explore.

The higher we traveled, the deeper became the snow, until we reached a point where some two feet of crusted white made walking difficult for both of us. We were out to enjoy ourselves, not bent upon completing an endurance test, so we descended again, dropping down a fairly gentle slope until we reached a wide, plateaulike valley at about the fifteen-hundred-foot level. The lower elevation and full exposure to sunlight had caused the snow to melt to such a degree that much of the land was visible, weeping still, but getting ready for the return of warm weather.

Yukon, obviously glad to find bare ground on which to wet and scratch with his vigorous back legs, danced around, sniffing and wetting and scratching up small clods of mud that threatened to splatter my person if I wasn't careful. Because of this, I hung back, letting him get rather farther away from me than was my habit.

While he was wetting a small bush that evidently offered some special attraction, a low-to-the-ground yellowish beast came hurtling out of its lair within a pile of boulders, growling savagely and throwing itself at Yukon. The attack was so swift and unexpected that the dog only just managed to lower his raised leg before the chunky savage bit his left front paw and hung on.

Perhaps another dog might have yelped and tried to back away. This was not Yukon's way. Totally silent, as was his habit when in action, he reached down with jaws agape and fangs gleaming to grasp the badger's head and to bite hard, producing a crunching sound audible to me ten yards away. The badger let go immediately, whereupon Yukon shook it with such violence that the body became a blur. Again I heard a sound, this time a sharp click. The neck vertebra had snapped. That badger died quickly.

This was my first experience with this species. Unless this one was particularly belligerent for reasons unknown, I concluded that badgers have a surplus of courage and a scarcity of brains; nothing that I have learned about the species since then has caused me to change this view. The badger is to be admired because of its tenacity, rugged strength, and ferocity and its inherent ability to pick a living under almost any conditions, appeasing its constant hunger with fresh meat or eggs whenever it can get them or with the rankest of carrion if nothing better is available, but it is perhaps the most foolhardy animal I have ever met.

Why that particular badger decided to attack Yukon must remain an open question. Initially I became worried in case it was rabid, but on my examining the body, this proved to be in such prime condition that rabies could be quickly dismissed. It may be that it felt threatened by Yukon's proximity to its den, or it may be that this one animal was more bad-tempered and daring than most. Whatever the reason, it died because of it.

Yukon was so excited by the kill that he ignored his bleeding toe and was not at first disposed to give up his prize, retreating from me with the badger between his teeth when I went to take it from him and

causing me to speak sternly to him before he sur-
rendered it. Only then did he concern himself with
his wound, but now he began to lick away the blood
with such evident gusto, enjoying his own taste, that
he at first refused me permission to look at it.

Back in camp later that afternoon, after Yukon's
toe had been cleaned and soaked with permanganate
of potash, I weighed the badger on a portable scale;
it registered twenty-four pounds three ounces, or almost exactly one-fifth of Yukon's weight. The creature's temerity was astounding!

While Yukon watched intently and drooled copiously, I skinned the animal, burned its stomach and
intestines, and cut up the meat. Later I roasted one
haunch over the open fire, but its taste was so strong
that I was happy to settle for a couple of pan-fried
kokanee. Yukon wasn't so fussy. He gorged on the
raw meat of his foe.

The dog's wound was not altogether serious, but it
was bad enough to cause him to limp for several
weeks, occasionally breaking open and bleeding quite
profusely, slowing him down to some extent. When it
eventually healed, the nail didn't grow back, and as
a result, the imprint of his left paw was to be forever
distinctive.

Ordinarily, on soft surfaces such as mud or compacted snow, the tracks of dog and wolf show clearly
the marks left by each of the claws; from that time
on, the imprints made by Yukon's front paw showed
only three claw indentations.

After supper that evening I busied myself scraping
the last remnants of fat and meat from the badger
skin before rubbing coarse salt into it to preserve it
until such time as I could tan it properly. When this
was done, the hide was folded flesh side to flesh side,
wrapped in canvas, and stowed away in the trunk of
the car. Yukon, in the meantime, had been busy licking off the permanganate from his toe, grimacing and
drooling at the acrid taste, but persisting until only a
trace of purple remained. Afterward he rose,
stretched, yawned noisily and prodigiously, and went

to lie down in front of the tent doorway, there to nap while I did the washing up.

By this stage of our wandering I had bought a folding camp stool and one of those light aluminum-framed folding armchairs that are so much in vogue today for use on lawns or for patio barbecues, and if such additional impedimenta may make it appear as though I had become effete and overly enamored with comfort, be assured that this was not the case. I was supremely conscious of the need to keep equipment down to a minimum and quite prepared to do without such comforts during relatively short field trips, but on protracted journeys I had discovered that the always damp ground offered serious inconvenience to my person and clothing. The meager "furniture" of my camp was light and easy to carry, and though it did become a nuisance on occasion, this was more than offset by the benefits offered, especially when I relaxed in front of the campfire at night.

When all chores were completed that evening, I trotted out the armchair and placed it under a tripod fashioned by tying together the tops of three ten-foot saplings from which the kerosene lantern was suspended. Sitting comfortably near the glowing campfire, I settled down to read Thoreau's *Walden,* only slightly distracted by Yukon's gentle snoring.

Somewhere within the darkening forest two great gray owls were calling to each other, perhaps already beginning their courting rituals. Their voices were soft, yet vigorously resonant; each bird in turn uttered its normal three-syllable call, *whooo . . . ooo . . . ooo,* paused, repeated the song, and waited for the other to reply. Occasionally one of the big night raptors gave vent to a single, rather elongated and tremulous *whooooo. . . .* It was nice music to read by.

At full dark the stars crept one by one into the sky, like static fireflies on a field of black loam. Yukon rose, stretched again, and marched purposefully into the tent; inside, he threw himself down with that always astounding abandon of his that produced a loud thump and suggested he was trying, by sheer force, to indent the ground to fit the contours of his body.

I was thinking of emulating his good example and seeking my own bed (we were leaving very early in the morning) when I found a particular passage in *Walden* that Thoreau might have written with us in mind:

> Remember thy creator in the days of thy youth. Rise free from care before the dawn, and seek adventures. Let the noon find thee by other lakes, and the night overtake thee everywhere at home. There are no larger fields than these, no worthier games than may here be played. Grow wild according to thy nature, like these sedges and brakes, which will never become English hay. Let the thunder rumble; what if it threaten to ruin farmers' crops? That is not its errand to thee. Take shelter under the cloud, while they flee to carts and sheds. Let not to get a living be thy trade, but thy sport. Enjoy the land, but own it not. Through want of enterprize and faith men are where they are, buying and selling, and spending their lives like serfs.

Noon the next day found us beside one of those "other lakes," but only briefly. The water was so calm and pellucid, so tempting that I took down the canoe and launched it, each of us relaxing in our own way while we floated idly and blissfully, watching the wilderness as it responded to the blandishments of a neophyte spring. We had traveled two hundred miles since leaving the campsite.

Two hours later we were on our way again, and when we reached a major north-south highway, we turned right, northward, keeping on this route until night overtook us. Now we stopped for a quick cold supper on the edge of the road, just inside the shelter of the forest. Having eaten, we dozed for an hour, then on again, through the night, watching it become pale.

When daylight came, I stopped outside a small

roadside café whose proprietor was just opening for business. Here I ordered bacon and eggs and, while these were being prepared, took two raw hamburgers to Yukon, who ate them on the front seat of the car. We were within four miles of 100 Mile House in British Columbia's Caribou region, where winter was still resisting spring; it was not severely cold, but the snow was deep, and there was enough frost in the air to keep the waterways frozen. These conditions decided me to look for a piece of wild country in which to camp while waiting for the spring breakup.

I consulted the map for the first time since we had started on our journey, selecting a goal at random. The survey map showed a large area of wilderness north of a gravel road that starts at Williams Lake and goes west until it ends at Bella Coola, on the Pacific shores. Somewhere in that region I thought I could find a sheltered campsite where we could spend a month or so, employing ourselves wilderness watching while waiting for true spring to arrive and for the rushing waters of breakup to subside.

After passing through 100 Mile House, we drove over fifty-six miles of the Caribou Highway before entering Williams Lake, going through this town and picking up the Bella Coola road. Less than an hour later we arrived at Riske Creek. It was midmorning. I liked Riske Creek, and decided to look for what we wanted in this area.

The community was small in those days, not much more than a cluster of log and frame houses built haphazardly on both sides of the roadway, dominated by an old-fashioned general store that did double duty as a trading post. This establishment was run by a man whose name was either Beecher, or Becher, I am not now sure. He was an old-timer in the region, helpful and friendly, though we didn't talk at length because he was busy dealing with a number of Chilcotin Indians (the name in their language means "inhabitants of the Young Man's River") who had come in to dispose of their winter's catch of fur and to trade for supplies.

After exchanging an initial greeting with the trader, I busied myself inspecting his store of goods, picking out needed items, and stacking them on the counter. Presently I became interested in the dialogue of the Chilcotins and the trader as each bundle of furs was placed on a long table, opened, and examined in turn. Typically, the conversation, conducted in a sort of pidgin English that was common in that day, went something like this.

The trader, opening the bundle: "You catch lots fur?"

The Indian, enthusiastic: "You betcha. Lots good fur."

The trader, perhaps examining some weasel skins: "Pay you dollar and a half for these furs."

The Indian, scowling fearfully: "Too little. Two dollar fifty cents more better."

Trader: "One dollar seventy-five."

Indian: "No. Two dollar twenty-five cents more better."

So it went, the Trader working his way up and the Chilcotin working his way down. When the trader settled for two dollars, a bargain was struck. But this didn't end the matter. The bargaining began anew as the Indian took supplies from the shelves and the two argued over their cost. As I was to discover, not a single item was priced accurately, each being deliberately inflated in expectation of the haggling that was to develop when each native took his turn at the counter and entered into the spirit of a game they dearly loved to play. Later, when my turn came, the trader told me that all prices were inflated twenty-five percent and that all bargaining stopped when this figure had been reduced to the true cost of the goods. The Indians were perfectly aware of this; even so, they tried to drive the prices down still further, but on receiving two firm headshakes, they settled for the fair price.

In between bargaining bouts with his swarthy and colorful customers, the trader and I talked, and on learning of my needs, he advised me to drive along a logging road that wound its narrow way northward a few miles west of Riske Creek. There, he said, I would find plenty of good camping places where Yukon and I could spend our time undisturbed.

Before leaving with my purchases of staple foods, I bought one of those small airtight stoves made of sheet metal; these are not my favorite heaters because they can become dangerously hot, but they do have the advantage of being light and easily transportable. Enough five-inch metal pipe was purchased to vent the stove high above the tent peak to ensure that stray sparks did not land on the canvas.

The logging road was narrow, winding, uneven and little used. It became virtually impassible after seven miles, clogged with heavy snow that hid a treacherous bottom. I was relieved to find a turnaround where the hidden ground was rocky and not likely to become a bog later on, when the big melt arrived. After I had shoveled snow off an area large enough to accomodate the car and tent, we made camp; we would use this as a base until we found a good, more permanent campsite away from the logging road.

Having grubbed out enough flat pieces of granite to make a base for the stove, protecting the canvas floor of the tent from the heat, I laid them as evenly as possible and placed the heater on top of them before connecting the stovepipe and leading it through an asbestos collar fitted for this purpose in the back wall. An elbow outside aimed upward and to this were connected three eighteen-inch lengths of pipe that were guyed with wire to adjacent trees.

As I worked, Yukon protested because he was tied to the rear bumper of the car; he was impatient to be set free and complained loudly, telling me it was time to eat. But first we needed firewood, and for this chore I needed his help.

Having unfastened him after I had finished installing the stove, we entered the forest in search of fuel, and to spend about half an hour cutting and hauling deadwood. The smaller logs he pulled out on his own, one at a time, hitched to his burden by the traces from the sled, which I had brought with me after cutting them down in length. The leading ends of the strong leather straps were fastened to his pulling collar and to his body harness with D rings and snap fasteners; the trailing ends were joined by a light chain that was tied around the thin end of the log. Since the butt end of the load was heavier than its top, this kept the chain end slightly raised, clearing the ground and allowing Yukon to pull the length of deadwood through the brush without getting caught up on obstructions. While he romped away with his load, I walked behind, carrying a similar-sized length on one shoulder, but the bigger logs we hauled out together. For these I hitched myself to the load with a rope and helped the dog pull.

It was late evening when the fires were started, one in the stove inside the tent, another outside, contained in a ring of rocks, over which supper was cooked. I has bought two big frozen steaks, one for each of us, which were now placed on a portable grill over a bed of coals, for Yukon, strangely, liked his steaks cooked medium-well, the fatty parts burned black. All other meat he engulfed raw, but he was a gourmet when it came to beefsteaks.

We slept well and snug that night, not awakening until the sun was up. The new day held promise of warmth.

We had breakfast outside the tent before a big crackling fire entertained by the antics of five gray jays, whose one and only thought was to beg food from me, quite unafraid of Yukon. He was used to the presence of these birds by now and would mostly ignore them. But when one, bolder than the rest, landed on my shoulder, he became jealous.

He was lying behind me, using me to shelter him from the heat of the fire, which made him uncomfortable. Thus, I was not aware of his intentions when the bird fluttered down, hovered a moment, and then perched on my right shoulder, where it peered intently at the bannock and marmalade I was eating.

After breaking off a piece of bread, I was reaching

up to give it to the bird when I was struck violently in the back with enough force to knock me off the stool. Unknown to me, Yukon had been unable to control his jealousy when he saw my hand reaching up with food for the bird.

With characteristic speed and with his usual and total commitment to the job at hand when he went into action, he must have picked himself up off the ground and dived for the jay at one and the same time, inadvertently dealing me one of his powerful chest punches. The startled whisky jack squawked loudly as it flew away.

No less startled, trying in a confused way to understand what had happened, I was about to pick myself up when Yukon, immediately contrite, came to apologize, making me at once aware that *he* had been the culprit. He intended to lick my face, but I reacted in anger and lashed out with open hand to land a blow on the side of his head. The hurt I inflicted on him was emotional. For the first time in our relationship I had struck him in anger. He backed up, whined, looked at me searchingly, detected my annoyance, and turned swiftly to run into the forest. He refused to return when I called to him.

It was now my turn to become contrite and worried. I was also rather ashamed of my action, especially when I recalled that on a few occasions when I had accidentally hurt him, his reactions had always been controlled; he had growled and snapped, but always pulled his bite, following it up swiftly with manifestations of friendship.

Two hours later he was still away. Was it possible, I asked myself, that one hasty and ill-considered slap could have endangered our relationship? I tried to put this thought out of my mind, telling myself that our friendship would surely not founder because of such an incident. But at the same time I was acutely aware of Yukon's sensitivity; knowing him as well as I did, I could understand his hurt. He had long ago given me his complete trust, which was something he had never offered to any man before, and it was not impossible that he might now feel himself betrayed, that he might revert and become once again the antisocial beast I had first seen in the back of Alfred's pickup truck.

We were in strange country; there was a chance that confused and upset, he would try to return to the homestead, more than two thousand miles away. These and a number of equally depressing imaginings combined to cause the morning to pass slowly and unpleasantly.

When he hadn't come back by noon, I couldn't stand to be inactive any longer. I would follow his spoor. I put food in a small packsack together with a flashlight, in case his trail led me too far from base to allow a return before night; then I strapped on the snowshoes and left.

At first his spoor was easy to follow; he had gone almost due west in a practically straight line. But after half an hour his tracks became confused in a more open area full of snowshoe hare trails. He had evidently done some hunting here, following first one spoor, then another, going all over the place as he worked his way toward a section of forest where hemlocks and cedars predominated.

Within the umbrellalike shelter made by the lower branches of a large cedar lay the remains of a kill he had made. The snow was flattened and bloody, bits of paper-thin hide were scattered about, and the hare's fine white hairs covered much of the killing ground. Lying there eating his prize, Yukon had left a large depression in the snow, the bottom of which was actually glazed by his body heat, which turned the crystals into ice. The kill was recent, the blood was still wet, and one bit of hide I picked up was still supple. Leading away from the tree, the dog's tracks continued in a westerly direction, and carmine stains in the left-front pugmark showed that his wound had opened again.

I whistled and called, listening for him, but the only sound audible above the usual soft noises of the forest was a faint, continuous susurrus coming from the northwest that I felt sure was made by running water.

Yukon's line of travel appeared to be toward this sound, and as I followed his tracks, I began to feel more confident, believing that he would return to the campsite after he enjoyed his run. It wasn't a matter of logic; rather, it was a *sensing,* an inner conviction perhaps stemming from my knowledge of the dog and from the faith that I had in our relationship. One hasty blow struck in momentary anger could not possibly unravel the bonds that held us together.

I wasn't concerned about his getting lost now. His superb intelligence and his fine homing sense could be trusted to bring him back to the camp after he had his fill of running. Yet I was not wholly relaxed, for there were certain possible eventualities that could put the dog in jeopardy.

There were many wolves in this country. If Yukon ran into a pack, its members could turn on him, and he wouldn't stand a chance against them. I felt sure he could take on a single wolf, but not a number of them. Then, too, the grizzly bears would by this time be getting restless in their dens; it wouldn't do for Yukon to blunder into some cave following a bear's scent and find himself at close quarters with an angry grizzly. But perhaps the greatest cause of my concern was that the ice covering the waterways was weakening, becoming treacherous. If he broke through in deep water, he would surely freeze to death should he be unable to get out quickly—freezing, not drowning, is the greatest danger facing those who break through the ice. Immersion in water a degree or two above freezing will kill a mammal (man included) within three to five minutes. People and animals drown only if they break through and fall into fast moving water that sweeps them under the ice, depriving them of air.

Continuing to move toward the sound of running water, unmistakable now, I tried to tell myself that I was fretting too much about Yukon, that he could take good care of himself, that, in fact, he was much better able to survive in the wilderness than I was. But I couldn't talk myself out of worrying.

I presently noted that his toe had stopped bleeding

and that he had lengthened his stride at a place where the grade dropped gently and where the evergreens began to thin out, to be replaced by clusters of poplars among which grew an occasional birch. This was typical vegetation adjacent to a body of water. The rushing sound was loud now.

Squeezing through a thick stand of young cedars, I broke out of the forest onto an area of level land, a natural meadow, treed at three of its boundaries and ending abruptly at the banks of a wide creek that curved sharply northward, before plunging over a rocky, ice-encrusted ledge for a distance of about fifteen feet. The water rushed over this ledge and dropped into a round, wide pool before continuing in a northerly direction. It was this sound that I had been hearing all along.

The stream, which was a fast one, accounting for the fact that it was not completely frozen over, had probably remained open in the center all winter long. Walking to the edge, I saw that less than four or five inches of water spilled out from midchannel, slabs of ice jammed against both shores. In the roiling pool below, thick chunks of ice bigger than tabletops bobbed up and down or tumbled lazily; some of these had wedged themselves against the shore, steepled like miniature rooftops.

The warmer March sunshine had already melted most of the snow on the meadow, the released moisture running into the creek to swell the rushing waters; the grassy little clearing was remarkably dry, except for a few boggy areas.

The place was a natural sun trap and an ideal campground; here Yukon and I could spend our time in comfort.

Only now did I realize that I had quite forgotten Yukon's absence while in contemplation of the beautiful clearing. I was so used to having the big dog around and to planning for both of us that I had unconsciously taken him into my calculations while surveying the campsite.

"Where the heck are you, Yukon?" I spoke aloud, practically a plea.

Searching the snowless ground near me, I found his spoor again on a patch of muddy ground. He had evidently wetted here and then scratched, scattering soil and grasses. Afterward he ran along the bank, going upstream and heading toward a heavily forested area that led to higher ground from which the creek emerged.

I was still wearing the snowshoes, so I backtracked to the deeper snow, detoured around the clearing, and picked up the trail again beside the waterway, soon entering a forest of tall, arrowlike lodgepole pines, a pure stand that appeared to continue toward the south. Here Yukon's tracks ran in all directions; he had again been tempted to hunt snowshoe hares.

Enough was enough! Yukon had too much stamina for me to hope to catch up with him. I stopped beside the stream, noting that within the shelter of the pines it was heavier with ice and was open only in the center, where a narrow ribbon of water moved swiftly toward the downstream falls.

I filled my pipe and lit it, remaining still for a time in the hope of hearing Yukon as he charged after some luckless hare. Chickadees called softly, the stream was less noisy, emitting more of a loud murmur than the steady, cascading noise it made near the falls, the breeze stirred through the treetops, and a woodpecker battered at a pine somewhere nearby; apart from these sounds the forest was quiet.

All at once I got the feeling that I was being watched, the kind of thing that caused a person to turn around apprehensively when walking alone down a darkened street or that is felt sometimes in a crowded room, compelling one to turn around and look directly into the eyes of another. Without moving my feet, swinging from the hips and neck, I searched the forest behind me, twice. Nothing was to be seen. I was imagining things.

I started back, but before I had gone more than a dozen paces, Yukon's *wooo . . . woooing* call made me turn around so quickly that one snowshoe hit the other and I stumbled to my knees. It was then that he came to me, rushing up madly, making his plaintive howl-bark, and wagging his tail furiously. So enthusiastic was he that he knocked me flat on my back in the snow, then stood on my chest with his front paws and began to lick my face all over, an action that I viewed with decidedly mixed feelings because his jaws and chin were all bloody from his hunt. But we made our peace, apologizing profusely to each other. Afterward we returned to the car-camp, arriving in late evening.

The next day was a busy one; it began before dawn and didn't end until almost midnight, but when we went to bed that night we were comfortably encamped about fifty yards from the creek, just within the shelter of the lodgepole forest, the meadow outside the tent doorway.

Four times we journeyed between car and meadow, carrying our supplies and impedimenta by means of a hastily made travois, a rather cumbersome affair that nevertheless cut our trips in half and allowed us to make good time along the trail, both of us pulling. I was harnessed to the top V end, while Yukon was hitched ahead of me, his traces fastened to the poles that protruded in front of my oody. It was the first time we had tried this method of portaging, and it proved so successful that we were to use it many times in the future when faced with a long haul. Even the canoe was carried the four miles between car and meadow by this means, its interior loaded with the last supplies.

I had always carried the canoe on my back, but now I tried the travois, only half expecting success. The bows were firmly secured to a crosspole a little more than midway up the legs of the travois, while the stern was fitted with a slinglike harness on either side of which two backward-slanting poles were lashed. These acted like skids. It took two hours to get the canoe to camp, and there were a few awkward places where the trail had to be widened to allow the sixteen-foot boat to turn; by and large, though, the system worked well.

Bounded on the east by the Caribou Mountains and on the west by the Coast Range, much of the Fraser Plateau is still wilderness country, a fourteen-thousand-mile region further delineated in the north by the highway that runs from Prince George to Prince Rupert and in the south by the gravel road that links Williams Lake and Bella Coola. The water ways that thread through this tableland drain into the wild and twisting Fraser River, which eventually empties into the Pacific Ocean at Vancouver.

Camped on the southeastern edge of this vast wilderness, some sixteen miles northwest of Riske Creek and about twenty-five miles east of Alexis Creek, Yukon and I found ourselves in a veritable paradise of nature. A notation in my logbook made a week after we moved into the meadow may be of interest:

What a fabulous, wonderful land! Not a sound of humanity is to be heard, not a sign of my own species have we yet glimpsed. The sounds are pure wild, so are the sights. Distant mountains appear to surround the plateau, but this is not nearly so flat as its name suggests. There are large, fairly level areas, it is true, but there are rolling heights, smallish mountains, and at least one tall one that we can see from our meadow. I believe it is White Mountain, but the map doesn't give its height—6000 feet? [Later] I have taken a compass bearing; it *is* White Mountain. At its skirts runs the Chilcotin River, which flows southeastwardly before it empties into the Fraser. Our creek twists and turns like a snake, but the map shows that it empties into the Nazko River, which flows north, turns around to the east, and also joins the mighty Fraser.

Our creek doesn't have a name. I shall call it Yukon Creek, even if it is never so entered on a map.

So far we've only explored within a fifteen to twenty mile radius of our camp for we're at that in-between time, neither winter nor spring, and this makes for hard and treacherous going. Even so, we've already encountered a number of moose, one fox, a chattering pine marten, two coyotes, and a bobcat that nearly committed suicide by almost waiting too long when Yukon took after it. It was too close! He'd have killed it, I'm sure, but it was a big tom and might have scratched him up some. Next week we're going to travel light and try to reach the headwaters of the Nazko River, about thirty miles.

For seven weeks we explored parts of the plateau, wandering at will, sometimes taking day trips, on other occasions sleeping out, huddling together under a lean-to shelter floored with evergreen boughs and kept reasonably comfortable by a big fire. Day by day, winter gave ground to spring; then, at last, the land wept clear, cold tears, and the migrant birds began to arrive.

One morning in April I woke up to the honking of Canada geese and was just in time to emerge from the tent to see three big ragged wedges as they flew over our meadow not more than two hundred feet up. A few days later the loons came and cackled deliriously during an entire night, and Yukon joined them, singing his own haunting melody that elicited replies from two packs of wolves, one probably not more than half a mile away, north of us, the other more distant and to the west.

Twice during our stay we went out to get supplies at Riske Creek. On the second journey I left the car parked on the gravel road, afraid to take it back up the logging road because the bottom was a virtual bog which we had been lucky to negotiate on the way out. As we were walking back in early afternoon, a mother black bear with two cubs treed herself and her family when we appeared unexpectedly around a bend in the road. The three sat on their perches, peering down at us and making lip-smacking sounds that were supposed to intimidate. Yukon would have tried to climb the tree, pack and all, had I let him off his lead.

May arrived. With it came an unexpected hot spell tht brought the mosquitoes and an early crop of blackflies. By now the creek had settled down to a purposeful flow, still augmented by floodwaters, but only moderately so, the noise of the falls being much more subdued.

It was time to travel again, to seek and to explore new lands.

Chapter 11

The Nass River begins to collect its waters at a small lake located in a fairly wide valley within the territory of the Klappan Mountains in northwestern British Columbia. About 125 miles due west of the kidney-shaped body of water, across the Alaska border, is Wrangell; some forty miles north-northeast lies the Spatsizi Plateau. From its birthplace, the Nass flows southwest for more than two hundred twisting miles to empty itself into the Pacific Ocean just north of Prince Rupert and almost opposite the tip of the Alaska Panhandle.

At most times the river is fairly peaceful, but although it is always more leisurely than some of its turbulent neighbors, the Nass becomes boisterous in the spring after it has gorged on the meltwaters that run copiously from the lowlands and from the snow-capped mountains.

The river wanders through an area of the north where the snow falls often and lies deep on the ground for long periods of time. Usually by the first week of September an advance guard of white starts to dust the mountaintops; by November the forest floor is covered to a depth of several feet, and by the time spring arrives the land must shake itself free from accumulations that are almost as incredible as they are real. Totals of three hundred and four hundred inches of whitefall are not uncommon during a Nass winter, heavy, mushy snow that tears loose great lumps of mountainside and sets in motion avalanches that plow ragged swaths through the thickly growing spruces and lodgepole pines.

The deep forests that cover the comparatively flat valleys discourage intrusion in spring and summer; not because of undergrowth, for only a few shrubs and seedling trees can survive within the penumbra that exists under the green canopy, but because of the deadfall timber that litters the understory.

In much of this wilderness the silva is undisturbed by man. The trees have grown tall and straight, each jostling its neighbor; all of them must struggle to live, competing for the right to thrust their evergreen heads into the sunshine they must have if they are to survive. Seeing this tight-packed and luxuriant mass of growth, a newcomer to these forests might well conclude that such abandoned vegetation must eventually result in the total destruction of all the trees, that such chaotic overcrowding must choke them all to death. But there is order here, even if this is not readily apparent, for the wilderness is everywhere controlled by a natural, efficient process of renewal that has kept all its species healthy for thousands of years.

Old and weakened trees, young trees that have not managed to thrust upward between the trunks and foliage of older and healthier individuals, or trees that have grown twisted and stunted are all, in due time, toppled to the ground by gusting winds or by disease. Insects, finding a weak place on some great forest patriarch, nip persistently into its tissues and eventually create long tunnels in its wood that are further enlarged by woodpeckers who come to feast on the insects; sooner or later such a tree succumbs to

206

its wounds. Snow loads weighing many tons festoon the treetops each winter and become heavier when a warm chinook wind blows out of the west, converting some of the snow into moisture; the dripping water works into the bark and into cracks of ailing trees, and when the chinook passes and the cold returns, the water becomes ice again and expands and rips apart branch or trunk with explosive force.

In these ways is the forest pruned regularly during all seasons. The resulting debris falls to the ground and creates a tangle of trunks and branches and mulching needles that is stacked in layers three and four feet deep, a vast natural cheval-de-frise covered in thick moss, fungi, and ferns, all of which accelerate the decomposition of the deadwood, which in time is converted into organic matter and returned to the soil.

It is easy to fall and twist an ankle, perhaps even break a leg, when one traverses such a place in spring, summer, and autumn, for the moss conceals openings in the criss-cross of rotting timbers. In winter, with the use of snowshoes, the going is safer, but no less difficult. The deep snow is cloying stuff that sits on the webs and forms ice lumps under the heels, forcing a traveler to stop often to clear the ice from between moccasin and webbing or to shake off accumulations of snow that weigh down the feet. Ten minutes of such going is enough to cause the sweat to run freely; an hour of this kind of travel demands a rest stop when, perhaps as one leans against the bowl of a big spruce or pine, the stillness of the forest is quickly felt.

At any season this land is quiet. Large animals usually avoid the entanglement of the trees because there is little food there to reward them for the rough going; red squirrels make a good living here, as do the nocturnal flying squirrels, mice, and voles. Hunting these are the weasels, pine martens, and the owls, but except for the shrill red squirrel, most of the day animals are predominantly quiet. At night only the hoot of the owl is likely to be heard.

There are birds in these forests in daytime, of course, but it often seems as though even these are avoiding the somber underworld. High above, invisible from the forest floor, eagles pipe their shrill calls as they fly over to fish in the waters of the Nass; occasionally the swift spruce grouse crashes away through the forest or voices its peeping call. Chickadees speak musically, but softly, as they search the bark of the trees for insects, and the occasionally strident woodpeckers further add their voices to the wilderness and furnish percussion when they batter at some insect-ridden tree.

Between spring and fall the sweet melody of a hermit thrush brings moments of cheer to this otherwise lugubrious wildness. But despite the sporadic calls of the birds, the most constant sound heard in the forests of the Nass the year around is made by the wind as it encounters the treetops, sometimes moaning, often howling, now and then sighing gently, its dirge accompanied during the warm months by the susurrus of the insects.

In the spring of the year the world of the evergreens is virtually impassable to all but the birds, the insects, and the small animals. The forest floor is soaked by meltwater that runs under the trellis of deadfalls and seeps from compacted masses of slowly receding snow. Most animals tend to travel along the banks of the river then, and man, if he ventures into this wilderness, must also follow the Nass, be it on foot or by canoe.

During this season the waters run fast and deep, and the Nass is in good voice, the rumble of its passage audible for a mile or more. Gone are the quiet shallows of summer, those places of round, smooth stones interrupted at intervals by deep pools that are the home of medium-size rainbow and cutthroat trout; gone, too, are the sandy beaches where the tracks of grizzly and black bear, wolf, and moose are often encountered later on. The high banks remain, and these are threaded by numerous game trails made by successions of animals that have traveled them through the ages.

In some places detours must be effected when the

swollen river has stolen land from the adjacent forest, undermining the banks and uprooting trees, which fall into the river. Some of these become sweepers, still anchored to the bank by their roots, their trunks and crowns submerged, playthings of the current that causes them to sweep back and forth, or up and down, sometimes coming to the surface only to disappear again under the water. One sweeper encountered on a wide river can be avoided easily enough by an alert canoeist, but a number of them holding onto both banks are hazards that can rip the bottom out of a canoe or turn the boat over, unless its handler is quick and skillful.

This, then, is the country into which Yukon and I penetrated in mid-May. We did not, naturally, encounter it all at once, but rather a little at a time, like a bather who advances hesitantly into the water, first putting in his toes, then inching forward slowly.

From Riske Creek we retraced our way to Williams Lake and headed north to Prince George, where we turned west along the Yellowhead route that ends at Prince Rupert on the Pacific coast, for I had a vague notion that we might explore some of the coastal zones. As it turned out, the northern interior of British Columbia exerted a greater influence on me; the Prince Rupert idea was scrapped.

Today the Yellowhead route is a smoothly paved highway that passes through spectacular country, but in those days, though the scenery was perhaps grander than now because there was less development along the way, the road was a much humbler affair that in places seemed to want to disappear altogether. Passing through Vanderhoof, we entered the Bulkley Valley with its many lakes and homestead farms. This area tempted me, but I had set my heart on going deep into the wilderness; there were too many people and towns and roadways here. This was no country for Yukon; it was too settled and open and would not offer him the freedom and challenge that his wolf nature required.

Stopping in Burns Lake for a meal, I got into conversation with a guide who at first thought he might get me as a customer for a fishing trip. Talking over coffee while looking at my survey maps of the region, this man dismissed the area of the Nass River on the basis that it was "too darned uncivilized." He recommended Babine Lake because it was easily accessible, and there was a place he knew of near Topley Landing where there was a log cabin that could be rented at "a real good rate." Of course, it turned out that it was *his* cabin. This conversation helped me make up my mind. We would go visit the Nass Valley.

At New Hazelton, where the Bulkley River joins the turbulent Skeena River, which empties into the ocean at Prince Rupert, I sought more information and learned that there was a restricted road leading north from Terrace that eventually linked up with the Nass. "It's just past the volcano," said my informant.

A volcano? *That* interested me. But I couldn't learn too much about this fascinating and unexpected piece of news. It was thought to be extinct, I was told, and there was a big area of lava over which the logging road traveled. But it was doubtful that I could get permission to use the road at this time of the year and even if I could, I'd find it muddy and rutted.

Back in the car, I subjected the one-inch to 4-mile survey map to close scrutiny. Sure enough, a volcano was marked on it, and so was the lava bed through which ran the Nass River.

"That's where we're going, Yukon. Even if we've got to carry the canoe between us all the way," I told my friend.

He wagged his tail, reaching across and licked my face, then returned to the engrossing itch he had been nibbling at when I interrupted him. I could tell from his reaction and from his behavior in the car that he was bored and had already had enough of automobile travel. So had I, but with fewer than one hundred miles to go before we reached Terrace, I decided we would keep going rather than find a campsite nearby where we could take a short break.

We spent that night in Terrace. The next morning,

early, I visited the logging company's offices to see about a permit to use the road and received one after a fairly long wait. I could use the road at my own risk, it was explained to me. It would be a rough trip, and I would run the risk of getting bogged down in places. So much was made of this that I almost backed out of the plan and might have done so if a driver hadn't come into the office just then. He had evidently come from a place called Aiyansh and he said the road wasn't in bad shape to there. He then made a remark that was quite without meaning to me: "The oolachans are running on the Nass."

Later I learned that oolachans (more properly eulachons) are a species of seagoing smelts (*Thaleichthys pacificus*) that enters rivers in large number every spring in order to spawn, evidently dying after spawning, like the salmon. The little fish, eight or nine inches long and silvery gray in color, are extremely rich in oil and were once the source of a brisk trade. Coastal Indians, and those other tribes that inhabited more inland areas along the migratory route of these fish, rendered them down for their fat, which was beaten vigorously until it resembled lard and traded to inland natives for tools and other desirable items. To this day, Tsimshian and Niska Indians occupying the Skeena and Nass valleys take large quantities of these fish, although the trade has died down and most of the fat and the fried fish are consumed locally. In 1877 the government of Canada built Grease Harbour, an oolachan oil factory on the Nass River, some fifteen miles north of the lava beds, which, in 1903, shipped out no less than six hundred tons of oolachan oil. Today the factory is inoperative, but the "grease trails" used by the native traders when carrying their product into the interior are still usable in places.

Becoming almost as interested in the oolachan as I was in the volcano, I rooted out a British Columbia biologist and plied him with questions, but on hearing that these fish were once used as candles and were also known as candlefish, I decided that my leg was being pulled. It was not. I can personally testify that the oolachan, when dried, will indeed give a fairly good light. This is even better if the fish is wrapped around a wick.

By now I was in a froth to get going, planning to go directly to Grease Harbour, so as not to miss the oolachan run, then return to explore the volcano and lava bed at my leisure.

The logging road was certainly not good, but neither was it as bad as it was made out to be by the company official. With Yukon sitting in his accustomed place on the front seat, head hanging out the window, we drove at an average speed of fifteen miles an hour through mud that in places was four or five inches deep and through streamlets that found their way over the road, creating minor washouts, for the winding route crossed seemingly innumerable small rivers and creeks.

Within the hour we reached Kitsumkalum Lake, which is fed by a river of the same name that trundles southward and empties into the Skeena. Because its waters carry large quantities of silt washed down from the mountains, Kitsumkalum Lake is light aquamarine in color, a delicate shade of green-blue that, when seen from afar with the sun shining on it, is indescribably beautiful. The traveler is compelled to stop beside this inviting water; if he is any sort of an angler, he must try his luck and be disappointed, as I was, because the water in the lake is too heavily silted and opaque to suit most fish. But this does not diminish the allure of Kitsumkalum.

From the shores of the blue water the view is almost too perfect, too panoramic. Verdant mountains climb gently from the water's edge, become steeper, lose their green covering, and end at the blue ice of a small glacier atop Mount Garland. The placid lake with its tinted water acts as a giant mirror and reflects the entire scene.

About an hour after leaving Kitsumkalum, but only fifteen miles away, we encountered Lava Lake, which is long and thin and receives its waters from postvolcanic springs and from the western slopes of Alder

Mountain. This lake is shaped like a shallow S, runs north and south, and is six miles long by perhaps half a mile wide. At its northern end is a small lava bed: scrubby, mixed forest surrounds this on all sides, grasses and ferns and mosses carpet the ground in open places, hiding the dark gray pumice. It is ten miles from here to the Nass River and to the Indian village of Aiyansh.

The road was better now because it passed over the lava, and crushed pumice had been used to make almost as smooth as blacktop, but when we reached the main bed and saw the Nass River for the first time, we were to learn from a group of Niska teenagers that the going was bad further north and that the trail to Grease Harbour was too narrow and muddy for the car.

The three lads were from Aiyansh, and they were even then returning from the river with sacks full of oolachans. I was about to leave the car to take a look at their catch when Yukon began to growl and to show his teeth, prepared to jump out when I opened the door. This was not usual behavior on his part: I put his lead on and tied it to the steering wheel before stepping onto the road.

The Niska teenagers were shy, but friendly; they would have given me a sample of the fish, of which they had taken about one hundred pounds between them, but I wanted to walk down to the river and get some of my own. One of the boys, who looked to be about fifteen or sixteen, offered to take me down and to show me how they caught the fish, whereupon a brisk argument developed in the Niska tongue. It seemed that Jimmy, the would-be guide, wanted the others to take his load of fish back to the village while he led me to the river. To settle the argument, I gave each boy a dollar, paying the other two to take Jimmy's load and the guide to show me the ropes. Everybody was now happy. But there was still Yukon to deal with.

Out of the car, the dog would not make friends with the Indian boy. The best I could do was to make him stop growling and to tolerate the lad's presence, but he would neither wag his tail nor allow Jimmy to approach him. Since he had never done this before, I concluded that it was memory of Alfred that caused him to react in this fashion with the Indians. In time I learned that my surmise was correct.

Yukon was a confirmed Indian hater. Wondering what it was about other Indians that caused him to remember the bad times he had experienced in the village in which he was born, I concluded that the only feasible explanation was the scent of the people. I do not mean by this that the Indians smelled bad; it was more a case of association of odors.

Every organism has its own peculiar scent. To the sensitive nostrils of a dog, all garage mechanics, for instance, smell more or less alike, as do all butchers, and so forth; Indians in those days lived within their own close-knit communities, more or less isolated. All of them trapped, fished, lived, and worked in buildings that were not partitioned off into different rooms; thus, the odors of their trades permeated clothing and hair and body, and their general scent, with variations caused by personal habits and hygiene, was distinctive.

Jimmy was not the talkative sort at first. He smiled a good deal and replied in monosyllables when spoken to, but he didn't volunteer information. As we walked over the lava, I asked questions.

"How many oolachans are there in the river?"

"Plenty."

"How many people live in Aiyansh?"

"Some."

"Were you born here?"

"Yes."

"Do you go to school?"

"No."

"Do you work?"

"Yes."

"What do you do?"

"Trap some. Fish."

Having elicited a three-word reply, I rested on my

laurels. It was not until the next day, after Jimmy had helped me make camp that night and come to chop wood in the morning, that he really started to talk. Then he wouldn't shut up.

That afternoon he demonstrated the method he used for catching oolachans. It was *not* complicated. In fact, the fish just about gave themselves up. I had never seen anything quite like the teeming thousands of darting, glittering fish that filled the Nass from bank to bank. Racing upstream, jostling one another, jumping out of the water, becoming pushed too far up the bank so they swam half out of the water, the oolachans could be scooped up by hand. That was Jimmy's method.

I tried it, got three fish in one swipe, and found that though they were covered in small scales, their bodies were rough to the touch, almost like the skin on baby sharks, easy to hold onto, and not slippery like other fish. In five minutes we had pulled some three dozen out of the water.

This was more than enough, but Jimmy was all set to go on doing it until nightfall. I explained that I didn't want so many. With a smile and a clipped "OK" the lad started gathering our catch from where they lay gasping on the riverbank, stringing them through the gills on several flexible willow wands. We returned to the car, drove it off the road, and set up a temporary camp within the shelter of a clump of mixed trees. Jimmy had supper of broiled oolachans with us that night.

The fish are reasonably good done in this way, but they disintegrate into a mush if pan-fried, because of the oil in their bodies, I would think. They are not my favorite species, but there is no denying that they are rich in nutrients. Jimmy tucked into them like a Russian gourmet eating caviar. I saved half a dozen to experiment with, splitting them and setting them out on a drying rack near the fire, hoping to convert them into candles. Yukon loved the greasy little fish. He ate fourteen at one sitting, raw.

When Jimmy arrived next morning, Yukon was more

tolerant of him, remaining now merely aloof while the lad dragged deadwood out of the bush, cut it up with a bow saw, and stacked it for me. He was nothing if not enthusiastic! Within an hour he provided more firewood than I was likely to need for my short stay here, but since he so evidently wanted to do it, I made only mild protests. Afterward we walked down to the Nass again, and Jimmy was soon plucking oolachans out of the water, up to his knees in the cold wet, without bothering either to roll up his pant legs or to remove his moccasins. While he amused himself and while Yukon was extremely busy putting his mark on as many trees and shrubs as possible, I looked speculatively at the swollen river, debating our next moves.

A few minutes later Yukon came to me limping. The lava had cut the pad of his rear hind paw, and he had a number of scratches on the others. Obviously he couldn't run over the glass-sharp pumice without protection. I had brought his moccasins with us, canvas shoes that fitted the contours of his feet and were secured to his legs with purse strings; normally, these were used during snowtime, especially in fall and spring when the snow was wet and would form ice balls between his toes. Now I put them on him. He always disliked them but bore them fairly stoically in wintertime; in spring he wasn't so stoic, and I had to speak sternly to stop him from chewing them off. They served their purpose, but three days later they were cut to ribbons anyway, the canvas not being proof against the sharp lava.

After concluding that the Nass was running too swiftly for comfortable, upstream paddling, and since we had not yet explored the volcano itself or properly seen Lava Lake, I decided to drive back there and camp in the area for a week or two. Jimmy, by now almost a camp fixture, offered to come, too, to help with the chores, but I was loath to allow him to do so. It was ten miles to the northern tip of the lake and too far, I thought, for him to travel twice a day.

"Gotta bicycle," he said, nodding his head in such

a manner as to indicate that the matter was entirely settled.

It was. For a fee of three dollars per diem, he would ride over and be the chore boy, guide, and general factotum. I didn't need him, but I rather suspected he needed us; we were, after all, an unusual event in his young life, a matter of new interest. And he certainly needed the money, little enough though it was. He made himself very useful, and he and Yukon became reasonably good friends during the ten days we camped near Lava Lake. But Jimmy's idea of a bicycle was not mine; it was the most beaten-up, abused, twisted-wheeled machine I have ever seen, and it didn't have tires. Still Jimmy loved it.

The creek that flows into Lava Lake at its northernmost tip come spilling down from the flanks of a mountain the peak of which stands guard five miles west of the roadway. The mountain has no name; neither has the creek been christened. In fact, few of the mountains that form the Nass Range have been individually named, being shown on the map under the general title Hazelton Mountains. This may be because they are so overshadowed by the rather formidable Coast Mountains with their huge glaciers and broad bases, or it may be that the surveyors simply ran out of names when they reached the humbler mountains that at this point keep the Skeena and Nass rivers apart.

However this may be, the unidentified creek passed under the gravel road by means of three corrugated iron culverts and shoutly thereafter merged its waters with those of Lava Lake. It is such an insignificant little creek that it could be easily overlooked if not for the fact that the tiny lagoon it has carved for itself out of the lava, just before it dives under the roadway, cries out for attention.

This pool, no more than thirty feet long by about twelve feet wide, is filled with crystal-clear water and dotted with forms of naturally sculpted lava on which grow small willows, ferns, wild grasses, and a variety of mosses and fungi. To see this pool is to want to keep it, somehow to pick it up, take it away, and place it beside a small white cottage in the country where one would live content until the end of time; no Japanese gardener could compete with this naturally designed pool lighted by shafts of sunlight slanting through trees that, twisted and scraggly because of their insecure hold on the lava, line the creek on both sides and lean toward the middle of the pool, forming an archway. On the north bank of the creek the vegetation is more sparse, the pumice more jagged and dark, a somber contrast with the vivid greens and yellows that dot the pool.

Sticking out of the pellucid water, a dozen or more pieces of lava are each shaped differently, each having its own form and line: a dog's head, or it could be a wolf's; a Greek urn with broken lip; a roughhewn heron standing on one leg, beak rather thick and foreshortened. All the shapes stand out in three dimensions, seem actually to live as the dancing light and the slowly flowing water endow them with movement.

For an hour I became lost in comtemplation and might have stayed longer if a varied thrush had not dropped down from the trees to land on the head of the dog, there to sit and sing its clear and lovely melody. Yukon and Jimmy were hauling firewood out of the bush at my suggestion, although I went with them the first time to make sure that Yukon behaved himself in harness and to tell the boy that on no account should he yell at the dog or threaten him with stick or fist. Probably because he was always pleased to work, Yukon behaved admirably; he did not act as joyfully as when he and I did this chore, but he followed the Niska willingly enough going into the forest, then allowed the lad to hitch him to the butt end of each log. When that was done, Yukon needed no further human assistance. With one great lunge he'd start the log moving and would keep it going fast enough to slide it out of the bush regardless of small obstacles.

When the varied thrush flitted down from the lava

statue and slaked its thirst, it sang once more and left, breaking my spell. It was early afternoon, and the tent had still to be set up, guyed with lumps of lava because the pegs would not penetrate the burned rock, and there was a ring of lava to be made to contain the campfire. Afterward Jimmy was going to ride his disgraceful bicycle back to Aiyansh, and Yukon and I were going to climb the mountain's flanks and visit the volcano that had erupted out of the lower slope of the mountain at an elevation of two thousand feet.

We had come here from the Nass, tying Jimmy's wreck behind the car and giving the lad a ride in the back seat, perched on top of our gear. Because I had by now formulated a long-range plan, I concluded a business arrangement with the Niska. Yukon and I would, in due course, go to seek the source of the Nass River, leaving the car behind at the lava flats; for ten dollars down and another ten dollars when we came out (if the car was not molested) Jimmy would act as guardian of my vehicle. But first we would spend some time beside Lava Lake; then, before setting out, we would drive to Terrace to buy enough food supplies to last, if need be, until the following spring, for we might have to winter in the mountains.

Now that we were here, away from people except for the Niskas in the village, and Jimmy, of course, I was in no great hurry to depart. In any event, it would be sensible to wait until most of the floodwaters had passed down the Nass, returning a normal level and flow to the river, for I was going to have a big load and I wasn't anxious to punish myself unduly, particularly in view of the fact that I had not done any great amount of paddling since the previous summer.

When Jimmy left for home, I called Yukon, and we set off, following the south bank of the creek at a leisurely pace, climbing the gentle slope that would lead us to the place where the volcano yawns with black mouth at the blue sky.

It is not much of a crater. It was probably not much of a volcano during its days of fire and brimstone. Yet it managed to spread its molten matter over an area of one hundred square miles, more or less, flowing downslope in a south-southwesterly direction, spreading, then turning and continuing on a northwesterly course along a narrow valley to spread itself over a comparatively wide, flat area immediately north of the Nass delta; the main flow spread east, the secondary flow entered the river and climbed its west bank, no doubt for a time diverting the Nass, until the erosive waters bit into the clinkerlike lava to carve a new channel.

Almost a century has passed since then. About fifty percent of the lava bed is now covered by vegetation, much of it still scrubby: willows, spruces, larches, and some lodgepole pines mingling with aspens and birches and with many bushes and plants. The open places are green with grass and colored by the flowers of each season, but here and there dark, dimpled patches of lava protrude.

In fewer than one hundred years, no time at all, in terms of evolution, but after the guts of the earth erupted to spread themselves molten and burning over this piece of wilderness, the green things have come to reclaim much of the land. Spearheading this slow march of life came the lichens, the nonplants that can take life from the air and from water and cover bare rock with matter and make new soil in which fallen seeds of other species can germinate.

LOGBOOK ENTRY: Night. Black night relieved only by the flickering of the campfire. Darkness under a volcano; no wind, hardly any sound except for the murmuring of the restless creek and the deep breathing of the wolf-dog. With full belly, sipping coffee, I sit and listen to the wilderness, thinking about tomorrow and about the ten-mile walk to the lava flats with Yukon, to meet Jimmy and to visit his village.

Morning. Brilliant sunshine, dark blue sky, coffee in the pot and bacon in the pan, three extra slices for Yukon's token breakfast. A varied thrush (is it yesterday's bird?) greets the warm sun that will soon now put vigor into the insects and cause them to take wing so that the bird can break its own fast. Yukon killed something last night. I don't know what it was, except that it was small. He suddenly jumped up and ran into the night and didn't come back for half an hour; when he returned his lips and muzzle were bloody—probably a rabbit. Now he's hardly interested in the smell of bacon. But he accepts the food, nevertheless, eats it slowly. I eat mine quickly, for I have just been reminded of the devil's club thorns that are still buried in my hand; it was too dark and too late to take them out last night.

Devil's club, aptly named plant; taller than a man, some of them, each trunk and stem bristling with long yellowish spines, each leaf festooned on the underside with thin thorns; maple-shaped, giant leaves that turn their faces to catch the dim light that filters through the trees within the shadows of which grows *Oplopanax horridus*. I met them last year, discovering the species after personal and painful contact. I noted them yesterday, as we climbed toward the volcano, and avoided them mostly; but when Yukon was about to dart right through the middle of a patch, I lunged for him, grabbing his collar, and my hand brushed against one stem, turning the knuckles into pin-cushions. Later . . . operation over; we can leave.

We left the campsite at eight o'clock, walking uphill along the slope of yet one more unnamed mountain, the peak of which is 4,550 feet high. Yukon, running too far ahead, was reluctant to stop and return when I whistled for him; he had scented something interesting and was liable to dash away in pursuit. I put him on the lead and secured its looped end to a snap fastener fixed to my belt for this purpose.

We could have driven to the Nass; but we weren't in a hurry, and Yukon, no less than I, was tired of the bone-rattling drive we had endured getting here. For this reason we were cutting across country, keeping to about the thousand-foot level.

An hour later we reached a sloping ledge that made walking easier. A short time after that our way was barred by the Tseax River, and we had to detour until we found a place where the water was shallow and the banks wide, making the flow less swift and easily fordable. Even so, it was thigh-deep on me and covered Yukon's back and most of his neck, leaving only his head out of the ice-cold water. He half waded and half dog-paddled across, seeming to enjoy the experience. This river has its source in two tiny lakes near the peak of the mountain and becomes almost dry during the summer months; it empties into the Nass.

My legs ached after being immersed in ice water, but the blood soon flooded hot again and brought a tingle to the skin. Yukon wet me all over by stopping (which forced me to stop, since he was still fastened to me) and shaking the moisture from his shaggy coat. I was always amazed at the ease with which he (and the other dogs, of course) could rid himself of water. With his woolly, lanolin-heavy undercoat, the moisture was never able to soak down to his skin, being trapped in the first layer of wool and on the long guard hairs; a couple of shakes, and he looked almost dry, giving me a cold shower that soaked my shirt. But on a day when the sun is high and warm, when the body is enjoying the physical conquest of land, and the mind is free to pursue whatever takes its fancy, a brief wetting is of no consequence.

About half an hour after crossing the Tseax we encountered a fairly large open meadow dotted with a number of good-size boulders and several areas of pinkish scree. It was an inviting place; I decided to linger awhile, to smoke a pipe while resting on the grass. Before doing so, I removed Yukon's lead absentmindedly as I looked around.

Free, Yukon streaked toward a talus slope at the foot of a small cliff, his demeanor telling me that something that rated at least Great-Great interest on his reaction chart had drawn him away. Since experience had taught me that it was useless to call him when he exhibited that kind of excitement, I let him go.

Within seconds I saw the attraction: a groundhog, a big one, that had been feeding in the open and had not noticed our arrival because he was upwind from us. The rodent obviously heard Yukon's galloping feet as soon as the dog took off; it was now running toward the talus with that curious humping gait characteristic of the species. It seemed that it was going to make it, too. Yukon was a good eighty yards away; the groundhog was within fifteen yards of the slope.

As I watched the chase, my attention was suddenly taken by a shape that appeared on the left, about one hundred feet in the air. It was an eagle. At first glance I assumed it to be an immature bald eagle, which species does not show the distinctive white on head and tail when young, but there was something different about this bird. I looked through the field glasses. To my amazement and delight, it turned out to be a golden eagle, the first that I had seen in North America—during the last twenty-four years of wilderness watching, I have seen only six of these great birds.

Flying an erratic course through the thin timber, the eagle was not quite diving, yet it was descending steeply and fast, following the contours of the slope and presently dropping to about fifty feet above the ground. It was evidently aiming at the groundhog, ignoring Yukon.

Yukon, at full stretch now, was aware that the bird was beating him to the prize and was probably aware that the groundhog would get away from him in any event. The quarry, terrified, ran a straight course for the talus, where no doubt lay its burrow, and the great eagle, with a wingspan of more than six feet, went into a dive.

Now the raptor folded its wings and launched itself downward. Yukon accelerated, running so that his

THE NORTH RUNNER

belly seemed about to touch the ground. The groundhog was still holding a straight course.

Down came the eagle, a blur of dark brown. Suddenly the great taloned feet shot forward to make a
V with the angle of the eagle's neck and chest. A thud
as the bird hit the rodent; a scream from the groundhog, pierced by the talons. One heartbeat later the
eagle lay sprawled on the grass, both claws fastened
inexorably in the groundhog's body.

Yukon was getting closer, perhaps thirty yards
away. He would reach the two; he would kill the eagle
and might get clawed by the steely hooks. Then the
eagle let go with one foot, righted itself, flapped its
great wings and lifted, pulling the body of the still-
struggling rodent up into space while beating frantically with big wings. Yukon was closing fast. It was
another race. The eagle rose in seeming slow motion,
weighted down by the groundhog, which must have
been twelve or fifteen pounds.

Right up to the last split second the drama endured.
Yukon launched himself straight up, stretching every
muscle and sinew so that he almost hung in the air as
though all movement had become frozen. The eagle
moved upward and to the right, slowly.

I heard the snap of Yukon's jaws missing their target, clicking tooth against tooth, as the big dog dropped
back to the ground. The eagle had won its prize. It
was now in full flight and gaining height rapidly. Soon
it disappeared over the top of the mountain. Yukon,
crestfallen, came walking back to me, as though apologizing for missing twice.

We resumed our walk toward the Nass, but I could
not help wondering what would have happened between Yukon and the eagle if the bird hadn't pulled
off its risky gambit.

Jimmy was waiting for us when we broke out of the
forest and onto the lava bed; he watched from about
fifty yards away while I put shoes on my friend; then
he walked slowly toward us, an old dip net in his right
hand. He was evidently intent on catching more

224

oolachans, I thought. But he disabused me of this concept when we met midway to the river.

"Run's about over," he said.

For a moment I wondered what he was talking about; then I realized that he was referring to the fish. It seemed unlikely that yesterday's teeming thousands could have gone by. But they had; a few of the silvery smelts were still making their way upstream, but the run was down to a trickle. The stragglers were safe, too elusive to catch now that they had maneuvering room.

Chapter 12

Early on the morning of June 7 Jimmy came to help pack the canoe and to see us off. He had a small and scrucy haversack slung around his neck, but he made no reference to it as we carried load after load to the water's edge. When all the stores and equipment were stacked beside the riverbank, I launched the canoe, let it swing broadside-on to a deadfall tree that jutted into the water, and tied it firmly fore and aft. Using the tree as a dock, I stowed things while Jimmy carried them to me. And what a load it was!

By the time we were done, and when Yukon and I took our places in bow and stern, the Chestnut was loaded with almost seven hundred pounds of stores and passengers, close to its maximum capacity. There was only just room enough left for Yukon to sit forward and for me to kneel aft, but the craft was well trimmed, just slightly heavy in the stern for better control, and no part of the load jutted above the gunwales more than four inches.

Jimmy untied the mooring lines, coiled them, and stowed them, while I held onto the tree; then he shuffled along the log and stopped by the stern, leaning forward. In an embarrassed way, he opened his haversack and brought out a brown paper parcel tied with string, offering it to me and smiling shyly.

"Salmon. Smoked. For you," he muttered in that clipped manner he had of speaking.

I thanked him briefly, knowing that to say more would only embarrass him further, although I was touched by the gesture. In silence he pushed the canoe into the Nass and stood watching as I paddled away from the log and turned the bow upstream. After getting the canoe under way against the current with a dozen vigorous strokes, I paused, waved the paddle briefly, and yelled "Good-bye Jimmy"; faintly, because he spoke in his usual soft voice, came his reply: "Good luck." As though not to be outdone by the humans, Yukon raised his head and howled.

The river wasn't wild now, but the current was strong enough to make for continuous paddling if we weren't to lose way. At first I kept the craft in midstream, but later, experimenting, I found there was less current closer to the banks; I also noted that the big load helped rather than hindered, making the canoe much stabler and easier to push through the occasional riffles that we encountered. But paddling was nevertheless hard work. An hour after setting out I needed a rest, and seeing a large mud-anchored log sticking out into the river some ten feet from the west bank, I steered for it and grabbed it, then held the canoe against it by lifting one leg out of the craft and hooking my heel over the log, telling Yukon to "stay" in case he decided it was time to land and explore.

I rested there for ten minutes, smoking my pipe and thinking of the early voyageurs, who daily would start out before first light and who would keep going until eight or nine at night. They also rested every hour, but whereas I was a free agent and at liberty to stop when and where I liked for as long as it pleased me, they were committed to get their loads to destination with the least possible delay. The sixteen-foot Chestnut weighted sixty-five pounds empty, while the north canoe of the fur trade route, made of birch bark over wooden ribs, was twenty-five feet long and weighed three hundred pounds without cargo or passengers and the big thirty-six-foot-long *canot de maître* weighed six hundred pounds unladen. The north canoe, carrying a crew of five or six, could handle some three thousand pounds of freight as well as its crew; this meant that each man worked to propel an individual load of about seven hundred pounds—assuming the average weight of each voyageur to be 180 pounds.

By the time I'd finished making these mental calculations the pipeful of tobacco was down to a sputtering dottle; knocking this into the water, I lifted my leg back into the canoe and pushed away.

We reached Grease Harbour three hours after we left the lava beds and since this village is fifteen miles from our starting point, our average speed was five miles an hour. If we could keep that up for eight hours a day and always provided we did not encounter unforeseen obstacles, I thought we could probably reach the source of the Nass in five days, six the most, but I had no intention of trying to complete the journey in that time. It was perhaps theoretically possible to do it under ideal conditions, but there was no point to it; we had plenty of time and plenty of food. Besides, we were due some leisure.

I had intended to stop at Grease Harbor to look at the oolachan oil factory, but as we neared the village, a pack of snarling, yapping dogs rushed down to the riverbank, followed by two Niska men. I waved, they ignored my greeting, standing to scowl at us as we approached. It seemed that the owners were as surly as the curs. I kept on going, steering toward the west bank and continuing to paddle for another half an hour before taking ten minutes rest. This time the canoe was beached, and Yukon was allowed to go ashore to relieve himself; so was I.

We made camp that afternoon on Cottonwood Island, a tiny islet in the middle of the river some thirty-five miles from our starting point. Our rate of progress had fallen; it took almost nine hours to reach Cottonwood, making our average for the day not quite four miles an hour, which punched holes in my earlier estimate of five or six days to reach the source of the Nass.

After camp was made and Yukon was free to go where he pleased and to do as he wished on our little island, I took the fishing rod and some small spoons and tried the river, casting in a sheltered area where a small promontory of the island projected into the water. Within a few minutes a strong strike almost jerked the rod out of my hands, but the fish came in like an old boot; it turned out to be a fairly large squawfish (*Ptychocheilus oregonensis*) that, when weighed later, scaled five and a half pounds. These fish are edible, but bony; this one would do for supper if I couldn't hook into a trout or two, but if my luck was good, Yukon, who liked any kind of fish, bones and all, provided he got it raw, would dine on squawfish on his own. And so he did, for I caught a plump one-pound cutthroat a little time later.

That night, sitting beside a smoky fire intended to keep the mosquitoes away, I did some thinking about our food supplies while Yukon pranced around his new domain, amusing himself in various ways. My plans were still rather vague, but I was determined now to winter in this wilderness, either building a small log shanty for our use or, if luck was with us, finding an abandoned miner's or trapper's cabin that could be made habitable. Such dwellings are by no means rare in the hinterlands of the north.

I was because of my intention to spend the winter in the country of the Nass that I had bought so much food, its weight totaling 335 pounds.* This was a big load for one man and one dog to handle during portages, especially when added to all our other gear, yet there was no help for it; prune as I might, I could not in safety reduce it further. We hoped to live largely off the land, but I knew from past experience that those who depend for sustenance on nature's bounty do so on a feast-or-famine basis, for the wilderness can be as niggardly as it can be generous. What I was trying to determine that evening was the most likely region in which to winter, at the same time calculating the amount of food I was going to leave in a cache along the route, in case we needed supplies on our way out next spring.

In regard to these emergency needs, it seemed reasonable to leave behind ten pounds of rolled oats, five pounds of dried beans, two pounds of raisins, one pound of dried apples, one can of Borden's unsweetened milk, and one small can of corned beef. This would allow us to survive if for any reason we were short of food on our return, even if we had to walk out. Looking carefully at the maps by the light of the kerosene lantern, I tentatively decided to build the cache somewhere near the junction of the Nass and

---

* Supplies carried: 100 lbs. rolled oats; 100 lbs. all-purpose flour; 50 lbs. dried white beans; 40 lbs. raisins; 40 lbs. dried apples; 10 lbs. powdered skimmed milk; 5 lbs. coffee; 5 lbs. tea; 2 lbs. salt; 48 packages dried yeast; 5 lbs. lard; 5 lbs. sugar; 2 lbs. baking powder; 5 small cans corned beef; 2 cans survival rations from Ash-Jon Corp., Brooklyn, N.Y., containing 5 H.A. vitamin tables, 12 oz. malted milk tablets, 8 oz. c.c. bars and 2 oz. enriched tropical chocolate—each can supplying the needs of one man for 5 days; 5 cans, large Borden's unsweetened milk. Equipment: 2 axes; 1 bow saw; ropes, vrs.; tarpaulin; tent and fly tarp; small airtight wood heater with chimney pipe; rifle, .303; rifle, .22; 1 hammer; assorted nails, 3 lbs.; 2-inch wood auger; first-aid kit, including vitamin C tablets and fly repellent; 2 kerosene "barn" lanterns; 36 candles; 3 yards x 5 yards mosquito netting, in roll, for tentless camping; 2 bottles scotch whiskey; 3 canoe paddles; 1 ten-foot canoe pole with shod end; miscellaneous items.

Meziadin rivers, about forty miles north of Cottonwood Island and seventy-five miles north of Aiyansh, but final selection of the site could not be made in advance. The maps did not show every detail of the terrain, and even if the scale had been large enough for them to do so, they could not possibly anticipate variations in the country owing to weather conditions over the years (the maps had been produced in 1949) as well as more recent changes in the topography due to altered water levels.

Such things are always unpredictable, even in country that is intimately known to a traveler, because seasonal rainfall, erosion, vegetation growth, and wind conditions can alter an area almost overnight.

Yukon turned up to interrupt my meditation. He smelled like something dead, with good reason. His right side was dark and matted with some highly noxious, sticky substance that odorously proclaimed itself to be carrion juice. Evidently the dog had found it, rolled in it, and was now returning to me to apprise me of the fact, as proud of himself and his aroma as a woman who has just bought a new bottle of perfume and wants to make sure that her husband notices it. Something of a battle ensued, lasting fifteen minutes or so, Yukon being led into the water, soaked, and then lathered with some of our precious detergent, two plastic bottles of which I had brought along for just such emergencies and for the occasional laundering of extra-grubby clothes.

Long before leaving Europe for Canada, I had been puzzled by this canine habit of rolling in odoriferous substances, and although I had searched the literature and asked a number of mammalogists for an explanation, none had been forthcoming. More recently, while on the homestead, having watched the dogs do it, as well as a number of foxes and wolves, I found what I believed to be the reason for a habit that fills humans with disgust. It seemed to me that the only logical explanation for such behavior by carnivorous animals was the desire to mask their own odor, to camouflage themselves with the reek of carrion in order to give them a hunting advantage. I adhere to this view today.

When Yukon smelled tolerably like himself again, he was allowed to leave the water, shake himself well, and roll in the sand, while I, ducking the first shower, returned to my stool by the fire and tried to pick up the mental threads from where they had been dropped.

For some years now it has been easy for a man to place himself in the deep wilderness if he has the money to pay for a chartered aircraft and pilot. The plane will fly him in, complete with gear and food, and will return at a given date and time to pick him up and to take him out again.

There is great security in this; *somebody* knows where he is and will eventually return to collect him. That this is false security makes hardly any difference to our modern explorer, who views the matter as he would view a life insurance policy, forgetting, as most of us do when we buy from the salesman, that such a policy pays off only after death.

One hour—nay, one minute—can bring death in the wilderness, and whether this comes instantly or more slowly is material only in terms of the degree of suffering that must be endured. But still, a man feels better knowing that there is another man with a machine who will come to take him home at some future date.

It is another matter altogether when a man enters the wilderness the hard way, furnishing his own power to propel a canoe *up* river while being vitally aware that if something goes wrong, it may well have fatal results.

There is something particularly unnerving about the prospects of death unexplained and unattended, of a man's end coming to him when he is alone in some remote place, there to lie unburied and to become food for the animals of the wilderness, his only remains a few gnawed and bleached bones that will never be found. Did the early discoverers of North America feel this way, too, when they trudged across the Bering land bridge to thinly populate the northern wilds? One must feel awesome respect for those prehistoric travelers, and then, upon further reflection, one may wonder if they would have dared the frozen unknown without the half-wild dogs that carried their supplies.

The feats of the early Europeans who came to explore and map the sprawling wilderness are no less impressive. They were the pathfinders who opened the way for the colonists; many of them set out alone to search the vast land that lies above the thirtieth parallel. But not quite alone; they were also aided by the dogs of the northland.

The country into which Yukon and I penetrated that June was unknown only to us, for we went into it guided by survey maps that, though vague at times, could yet tell us where we were going in a general sense and what lay ahead in terms of rivers, lakes, mountains, and valleys.

It could be said that I undertook the journey in sheer ignorance, armed only with a talent for survival learned during years of war. This is in part true, but I had such confidence in Yukon that I believe I would have undertaken the trip even without maps. With him beside me, I always felt confident and never lacked companionship; without him, I do not believe I would have dared cut myself off from civilization and penetrate alone into a country where I would not be likely to encounter another human being.

I wonder sometimes whether *I* led him, or *he* led me. I was always aware that we each relied heavily on the other, but only much later did I come to understand just how great was my dependence on him, on his strength and endurance and courage and supersenses, and on his willingness to work. He was my "auxiliary engine" when we had to portage around rapids, over sand flats, or around swamp, and he was always eager to have his harness strapped to his back and to carry forty pounds between the canoe and the end of the detour, returning briskly by my side for another load. I was so conscious of his willingness that it made me feel somewhat guilty at times; to be fair to him, I always made sure that my own pack was the heavier. Between us, we could carry one hundred pounds of supplies and transport all our goods in four trips. Sometimes these were short and the work occupied an hour or so; on other occasions we might spend the entire day fetching and carrying and end up camping beside our pile of supplies.

Yukon slept with me inside the tent, but he was always on guard and ready to spring up and growl if a marauding animal was close to our camp, attracted by the smell of the food piled on shore or packed in the canoe, when we were only spending one night at a given location. On numerous occasions he alerted me to the presence of bears, several times when they were actually walking into camp. When this happened, I would yell loudly and punch at the canvas, and this usually sufficed to deter the would-be raiders; if it didn't, Yukon continued to growl, and then I would get out of the sleeping bag, pick up the rifle, and put the lead on the dog before unzippering the tent doorway. With the five-cell light clamped on the gun barrel, I would sweep the camp with light, one-handed, holding Yukon in check with the other. Only twice did we discover a bear persistent enough to linger after hearing the sound of the zipper, and both these animals sped away when I fired a shot in the air.

In this and so many other ways Yukon was to me what his kin had been to the newcomers to this land. He was also a living reminder of the great breed of dogs that made possible the harvesting of furs, carried people and supplies from Canada's Labrador to Alaska's Point Barrow, hauled the mail, and brought the law into the north when civilization made this a necessity. Without these dogs Byrd would not have reached the North Pole; neither would Amundsen have got to the South Pole. Without Yukon I would have not reached the source of the Nass River.

Yet the northern sled dog goes largely unsung. Often eaten by the men they served, most times going half starved and beaten unmercifully, they worked long hours in a degree of cold impossible to understand unless it has been actually experienced, and soon now, they will be no more.

Yukon, possessing all the qualities that made those dogs great, will always be for me the symbol of the many north runners without whom man might never have colonized the wilderness.

LOGBOOK ENTRY: We left Cottonwood Island at dawn after camping there for three days. Used hardly any rations because fishing was good and a bed of cattails on the east side of island yielded a good supply of tender shoots for salad. Yukon kept himself well fed by hunting mice and voles, at which he is amazingly expert. Predominant species: deer mice (*Peromyscus maniculatus macrorhinus*) and long-tailed vole (*Microtus longicaudus littoralis*); both are numerous on the spine of the island. Yukon keeps himself content by snacking, going off to catch a few mice or voles when he's hungry, then returning to lie down for a while until he feels like another snack. By suppertime he was so full he refused to share my meals! His technique: First the stalk, using nose and ears and walking lightly; then, detecting scent or sound, he bounds up and down, lifting all four feet off the ground and slapping at the vegetation with his front paws each time he lands. His success rate is astounding.

Encamped on Vandyke Island; 1:30 P.M. We made it here after eight hours, only about seventeen miles from Cottonwood, as near as I can judge. The first two hours went well, river slow and quite wide, but then we encountered a two-mile stretch studded with rocks sticking out of the water that caused the current to split every which way. Nasty. Had to line the canoe upriver for about a mile, but fortunately the west bank was clear of trees and bushes. Yukon enjoyed the run he had and got a snowshoe hare; he sulked a bit when I took it from him and tied it to my belt; we'll eat it for supper, stewed with beans—if they're soft enough; I've put about two pounds of them in a cotton bag, and we've been trailing them in the water since we left, soaking them. Must check on them now.

Vandyke is more than twice the size of Cottonwood; there are hares here. It looks like rain. Maybe we'll stay here until the weather clears.

Morning. Clouds cleared overnight. We're off again, and we ought to make Meziadin Lake by noon (twenty miles, give or take). Time now six A.M. Later . . . Meziadin by 2 P.M. No problems, just farther than I thought, I guess. Almost a problem, though. This morning a bull moose stepped out of the trees and gave us a look, but kept on walking to drink at water's edge. Yukon almost jumped overboard! I threw myself over the load and just managed to grab his tail before he left. Thank God the load is heavy and kept us on even keel. But it was a good lesson learned, for we're likely to encouter a variety of animals as we travel upriver and he'll probably react the same way. From now on I'm going to pass a rope through his collar, double it, and lead the two ends to the stern; this way I can pull him up short before he starts acting up and if (God forbid!) we should tip over for any reason, I can pull one end of the rope through his collar and set him free so he can swim ashore without getting tangled up.

Meziadin Lake is big, about twelve miles long by two miles wide at its widest point, and takes its waters from the Cambria and Longview ranges of the Coast Mountains. The lake looks like a crawling caterpillar, aiming northwest and gradually turning due west, where the Bear River emerges from Meziadin, cuts through Bear River Pass, and empties into the Portland Canal at the town of Stewart; this canal is natural, not man-made, and marks the boundary here between Alaska and British Columbia. Hyder, Alaska, is just across the way. Meziadin River empties into the Nass, so it looks as if the lake drains two ways. The river is about the shortest one I've ever seen, probably no more than six miles long, shaped like a dog's leg and wide near the lake, becoming straighter and narrower until it joins the Nass. At the river mouth there are three log buildings that are obviously in occasional use. I don't like this place much; it looks as though we could be disturbed by people; maybe they come from Stewart, use the lake as a resort. We'll stay tonight and leave in the morning and make the food cache higher up. *Note:* The temperature has dropped considerably, though the sun is full and the sky clear; obviously, we're being affected by the Cambria Glacier, which has a surface area of some 250 square miles in extent. And that's only *one* glacier, there are many others. No wonder the lake is so damned cold! But what a country! Just beautiful!

Next morning. Lovely day, warm in the sun, but chilly enough to keep the bugs down and to make for easy paddling. We are about to leave, and just in time too, for I can hear a motor uplake, coming our way. Motors should be forbidden in a place like this; they are sacrilegious! We're off now.

The food cache was built past the junction of the Nass and Bell-Irving rivers, some seventy-five miles north of Aiyansh, on the south shore and immediately beside the confluence of a creek that is shaped like a Y, the leg of which joins the Nass. This creek receives the waters it empties into the big river from a series of lakes that lie a couple of miles away. One of these, Yellen Lake (the only one named), interested me, and after using up two days building the cache, while Yukon spent most of his time chained up for fear that he might go on a long jaunt of his own while I was busy, I felt we both needed a reward, that some days exploring Yellen and the other bodies of water would be good for us.

We were now in country dominated by the Cassiar Mountains, in a wide valley of rolling, foothill type of country that was literally crisscrossed with waterways. The Y-shaped creek was navigable, if narrow and shallow in places. We followed the right fork of the Y and half an hour later nosed into Yellen Lake, which is one and a half miles long by half a mile wide and sited northwest to southeast. We would stay here a week or more, depending on how things went and on the fish-content in the water.

This meant unpacking the canoe and building a temporary cache; otherwise, while we were away from the tent, it was almost mathematically certain that a bear, either grizzly or black, would get wind of our supplies and would come and help itself to them; if this happened, not only would our food be ruined, but the tent would probably be clawed to ribbons.

It was midmorning before the canoe was unloaded, the tent pitched, and the supplies stacked near it, covered by the tarpaulin that normally protected them from the wet when we were traveling. Once more Yukon was chained up while I worked on the food cache. This was to be a simple affair, merely a platform on stilts where the supplies could be stacked and covered over by the canvas.

After digging four corner holes two feet deep and planting in these four poplar logs twelve feet long and five inches in diameter, I made a makeshift ladder, again using two poplar poles long enough to reach the top of the platform. Wide at the base and narrow at the top, the ladder was furnished with rungs made of poplar saplings lashed to grooves cut in the uprights so they would not slip. I had fashioned the same kind of thing at the other cache, leaving it there lying down for when it might be needed; now I used the new one to fasten a log frame around the four posts and then lash cross poles over this, making the platform. It was late afternoon when the last of the supplies had been hauled up by rope and covered by the tarpaulin. And I wasn't in the best of humors by this time, feeling that I had wasted most of a day, but when a little while later Yukon and I pushed away from shore and set out to explore the lake and to do some fishing, my good humor was restored. The water was almost teeming with kokanee, which is definitely my favorite fish. I caught twelve before putting the rod away.

I *think* we spent two weeks camped beside Yellen Lake, but I can't be sure, for I had lost track of the days. It was a wonderful couple of weeks, and I was sorely tempted to stay right there, build a cabin, and settle in until next year. But I really did want to see the source of the Nass, to have the satisfaction of following a river to its very beginning, something I had never done before.

Two days after reentering the Nass, we arrived at the confluence of Damdochax Creek, the point at which the Nass turns from a northeasterly course toward the northwest, for a time running parallel to the Telegraph Trail, which ends at the settlement of Telegraph Creek, almost two hundred miles away.

After turning into this riverlike creek, we followed it for eight or nine miles, and reached Damdochax Lake. Here was a surprise: At the junction of lake and creek were two excellent cabins. So good was their condition that I felt sure they were used as a fly-in camp by some big-game guide who brought in rich tourists to hunt and fish.

"Well, Yukon, we're going to call this home for a time. If the owner shows up and chucks us out, we'll find somewhere else or build our own place."

Yukon turned around in the bow and galloped over the top of our load, almost upsetting the canoe in his eagerness to come give me one of his sloppy caresses. It was hard not to yell at him, but there was no harm done, so I yielded to his blandishments; after he'd slurped against my face and made the canoe stern-heavy, I paddled the last few yards to a cleared space in front of the cabins where there was a rickety, but serviceable, dock. Yukon was ashore instantly, running to investigate the buildings and to soak them with his distinctive "calling card."

When the canoe was secure, I followed, tried the door of the first cabin, the larger of the two; it opened, and we entered. Inside were two double bunks, a table made of poles with a board top, and four home-made benches. On one wall was a cupboard containing a number of well-used pots and pans and some metal plates as well as knives and forks. But no food. On the table was a stub of candle stuck in a bottle under which was a faded piece of wrapping paper with something written on it in pencil. I had to take it to the door in order to read it.

"Welcome. Use the place, but leave it as you found it. W.H."

No date, no reference to the owner's future plans.

"I thank you, W.H., whoever you are," I muttered.

The cabin was sixteen feet wide by twenty-four feet long made of round logs throughout, even to the floor, except that there the logs had been hewn flat on top. One two-foot square window was let into the east wall, facing the lake, but it was covered by a square of three-quarter-inch plywood to keep out the animals. When I removed the cover, it was to find the glass very dirty and covered in cobwebs. Back inside, I saw what I had missed earlier because of the dim light, a sturdy cast-iron box stove in one corner, its chimney removed and set carefully against the wall, the hold through the lean-to roof covered by what appeared to be a large flat rock. The place was hot and stuffy, the dust lay thick on everything, but it was made to order. Two days later the cabin was spotless, and all my food and gear was inside it. It now remained to hunt out the holes by which the deer mice gained entry and to seal them with pieces of branch hammered firmly in place.

Judging by the heat and by the fact that some blueberries nearby were starting to turn dark, I supposed that the month was July; I guessed at the third, marking that date on the calendar I had brought with me but never used until now because it had been packed inside a tarpaulin-lashed bundle that I hadn't wanted to disturb during our journey.

By the end of the month Yukon and I had traveled to the small lake that gives birth to the Nass River; we had walked many miles along the Telegraph Trail, met a number of black bears, and grizzlies, and moose, and found a wolf rendezvous where the pack's five pups were spending part of the summer, waiting until they were strong enough to travel with the adults.

Between trips, I built a smokehouse out of poles, roofing it with an elementary thatch of cattail leaves that allowed the smoke to get out slowly; two racks were next installed, one above the other, for holding the fish and meat I planned to smoke for winter use. Yukon, meanwhile, was keeping himself well supplied, catching mice and groundhogs and hares and muskrats on quite a regular basis during our daily walks. The little animals I allowed him to eat on the spot; the bigger ones I always took from him so they could be skinned and gutted, then cooked to kill any parasites the carcasses might be harboring. When the quarry wasn't too mangled by his teeth, I shared part of his catch, although at that time of the summer I was quite content to eat fish, of which there was an abundance. Rarely did I return home empty-handed from a fishing trip, and more often than not I would stop fishing when I had enough for a couple of meals with a surplus left for smoke curing.

By now I was using the smaller cabin as a storehouse for my bulk supplies of flour and oats and beans, as well as for the smoked fish. This building was empty except for a couple of bunk beds at one end; there was no heater in it, and its floor had been covered with tin sheeting, presumably so that it coud be used as a storehouse while doing double duty as a summer bedroom for extra guests.

Once our provisions were secure from marauders, we took trips that lasted several days, traveling light, frequently without the tent, being satisfied at the end of day to lie before a good fire and to feel thankful for the chill nights that banished the vicious mosquitoes.

In this way we traveled to the source of the Nass River, taking five days to cover the sixty miles in the unladen canoe because of a set of fast rapids, located three miles north of where the Telegraph Trail veers sharply toward the west, and because of a large swamp almost five miles long that chokes the river with marsh grasses and cattails during the season of low water. Having done it once and taken twelve days to complete the round trip, I didn't particularly care to repeat the experience.

Instead, we explored a good part of the Telegraph Trail. When this turns away from the Nass, it runs more or less beside Muckaboo Creek, at the mouth of which a sharp two-mile drop creates another set of fast rapids; the trail runs through a valley on the northwestern side of the creek. About eight miles up, we found a tumbledown log cabin, which nothing could have induced me to approach had I suspected what was going to transpire, although Yukon, could he have recorded his feelings, would no doubt have disagreed with me vehemently.

Sometime before I was aware that the building lay ahead of us, Yukon began to show signs of excitement, the kind that usually signaled the presence of some large animal or at least the presence of something that merited Great interest. Before he could run ahead on his own, I snapped the lead to his collar. Presently I noticed the building but could not determine its condition at that distance.

The closer we got to the cabin, the more intense Yukon became, so much so that I began to wonder if we had stumbled on the residence of an Indian trapper. A short time later I saw that the building was virtually a wreck, still standing, but showing gaps in its walls and ragged holes where window and door had once been; I noticed something else, which was evidently the cause of Yukon's excitement—a terrible stench. And the closer we got to the cabin, the worse was the odor; even *my* inefficient nose could now identify the sweetly sick smell of putrefaction.

As we approached the gaping doorway, Yukon pulled hard at the lead, seeking to enter the building; I wasn't anxious to discover the source of the awful stink. About to turn away and retrace our route, I stopped. What if some unfortunate person lay dead inside that building? I regretted the question the moment it was silently phrased. Now I *had* to go in.

With great reluctance I allowed Yukon to drag me toward the doorway, but before we reached it, a swift gray animal came hurtling out of the gloomy interior, startling me so violently that I dropped the lead as I instinctively moved out of the creature's path.

It was a medium-sized coyote. Yukon closed with it in a trice, and for some moments that spent themselves like hours my ears were filled with the sounds of savage battle.

The growls and hysterical yaps came from the coyote; as usual, Yukon was silent, single-minded about the killing to the exclusion of all else, his inexorable jaws clamped tightly around the smaller animal's neck, just back of the head. The coyote's snarls became weaker; it started to thrash around violently, gasping for breath.

Yukon braced his front legs, hung on, biting deeper with every movement of the other's body; then, heaving mightily, he turned the coyote on its back, shifted his grip swiftly, and closed his fangs on the unfortunate animal's throat, cutting off its snarls.

I thought I had seen him in every kind of mood until that day, but this was something different, a chillingly intense killing passion never before displayed to me. I yelled at him, going as close as I dared and trying to find his lead, but it was between his legs, the end partly under the small wolf's twisted neck. I was not about to stick my hand down there, despite the fact that I felt sorry for the coyote and regretted the incident almost bitterly. Yukon's jaws were crimsoned by the other's blood. I could see the red pumping out slowly and dripping onto the ground.

Suddenly it was over; the coyote became silent, its body twitched, its bowels and bladder emptied; then it went limp, lips parted as though it were snarling silently, eyes staring right into mine, accusingly, I felt.

Yukon started to drag the carcass away, shaking it viciously, but I stepped behind him and picked up the lead when it emerged from under the dead wolf.

Pulling strongly at his neck, ignoring his resistance, and feeling almost like vomiting, I yelled at him, "Drop it! Now! You bloody butcher!"

That got through to him. He let go, licked his bloody chops, and wagged his tail, looking into my face almost like his old genial self, except for the crimson stains on muzzle, chest, and legs. I was confused, as much upset by the needless killing of the coyote as I was by the change in Yukon, but now that most of the excitement was over the awful stench of rotting meat made itself obvious again.

Having led Yukon some distance from the dead coyote and tied him to a tree, I returned to the cabin and forced myself to enter. The gush of stench was unendurable. I held my breath, walked a little closer to the dark mass on the floor in one corner, where the roof was partly collapsed so that it was necessary to bend low to see properly. It was a bear. It must have been dead for days; this is what the coyote had been feeding on so intently that it failed to notice our approach. I hurried outside, only vaguely wondering about the cause of the bear's death. It could have died of old age, disease, or perhaps it was injured in some way and had starved to death.

Yukon was whining loudly and pulling at the lead, eyes fixed on the dead wolf as though he would take a meal from its warm carcass if allowed to do so. The animal had been in good condition, but because it was summer, its coat was not prime, not worth skinning—not that I would have done so in any event, no matter how much its pelt would have fetched; it reeked too greatly of carrion for that.

Years later I learned that wolves will unhesitatingly kill coyotes whenever they get a chance to do so. I also learned that while wolf and dog will mate and breed, and while dog and coyote will do likewise, wolf and coyote will not do so in the wild. Evidently this is nature's way of keeping the species separate.

LOGBOOK ENTRY: The marks placed on the calendar show that tomorrow is Christmas Day. Maybe it is, or maybe it isn't, but that is when we are going to celebrate the festive season. Cliché or not, time most definitely does fly! At least, it does when one lives life right up to the hilt, when every day is full of interest and fascination. When I committed us to stay here after freeze-up, I wondered if I would become bored, if cabin fever would get to me. Not a bit of it! I have six books that I read according to mood: Thoreau's *Walden,* Steinbeck's *Sweet Thursday,* Darwin's *Origin of Species,* Claude A. Villey's *Biology,* Gordon MacCreagh's *White Waters and Black,* and Plato's *Republic.* Some might think this a strange mix; for me, it's just right. And I have Yukon for affection and companionship and talk. He's becoming educated, for I discuss all my six authors with him and even read excerpts aloud for his benefit. He listens intently, and he *never* argues. What better audience can a man have?

Christmas menu: fried Canada goose, stuffed with rolled oats, raisins, and blueberries; boiled bullhead lily roots for potatoes; wild onions simmered in powdered milk; and bannock bread. Dessert is my own version of rice pudding: rice boiled with powdered milk and raisins and sugar. Then coffee (precious stuff now) and two good tots of scotch whiskey. Yukon shared everything but the whiskey and the coffee; afterward we went out to walk the meal down.

I forgot to bring a thermometer, so have no idea what the temperature is, but as the hairs freeze inside my nose, it must be below zero, probably twenty to twenty-five degrees below zero Fahrenheit. The snow is *deep.* Yukon has quite a time of it leaping through the stuff if he gets off my snowshoe trails, but being as tough and big as he is, he still takes off for short trips on his own when I let him. Just now I won't let him away solo; there are two big packs of wolves in the area. I call them the Nass pack and the Skeena pack because though their ranges overlap in our territory, the two seem to spend most of their time in their respective river areas. The Skeena is only about twenty miles away as the raven flies (no crows here in winter) from Damdochax. The two rivers begin quite close to one another and thereafter run almost parallel, except that the Skeena flows farther south to empty in the sea below the Nass. The Nass wolves are more numerous; there are nine in the pack, seven in the Skeena pack. But they're big, bigger than Yukon, some of them; he wouldn't stand a chance among that lot. Last week the Nass pack was out on our lake, and I took a shot at one of them but missed. It was snowing hard, and the wolves were yapping, about seven hundred yards out on the ice and snow. Yukon got very excited and wanted to go out, but I tied him to the bunk and took the Lee-Enfield and went out to stand beside the cabin and lean against it to take steadier aim. It was an impossible shot without a scope, and I didn't expect to hit the one I was aiming at. But it sent them away. We've seen both packs quite a few times, but they always run from us. The rendezvous we found in July was in the territory of the Nass pack, so the pups must belong to it. I wonder how many of the young ones have survived?

Moose were plentiful in the autumn. I managed to shoot a young bull only two miles from Yellen. Yukon and I packed it in, but it took us one entire day to skin the animal where it was shot, cut it up, and haul it in on top of a makeshift sled I fashioned out of two upward-curving birch trunks spanned by four pieces of sapling.

I had planned to keep a daily record in this journal, but I've not been faithful to the promise. So much to keep me occupied! All I've managed is a series of longish entires every now and then, plus voluminous short notations of wildlife and geography. This is my first proper entry since September. I even forgot my birthday on the twelfth!

We've now been six months away from civilization. I don't miss it; Yukon never enjoyed it when he *did* meet it. What a dog! Early September, when there was an inch or two of snow in the valley but quite a lot on the peaks, we climbed Blackwater Mountain, which is just behind us, maybe three miles south of the lake. Halfway up Yukon registered Great-Great-Great interest and pulled me off our course toward a ravine littered with rocks. We were about four thousand feet up, in about eighteen inches of snow. Because of Yukon's interest, I unslung the rifle and worked the bolt, putting a cartridge in the breach. The clicking noise made by the gun produced a young mountain goat in the ravine, a billy. It was about one hundred yards away, maybe thirty feet above us. I shot it. Yukon looked at me and *wooo . . . woood*, as though he were saying, "Good shot. But you'd have gone right past it if it wasn't for me." Which was true!

Chapter 13

The high country was crying torrents the day the first wedges of Canada geese flew over Damdochax Lake and filled our valley with the age-old call of spring. On the darkling waters slabs of ice, some of them bigger than a tennis court, screaked and groaned as they rubbed and bumped each other in their anxiety to be set free, converted into liquid, or reduced sufficiently in size to allow them to slide through the mouth of the creek and be carried to the roaring, tumbling Nass. Behind our cabin, nine creeks running down the northeast face of Blackwater Mountain rioted exuberantly, producing a continuous rumble as each full-to-bursting channel hurried ice-cold water on its route down to the big river.

According to the markings on my calendar, it was April 14 when the geese arrived and flew low over the lake; they came following eight days of uninterrupted thaw under blue and sunny skies. Before then, alternating periods of melt and freeze brought a blush to the willows and alders, adding russet and yellow and orange hues to the green and white landscape, causing the lake ice to crack; and putting a hard crust on the snow. Now we could walk on top of even the deepest drifts with ease and without fear of breaking through to plunge waist-deep into the watery under-pack, although we kept off the crust during the middle hours of sunshine because the sun weakened the icy surface, which didn't become hard again until late afternoon. The snowshoes were all but abandoned at this time. When the snow softened, it turned mushy and made ice balls under the heels of the moccasins, at the same time refusing to pack properly and causing Yukon to break through repeatedly. Our old trails, thoroughly compacted after a whole winter's use, turned into ice paths rounded at the center and dropping off to the sides, their surfaces as shiny as glass.

Yukon had been very restless of late, unusually so. I was puzzled by his mood at first, but watching him carefully while trying to understand the cause of his unrest, I recalled that he had done a lot of howling during the last few weeks, especially at night, when he would awaken me repeatedly.

Three times in two weeks he had regurgitated part of his supper at my feet, which was something that he had done only on two previous occasions and while we were still living at the homestead, an act that, if rather revolting to human sensitivities, denoted his fealty and affection. It was the wolf in him that caused him to do this, prompted by a desire to share with me.

Wolves often carry meat back to their young, or to their mates, in their stomachs; they gorge at a kill, then return to their den or rendezvous to regurgitate for the benefit of the stay-at-homes, something that they can do with great facility. Almost invariably, if returning wolves are not carrying meat in their mouths following a successful hunt, the pups will rush to them and nip at their lips and cheeks in a frenzy of excitement, a behavior pattern that stimulates the act of regurgitation.

The first time that Yukon did this for me occurred after we had returned from the trapline one evening and I had fed him rather well on raw beaver meat, a reward for his labor that was emphasized after his meal by verbal praise and patting. Later, when I had finished my own supper, I sat down to read in the living room, and he came to me, pawed my knee, and whined, wagging his tail furiously. I put out a hand and patted his head absentmindedly, then slid my fingers down and pinched one of his cheeks, whereupon, still wagging his tail, he arched his back, made a slight noise deep in his throat, and deposited at my feet a mess of steaming, overly reddened, and slimy beaver meat.

I was touched by his generosity, yet I secretly wished that he had not been quite so enthusiastic in his show of affection, for I was now faced by the need to clean up the repulsive stuff. I hesitated, trying to decide how best to remove the gory offering, in my preoccupation failing to thank Yukon for his kindness, but as he continued to look intently into my eyes while wagging his tail expectantly, I realized that I was supposed to accept at least part of his gift, for to refuse it would be akin to a man tossing into the garbage a carefully chosen birthday gift offered by his wife!

I stood up, took a deep breath, held it, and went down on all fours, *pretending* to eat while producing great lip smackings and drooling sounds. Afterward I rose, took a couple of steps backward so as to put a little distance between myself and the "gift," and thanked Yukon solemnly. Wolf etiquette had been observed; Yukon was satisfied. He bowed, wagged, *wooo . . . woood,* and then settled down to cram back into his stomach that which he had so recently ejected, doing a thorough job. The second time he felt the need to offer me a token of his esteem, he deliverd it in exactly the same way and for similar reasons; he felt glad, happy to be with me, so he showed his feelings tangibly. As before, I pretended to eat of it (it was muskrat on this occasion), and when I was done, he again gobbled up the residue.

These same rituals were observed by both of us in the Damdochax cabin, but after the third time I was getting rather tired of the act and truly hoped that he would be just a little less demonstrative.

Mulling over these events while seeking to discover the cause of his restlessness and excitement, I realized that he was always deeply affected when the wolves howled at night, something that they did often during January and February. Looking through my notes, I was able to establish that each time he had regurgitated the wolves had howled from nearby the night before, and he had responded to their calls while sitting tight up against the door.

It seemed that Yukon was suffering from spring fever and that he was of a mind to run into the wilderness and to seek the affections of a female of his own kind. It also seemed as though some of the wolves were interested in him, for recently I had found fresh wolf tracks and copious urine stains in the area of the cabins; most of these were around the smaller cabin, with its odor of meat, but there were still enough big paw marks outside our own door to suggest that the wolves were almost certainly drawn there by Yukon's scent, although whether they were interested in him as a possible meal or because they detected his wolf strain was impossible to determine. Because of this, I made doubly sure that he stayed at home or close beside me when we went out. I didn't want him torn to pieces.

The winter treated us well. In early fall we had hunted small game to provide variation from moose meat—the goat had been consumed by then—and I also fished regularly, smoking most of the catch. At this time, too, I harvested a good supply of bullhead lily and cattail roots, both of which make a good substitute for potatoes, are rich in starch, and can be fried and ground up into flour.

Using the .22 rifle, I managed to shoot five Canada geese from among a flock that landed on the lake for a brief rest before winging southward; in the lowland forests, we hunted snowshoe hares and grouse, while higher up ptarmigan became our quarry.

This was hunting for meat, plain and simple, not

sport-shooting. Already we had used up a great deal of animal protein between us and I knew that if we were to survive during the deep winter, when game tends to seek shelter and can disappear from a region almost overnight, we were going to need a good reserve of meat.

Later, when the land was frozen and fresh vegetables were no longer available, I made a point of going out twice a week to cut down a small spruce tree from which the bark was peeled and the cambium layer scraped off; the resulting pulpy material, rich in vitamin C, was ingested raw as medicine against scurvy. Though evergreen cambium is not altogether unpleasant, I prefer using the pulp from poplar or birch, which tastes rather like cucumber, but these deciduous trees store their sap within the root system in winter and offer little vitamin C during the months of cold.

Evergreens, on the other hand, through a process known as winter hardening, are able to convert the interior of their cells into jelly; as a result, little water remains free inside each cell, and ice formation is halted, allowing the sap to circulate throughout the vascular systems of the trees all winter long. This accounts for the fact that such trees keep their leaves (needles) the year around and enables the evergreens to maintain a reduced rate of growth even during the coldest weather.

I had brought a fair supply of raisins and dried apples, but these were used sparingly, either as a dessert treat now and then or, mixed with raw oatmeal, as emergency rations during long trips, so I felt it was important to provide my system with a continuous supply of fresh vegetable matter. On the premise that it wouldn't do him any harm, I always mixed a ration of cambium pulp in Yukon's food whenever I ate some myself.

What with plenty of exercise every day, a ravenous appetite that was always satisfied, natural vitamin C, and the clean, crisp air of the north, I kept fit, without getting so much as a minor cold all winter long. As for Yukon, he was superbly healthy and as hard as iron.

Before the winter was halfway spent, our partnership had become so close that we could anticipate each other's needs and actions, especially when hunting. Yukon knew that if he flushed hare or grouse while I carried the gun, I would immediately seek to shoot it; he would wait for the shot and then dash in to retrieve or to complete the kill if the quarry was wounded. On those occasions when my aim or luck was bad, he attempted to rescue the situation, seeking to do the job himself and often succeeding where I had failed.

He was always an excellent hunter, but he soon became expert at flushing and running down hares and almost as good at hunting grouse and ptarmigan. He was best with blue and spruce grouse, birds of the deeper forests that spend much of their time on the ground and are proportionately easier to stalk than the wary ptarmigan, which favors more open places.

Watching him as he stalked grouse was an education in itself; I envied his dexterity and ability. Taking advantage of every bit of ground cover he could find, always remaining downwind of the quarry once he had scented it, he would approach with infinite patience and maximum caution until he felt he was close enough for a wild dash. Many of the birds escaped him, as one might expect, yet he managed to bring down his share, on several occasions pulling the bird out of the air by jumping, as he had done at the golden eagle.

His hunting skills became more and more important to us as winter wore on and the game began to thin out. Our stocks of frozen or smoked protein dwindled alarmingly under our ravenous assaults, and it became necessary to hunt almost every day. Sometimes we would prowl for hours through the valleys without discovering anything bigger than mice or squirrels, and then we would climb, seeking ptarmigan within the timber in midaltitudes, for by now these birds were also seeking the shelter of the trees. Without Yukon I would have failed to see the majority of the birds as they squatted rock still and camouflaged by their white plumage; they were indistinguishable against the snow to my inexpert eye, but their scent was inevitably picked up by the dog's sensitive nose.

While not hunting, when we just walked, which was something that I made sure we did every day, I learned about the wilderness and its many life-forms, reserving a time each evening for sitting by the light of the kerosene lantern, making copious notes of my observations as quickly as possible in order to conserve my supply of precious lamp fuel.

It was to take many years to correlate all these observations in a meaningful way and to begin to acquire an effectual understanding of the intricate checks and balances that govern the affairs of the wilderness and lead to the shaping of natural life. Indeed, I am still engaged in this task and have added considerably to the lexicon begun during those unforgettable months that Yukon and I spent in the wilderness of northern British Columbia.

I consciously learned a great deal every day, expanding my knowledge dramatically by the time that breakup arrived, but with such increased awareness came the realization that the more I learned, the more questions remained unanswered.

From books comes great knowledge, surely enough, but the best teacher of all is life itself when this can be observed in those regions where it remains undisturbed by the inroads of civilized technology. I was not then, and am not now, especially concerned with field dissection so as to observe the inner mechanics of living things, being able to learn about these from any good biological source book, but I was enraptured with the study of animal nature and with the relationship that each living thing maintains with its own species and with its environment as a whole. To begin to understand these things, I realized, the entire wilderness had to be studied, all of it: animals and plants and insects, the soils and the rocks and the waterways—an impossible task, of course, because one lifetime is insufficient to learn all that there is to know. But I keep trying, like a single ant attempting to empty a warehouse full of sugar by taking one grain at a time.

When the last ice melted and the pregnant waterways became delivered, the insects arrived: the blackflies and mosquitoes and deerflies and horseflies, an incessant torment of bugs that told me as much as anything else did that it was time to go.

The last day marked on the calendar was May 15. The next morning I packed the canoe, wrote a note for W. H., and left him a supply of beans and rolled oats, of which I had more than I needed for the return journey. When that was done, I went outside, closed the door, and made sure the latch was firmly in place before moving away from the building to stand for some minutes looking around, seeing the white-capped mountains, the green trees, the lake lying there placid as a mirror, reflecting the blue of the sky and the white of a few fluffy clouds. Near the far shore a loon was bobbing up and down, the male of a pair that was nesting there. All around the cabin, within the trees, the returned birds were singing their gladness at the season of plenty. It was hard to leave at this new and joyous time, but leave we had to.

We met the oolachans a few miles north of Grease Harbour, thousands of the little fish, seeming to fill the river from bank to bank as they raced north to their spawning beds. It just didn't seem possible that an entire year had passed since I last saw the interesting fish, but when we swept past Grease Harbour and what I presumed were the same dogs came snarling to the shore and three surly Niska men stared at us impassively and failed to return my waved greeting, it was as though I was suffering from déjà vu.

Some twenty minutes later, sweeping past the east side of the lava island that splits the Nass just above the place from which we had embarked last year, I caught sight of a group of Niskas at the water's edge, very close to the tree that had acted as our loading dock. The Indians were scooping up oolachans. Moments later we were close enough to enable me to recognize Jimmy and some of the others.

Jimmy was up to his knees in water, the disreputable dip net in his right hand bulging with a mess of struggling, glittering fish. The lad was looking our way, waving; I waved back, then steered for the shore. Before the bow could become scratched on the lava, Jimmy's small, callused hands reached for the craft, easing it over the glassine rock.

Yukon leaped out of the canoe before its nose was out of the water, dashed a little way upshore, then spun around and delighted Jimmy by greeting him like an old friend, becoming so effusive that he knocked the Indian lad down and then climbed on top of him the better to lick his face. But when the other Niskas approached him, grinning hugely, Yukon backed away, staring at them with that baleful expression he put on for strangers, causing the five teenagers to back away hurriedly.

Jimmy positively preened; that the big dog should single him out of the group for such special treatment, refusing to have anything to do with the other lads, gave him status in the eyes of his peers, made him a sort of unofficial *smoket,* which means "chief" in the Chinook jargon common on the coast and in some of the inland areas. Jimmy picked himself up, gathered his net and some oolachans that had spilled out of it, and came to greet me.

"Good trip on *Le-shimsh?*" he asked in his soft, strangely accented voice.

I nodded affirmatively, amazed at getting an entire sentence from him, even if a short one, but not knowing what he meant by *Le-shimsh.* When I asked him about the word, he told me that this is the name given to the Nass River by the Niskas. Later yet (almost ten years later) I learned that the word *Nass* is of Tlingit origin, meaning "stomach."

It transpired that when Captain George Vancouver

arrived off the mouth of this river on July 23, 1793, the local Tlingit Indians told him that the waterway was called by them *Ewen nass.* Vancouver did not know the meaning of the second word, but he did know that *ewen* meant "great," for he had already been referred to as the *ewen smoket,* or "great chief," of the white sailors. In fact, the two words mean "great stomach," presumably because the Tlingits of the region got so much of their food from the waters of the Nass estuary, through which travel salmon, oolachan, and steelhead trout.

"How's the car, Jimmy?" I asked after he had explained *Le-shimsh* to me.

"Car good. I keep all these bloody Indians away!"

It seemed that Jimmy had taken his job very seriously and that he had gained a good deal more confidence. While Yukon and I walked to where the vehicle had been left, I heard Jimmy organizing his companions, speaking in his fluid and musical native tongue; I presumed he was ordering them to unload our supplies and to carry them to the car. He was.

As the lad had said, the old and battered Chevrolet was as I had left it, but instead of finding it covered in pumice dust, its scratched and rusting body was as beautifully clean and shiny as the aging paint would allow. Evidently Jimmy had earned his money.

Within a short time he earned more, for the one thing omitted from my calculations while I planned our journey north was the car battery; having stood twelve months, it was completely lifeless. As cheerful as ever, and with his newfound confidence making him sound completely assured, Jimmy volunteered to walk to Aiyansh and to come back with his uncle, who had a truck and jumper cables.

Waiting for his return, I lifted the hood, poured river water into the battery, which was bone-dry, then unscrewed the air filter and poured some neat gasoline into the carburetor. When Jimmy and his uncle arrived in a rattletrap pickup truck, we connected the two batteries, and I turned the switch and pressed the starter. After whirring impotently a few times, the motor eventually caught, fired, coughed, and died; I put more gasoline into the carburetor, and we tried again. On the second attempt the engine fired almost immediately, ran raggedly for a time, and then coughed itself into silence. But the third try did it. The engine caught, ran at first like a badly syncopated drum roll, and finally settled to a steady beat.

Sensing from the look on his face that it would not be appropriate to pay Jimmy his wages in front of his uncle, I gave the adult Indian the five dollars he charged me for his service call and waited till the bone-shaker truck disappeared down the road before giving Jimmy his money: ten dollars for taking care of the car, another five dollars for fetching his uncle and helping unpack the canoe. The other lads each received one dollar, which was hardly fair, really, because they had done most of the work, but I made it up to them by distributing equally all my remaining stocks of raisins and dried apples.

The youngsters stood in a group, clutching bag or parcel and waving good-bye, yelling Yukon's name as the car pulled away, while the object of their enthusiastic adieus sat on the front seat with great dignity; he did unbend at last, though, sticking his head out of the window to look back at the young Niskas.

We reached Terrace at suppertime, eating in the car outside one of those instant-food places that do greasy chicken, leathery hamburgers, and stick-dry French fries. It was all very strange after a year's absence from the haunts of mankind, strange and *shoddy,* when compared to the clean beauty of the wilderness and to the calming sounds of the forest. The malady that afflicted me soon after entering the town would today be diagnosed as culture shock.

I bought a newspaper before stopping at the restaurant and as I masticated the tasteless food, I looked at the date; I was behind in my estimates of time by no fewer than nine days.

Trying to read the first news reports to reach me in

more than a year, I found little taste for them, and in less than five minutes I stepped out and crammed the journal into the nearest garbage container. Back in the car, sitting beside Yukon once more, I felt troubled, at a loss. What were we to do now? The dog was already restless, unable to sit for more than a few moments without rising, turning around on the narrow seat, and flopping down again to look at me intently. I gave him the second of the two hamburgers I had ordered for myself and could not now finish; while he was eating it, I took my wallet and counted the money it contained. The total was better than expected, almost $350, but not nearly enough to get us out of the clutches of civilization.

Suddenly I felt impelled to quit this town, to get back on the highway, and to drive where there were trees and green fields and fresh air. Without debating the matter further, I backed the car out of the parking lot and turned east, leaving Terrace behind soon after we crossed the ramshackle wooden bridge that spanned the Skeena River.

It took us seventeen days to reach Winnipeg, every one of them crowded with doubts and frustration. From town to city we went, stopping in each place just long enough to learn that none of the newspapers along our route needed editorial staff. During all this time Yukon was disconsolate, and my heart ached for him. If it was difficult for me to accept this sudden plunge into urban life, it was doubly hard for him to understand the causes for the change—being cooped up in the car day after day or spending time chained up in some garbage-strewn campsite when all he wanted was to be free to run again through the wild country. Those were not good days for either of us.

When we reached Winnipeg 1,693 miles later, my cash was down to $135, but by now I had made a decision, realizing that I must make a stand *somewhere*. I was firm in the determination either to find work in this city or to return to the homestead and hire out as a logger. One of those Scylla-Charybdis choices. If I took up logging, we would be able to live in the back-woods, but under severe restrictions and with little opportunity to earn more than a subsistence income; work in the city, conversely, offered a chance to free-lance and earn extra money, but we both would be locked into urban life for as long as it took me to accrue the capital needed to buy our freedom anew. Of the two choices, I preferred the latter, for it promised better and more immediate results, and I knew that I could personally stand the pace for as long as it took me to buy our independence; but Yukon would suffer intolerably, more than he had done in British Columbia, for there was no chance of finding such suitable quarters in Winnipeg.

After leaving Terrace, realizing that I would need at least one outfit of city clothes if I hoped to get a job as a journalist, I had bought in Prince George a jacket, slacks, two shirts, and a pair of shoes, the whole for fifty-two dollars. On arrival in Winnipeg I stopped at a service station, went into the washroom with my new wardrobe, and presently emerged more suitably dressed. At best, my new ensemble would have been described as humble; but it was better than my worn and not-so-clean bush clothes.

Togged out in this way, I left Yukon in the car outside the Smith Street offices of the Winnipeg *Tribune* and marched upstairs to seek audience with the managing editor of the daily.

Eric Wells was friendly when I was ushered into his office, but he wasn't too hopeful when he learned the reason for my visit. I don't think he was too impressed with my cover story about taking a year off to get to know Canada while writing free-lance articles.

It all depended on his city editor's needs, he explained, but as we continued to talk and it turned out that we knew journalists in common, he seemed to warm to the idea of hiring me.

He called city editor Vall Werrier to his office, introduced us, and suggested that there might be a place for me in the city room, at which Werrier frowned, shook his head with his eyes closed, then looked at Eric.

"I don't think I need anybody else just now," he said, inadvertently committing the greatest sin of them all, for no city editor has *ever* been known to think that he is employing enough reporters.

I felt confident at his reply. If he'd said he would like to think about the matter, my goose would have been good and properly cooked, because he could then have stalled long enough to force me to look elsewhere. In any event, thanks to Eric Wells, I got the job, and when I descended in the elevator to the ground floor, I did so with a sense of infinite relief.

Outside, I was about one minute ahead of an enormous policean who was alternately eyeing his watch, my car, and Yukon, all set to write me a parking ticket at the stroke of four o'clock.

"I'm just leaving," I told the blue-clad hulk.

Then, as an afterthought, I paused to ask him if he knew where I could find inexpensive lodgings in the downtown area where I would be allowed to keep the dog.

"You don't want much, do you? Who'n hell would want to take in that son of a bitch. Looks like he'd tear your arm off!"

But he did direct me to a part of town where there were a number of rooming houses. I was turned down five tmes in a row, inevitably being refused the moment the landlady caught sight of Yukon, whom I had brought with me, on his lead, in order to leave no doubt that I had a dog and to show clearly what kind of dog he was. I felt frankness was best in this case.

Dejected by the speedy refusals, I almost walked past the sixth Rooms for Rent sign on a house some doors away from our last shutout. The building looked as though it might well collapse at any moment; maybe this landlord was more desperate to rent? Yukon and I walked down the broken cement pathway to the front door, and I thumped on the wood with my knuckles.

The knock was answered by a slattern who could have hired out as a Halloween witch; prune-wrinkled, greasy gray hair in curlers, rouged like a neon sign, and with a cigarette hanging from the center of her tight-lipped mouth, she peered at us through the four or five-inch opening permitted by the safety chain.

"You wanna room, you'll havta keep the dawg in the yard. Ain't got no time to clean up dog dirt in the house, you know! An' it'll cost you an extra three bucks a week. OK?"

I was struck speechless, but I managed to nod. All the others had slammed their doors when asked for a room and shelter for the dog; this old harridan didn't wait for me to ask! Recovered, I told her Yukon preferred to be outside and wouldn't cause her trouble; to the contrary, he would be a good watchdog in her yard. The matter was thus settled, and she even agreed to give the dog his supper if I had to work late on assignment.

My room, at nine dollars a week, was what one would expect for the price. It was at the back of the house and overlooking the yard, which was good, because, when home, I could keep an eye on Yukon, but that was the room's best feature.

Despite the fact that Mrs. M. was a dreadful woman in many ways, overly fond of the bottle, slovenly, and with a mouth that would have silenced a longshoreman, I was grateful to her. She was essentially kind, and although neither my room nor Yukon's backyard offered much, they were to be home to both of us for some months.

The *Tribune* is an afternoon newspaper, and as a reporter I found that my duties weren't onerous, while my pay was considerably more than the meager wages I had earned at the British Columbia sweatshop. Soon I was saving money, doing my best to curtail social life, and making use of my spare time weekdays to free-lance for a series of noncompetitive business publications that were always looking for writers because they paid as little as possible; their only virtue, so far as I was concerned, lay in the fact that the stuff they

wanted was easy to write and could be obtained with
a minimum of effort.

Most weekends I was off duty, and I would take
Yukon on camping and fishing trips in Manitoba and
Ontario. We both lived for these outings, poor Yukon
most of all; but after a number of weeks, despite
my determination to remain uninvolved with other
people, I found myself coming under the spell of one
of the newspaper's librarians. Joan Gray was her
name, dark-haired and going prematurely gray, viva-
cious, calm, and charming (I am biased, of course, but
others would say the same about Joan.)

By autumn I knew I had a problem. I loved my
wolf-dog but I also loved Joan, the woman who was to
become my wife. The problem stemmed from the
fact that I knew I could not expect Joan to share with
Yukon and me the kind of life that we had lived.
Neither could I expect Yukon to share the kind of
suburban existence that seemed to be looming on
our horizon. What could be done?

I was not being deliberately cunning when I invited
Joan to join Yukon and me on a fishing trip in the
Lake of the Woods of Ontario, but I confess that I
hoped she would like that sort of thing. She had spent
half her life on a farm but had never gone fishing and
was not then familiar with the wilderness. As it turned
out, she loved it, but it was to be some time before
she became as whole-hearted about the wilds as I was.

In the meantime, there was Yukon to be considered.
Daily he was becoming more restive. When I faced
the fact that I was now intent on making a lasting
commitment to another person, I knew that the vaga-
bond existence the dog and I had been leading had
perforce to end. For a long time I was split down the
middle. I wanted to be with Joan and to work for her
and for our future together, yet I wanted to be with
Yukon, for whom I felt a deep loyalty. He wasn't a
tame house dog that could fit into suburban life and
be content with walks morning and night, on his lead,
over the sidewalks of a city. I didn't know what to do,
and as a result, I stalled both of them.

Joan spent that Christmas with her parents, who lived some twenty miles outside of Winnipeg, while I stayed in the city, doing a shift on the newpaper and celebrating the holiday in my room with Yukon. What a contrast this was with our last joyous Christmas together in the Damdochax Lake cabin!

Chapter 14

Except for the empty barn and the snow that covered the driveway, the homestead had not changed during the thirty-three months that we had been absent from it.

It was mid-January and mild for that time of the year when Yukon and I stepped out of the car and pushed our way through some two feet of snow to get to the house. The dog was wildly excited at being back; my own emotions were a compound of nostalgia, concern, and self-recrimination, the last generated by a sense of personal failure.

During the six-hour drive from Winnipeg, my mind had worked feverishly seeking a solution to the dilemma that faced all of us, but try as I might, I could think of nothing that would remedy our situation. Every course considered returned me to the one inescapable truth that I was trying to avoid: I must give up Yukon—or Joan. I couldn't bring myself to accept either alternative and felt disloyal to both.

So I had returned to the homestead, seeking there an inspiration that would solve my problems.

Leaving Yukon outside to reconnoiter the yard and outbuildings, I busied myself lighting the fires, anxious to put heat into the exceedingly cold house, the while trying to clear my mind of everything but the affairs of the moment, reminding myself sternly that we had come here to seek some peace and tranquillity and that we had three weeks of freedom during which we could run the north woods together, as we had of old. Surely, I thought, some solution would present itself during this time.

Being greedy for money when I went to work for the *Tribune,* I had felt put out that the newspaper did not pay overtime and instead compensated its staff with time off. More recently, having accumulated twenty-four days off during the last months, I blessed the system, for it now allowed me to take a holiday when I needed it and to return with Yukon to the homestead, at least giving him a break from his incarceration in Mrs. M.'s desolate yard.

The heat from both stoves, loaded with bone-dry tamarack logs cut months before we left the homestead, was filling the house, ridding the floors and walls of the frost accumulated during the winter; as the warmth soaked into my chilled body, it seemed to ease the sense of helplessness that had besieged me of late.

Turning away from the living-room heater, I walked to a window and looked out to see that Yukon was in the middle of the clearing and wading happily through chest-deep snow, evidently making for the forest. I moved toward the door instinctively, meaning to call him back, but I stopped. "Let him go," said a voice in my mind, "let him run wherever he pleases; he's due some freedom."

There was that determined look about him that one often sees in dogs when they set out intent upon a definite errand, trotting along purposefully without stopping to sniff or wet.

His line of travel would take him into the northeastern part of the forest, an area that had been logged many years earlier and that was now dressed by a mixture of evergreen and deciduous trees offering shelter to a variety of animals; hares were plentiful there, as were mice. Perhaps Yukon wanted to hunt, to earn his own living again, or maybe he was merely intent on rediscovering old haunts. It didn't matter; he was free to do as he pleased for the first time in many months.

The sun was beginning to edge toward the eastern treeline, creating long shadows on the snow and highlighting the spruces with a pinkish glow that spilled over the snow itself and made a charcoal sketch of Yukon's body. As I continued to watch him, and despite my resolve to the contrary, my mind returned to worry over the future. At the hub of the matter was Yukon's nature and ancestry. He was not as other dogs; he was *wild*. To attempt to subdue his wildness was to destroy the very qualities that made him such an extraordinary and magnificent animal.

Because I had wanted to believe it was possible, I had at first pretended to myself that he could learn to live in the city with Joan and me, perhaps somewhere on the outskirts, knowing, even as I dissimulated thus, that he could not, that he needed the wilderness if he was to survive as himself. Civilization was an environment alien to Yukon; he didn't understand it, he couldn't accept it, and he wouldn't be crushed by it. He would fight it, as he had fought Alfred, and he would become savage and dangerous again.

Indeed, he had already become dangerous! Five days before, he had attacked a man who stumbled against the yard fence, a drunk returning home from the bar via the alley that ran behind Mrs. M's house.

It was fortunate that I was home and that my room overlooked the yard; otherwise, he might well have killed the man, or else the victim's screams would have brought the police, and they would have undoubtedly shot Yukon.

I had just come home, from a late assignment and, as was my habit, had spent some time with Yukon in the yard before going up to my room. He had seemed distant and more than usually restless, failing to rise on his hind legs to lick my face, not pressing against me when I stroked his head and chest. Two days before this he had killed the neighbor's cat and eaten most of it, causing me considerable worry, not because he had killed the animal, for this was a natural thing for him to do, but because city dwellers do not understand these things and, rather naturally, look with horror upon a dog that will kill and eat their pets. In Yukon's mind, the cat might as easily have been a groundhog or hare running through the wilderness; to Mrs. M.'s neighbor, Yukon was a murderer that should be destroyed.

Coming so soon after the cat incident, Yukon's behavior toward me that night added greatly to my concern, but when I left him, I chose to believe that he was merely more restless than usual and that he would recover his equanimity when I took him for a day's outing in the winter forests that weekend.

The screaming started some fifteen minutes after I entered my room, a frenzied, terror-inspired shrieking that told me at once, without a shadow of doubt, that Yukon was attacking somebody. I was so sure of this that I didn't waste time looking out of the window; I ran out the room and down the stairs, taking them three at a time, then along the darkened corridor to the back door and outside.

Yukon had the man's forearm in his mouth and was pulling and shaking it savagely, his grim silence the more frightening in contrast with the hoarse scream of pain and terror coming from the man. The unfortunate victim was struggling wildly, but had already been pulled halfway over the fence.

Yelling as I ran, knowing that it wouldn't stop Yukon, but hoping my voice would give some encouragement to the man, I reached the dog and grabbed his collar, pulling him forward and twisting his head, not wanting to pull him back because I knew that to do so would cause his teeth to rip more cruelly through the flesh of his victim.

Yukon let go, but for an instant he seemed about to attack me. I held him more firmly, speaking to him quietly and trying to make my voice sound calm.

"OK, that's enough. Settle down now."

He recognized me. But I couldn't let him go or he would have charged the man again. I had to drag him away and secure him by his chain before returning to assist his victim.

Because of the time of year, the man was wearing a heavy topcoat, and this had protected him in some measure from Yukon's fearsome teeth; nevertheless, the arm was gushing blood so badly that a tourniquet was needed at once. All I had was my tie; I whipped it off and started to fasten it above the wounds, but the man was so hysterical he started to fight me, seeking to get away. It was then that I realized that he was very drunk.

After some moments I managed to calm the unfortunate man long enough to fasten the makeshift tourniquet above his elbow, cutting off the flow from the brachial artery.

The police and an ambulance arrived eventually, and the man was taken to hospital, leaving me to answer a lot of difficult questions, although the policeman taking my statement was understanding. The fact that the man was so drunk and that he had staggered against the fence minimized Yukon's crime, but I was warned that the dog must from now on remain tied and that it would be necessary for him to have a blood test so that he could be checked for rabies. Later I learned that the man's wounds needed twenty-three stitches and that his ulna had been fractured. Fortunately there would not be any lasting disability.

The next day, pleading personal reasons, I got leave to take my accumulated time off; then I talked the matter over with Joan.

"I don't think you're being fair to Yukon. He needs room to run. He's not a city dog, *you* know that!" she told me.

She didn't say so, but I knew that she thought that I was being selfish, putting my own feelings ahead of Yukon's happiness. And she was right, of course, but I could not bring myself to think of life without Yukon; neither could I accept the fact that he would be better off on some farm or perhaps with Bill, who had taken Rocky and Sooner. He was not the kind of dog able to thrive as a captive, even a more or less free sort.

The next day we left Winnipeg, and I sought desperately for a solution as I drove to the homestead, finding none, and continually returning to the crux: I wanted to have a wife *and* to keep Yukon with me; I wanted—no, *needed*—to live and work in the city, *and* I wanted to pursue an untrammeled life in the wilderness. It couldn't be done; I knew it.

Watching Yukon now as he jumped joyfully through the deep snow that covered the clearing, I asked myself aloud, "What the *hell* am I to do?"

After entering the forest, Yukon stayed away from the homestead for two days and three nights. He returned home early on the morning of the third day and awakened me by pounding on the door as he used to do. The agonizing that I had done during his absence may best be imagined. I remembered the bear drama—who could forget it with his drool as a constant reminder? —and I imagined all manner of dire things occurring to him, not with bears, perhaps, because they were still sleeping in their dens, but with wolves.

There had been wolf tracks in the snow in the yard when we arrived, and scats and urine marks. Each night since then the wolves had howled from different parts of the forest, which meant that there was more than one pack in our section of wilderness. There appeared to be several loners out there, too, judging by the single howls that often replied to the pack music. I had faith in Yukon's ability to take care of himself, yet I worried. Now he was back.

He greeted me effusively when he walked into the kitchen, giving me no chance to examine him, but since he looked all right, I gave up the attempt. When he was done standing up and licking and rubbing against me, I got a meal ready for him, assuming that he would be hungry and adding a beef bone to the canned food and dry rations in the dish. He sniffed at the meal, disdained it, but picked up the bone and took it to his favorite place beside the door, wagging his thanks. There he flopped down, licked the bone, and chewed halfheartedly, but soon went to sleep.

As I looked at him as he lay with his haunches turned under, his front paws stretched forward, and his head resting almost on top of the bone, it was easy to see that he was in top condition, obviously not hungry. His coat was somewhat unkempt and matted by a number of last year's burrs; otherwise, he was fine.

Stepping closer to him, at which his lids slitted as he looked at me momentarily, I noticed he smelled particularly "doggy," the odor characteristic of the male of the species that is accentuated when he is seized by the mating urge. The smell is particularly strong at this time, offensive to some human noses; it comes from a kind of musk manufactured in a pair of glands, one on each side of the anal sphincter, that routinely discharge small amounts of their content during defecation, increasing their output during periods of sexual arousal.

I wondered. . . . was his arousal merely the result of frustrated desire or had he scented a bitch wolf who was in estrus? Or was it possible that he had actually met a wolf bitch out there?

I felt a tiny glimmer of hope. Could this be? And if so, would it be the answer I had been searching for? Would Yukon be able to form his own pack and live the rest of his days in wild freedom?

At first I rejected this last concept. I found many reasons why it would not be desirable. It wouldn't be safe, for there was the ever-present risk of his stepping into a trap, or the other wolves might kill him; and I would never know what had happened to him. Of course, it was by no means certain that he had made contact with a wolf bitch; perhaps he had only found the scent of one and become excited by it.

I went into the living room, sat down by the heater, and forced myself to be objective as I examined the possibility of his having found a wild mate. There was really nothing so very unusual about this; Yukon himself was proof that dogs and wolves interbreed quite freely. Neither was it stretching coincidence to accept the premise that he might well have met a lone bitch in the forest, for there were many wolves in the region around the homestead.

At the end of half an hour of such reasoning I knew what I must do if something more were to result from his forest escapade. I owed it to him to give him the final choice.

I rose to put fresh wood on the fire, and Yukon woke up. He yawned noisily, gaping wide, then got to his feet and stretched. Finished, he came to me, and I patted his head and scratched his chest for a few moments; afterward he walked to the door and pawed it, asking to be let out.

As I went to open the door, I almost decided to go with him, knowing that he would have stayed with me. But I let him go. It was not in me to deny him that which I myself craved so much.

Between mid-January and early March, depending on latitude and weather conditions, wolves that have not yet selected mates, or those whose partners have died or been killed, begin to pair off in preparation for the breeding season that usually occurs during the last half of March. The packs become increasingly restless during late winter, howling often and traveling greater distances.

Unattached males and females belonging to individual packs are now likely to wander on their own, seeking a mate that is not already paired off and thus becoming temporary "lone wolves."

When two animals of opposite sexes meet at such times, they will probably pair off to form their own pack of two that will almost certainly become increased by the birth of pups sixty-three days after mating takes place. Before then, the two roam far and wide, depending for their food on small animals such as hares and mice and groundhogs while looking for a territory not already taken over by an existing pack.

Thus engaged, they frolic and play almost like puppies, courting each other, running a great deal and howling frequently, at times without any prompting, more often in reply to the voices of other wolves.

As the weight of the young in her belly increases, the bitch becomes more sober and starts to look for a suitable den in which to birth her pups. This may be a cave within a pile of rocks or an old and abandoned wolf den, or the bitch may decide to dig her own. However this may be, she is no longer the carefree, romping flirt of a few weeks before, and she is now likely to snarl a warning at her mate when he, ever ready to prolong the courting period, becomes overly exuberant.

Reviewing in this way my knowledge of the species the night after Yukon disappeared into the forest for the second time, I put on the snowshoes and went for a tramp through a wilderness that was lighted by the fullness of a silvered moon. As I walked, I thought about Yukon's relationship with Sussie, his solicitude for her, and his concern for the pups, and I remembered the sadness of it, the dreadful moment when I had to shoot her, and the death of the pups.

When I reached the flat place of granite where Yukon and I had rested so often in past summers, taking our ease at noontimes, I stopped, remembering the last occasion that we were here together, recalling once again the lake and the bushes and the shrubs and the pink granite and all those other intimate objects of this landscape in summer that will never fade from my memory.

A single wolf howled. Its ululating voice issued from the west, perhaps a quarter mile distant. Two howls replied to the solo, but these came from behind me and were more distant. For a time there was quiet. The wilderness, shrouded in its white cowl under the moonlight, seemed to be waiting for more of the wild songs. In the sky, the North Star pulsed directly over my head, and the Dipper looked so close that it seemed possible to reach up and touch its pointers. The two mournful voices, evidently raised in the area of the homestead, rose again in a prolonged song that echoed throughout the forest, a ghostly duet that to my imagination was destined to travel through space until it reached eternity and became preserved there for all time.

Four days after leaving the house for the second time, Yukon returned at dusk, but now he would not come inside. Wagging his tail and whining softly, he danced on the porch floor until I stepped out of the kitchen, then he rose on his hind legs and licked my face before walking outside, there to stand and look anxiously toward the northeast. I went to get the field glasses, joined him, and scanned the forest at the edge of the clearing. His trail was easily discernible in the gloom, but only the dark of the trees and the white of the snow were visible at the forest line.

Yukon sat on his haunches and looked at me intently, then turned his head to look at the darkening forest. Suddenly he howled, a long-drawn, deep cry that rose high, held an instant, and slowly came down the scale to end abruptly. Then, with the power to cause the hairs to stand stiff on the nape of my neck, Yukon's call was answered from just inside the shelter of the trees; a single voice, somewhat higher in pitch, rose loud and bell-like over the clearing. Before it ceased, Yukon howled again.

When it was over, he turned to me and whined, got up, and walked toward the well, behind which ran his trail. He stopped, looked back, and whined again, clearly undecided, but it was obvious that he wanted to go. Now I knew that he had found his bitch, just as I had found my woman; we were gripped by the same emotions, faced by indentical choices, and though neither one of us wanted to leave the other, the age-old forces at work within us could not be denied.

Yukon's life was out there in the forest, with his mate. Mine lay in the city, with Joan. This was right, as it should be, especially for him. He belonged to the wild as he had never belonged to me, and I could not deny him his right to live, or to die, in the wilderness that had created him.

Love, I realized at that moment, is whole only if it is capable of letting go; if it is able to release the object of its stimulation when such a sacrifice is necessary.

"Go, Yukon. Go to your lady."

He stood broadside-on to me, a dark outline against the white snow, his head turned my way and his triangular ears stiffly erect. His brush had been at half-mast, but when he heard my voice, it moved slowly upward and settled into its tightest curl. High-stepping, he left. Soon he was swallowed by the darkness.

I lingered, listening. Two voices were presently raised in the wolf song.

I never saw Yukon again. But I heard him and his wolf bitch sing often during the remainder of my stay at the homestead, and I saw the signs he left on three occasions when he visited the house and buildings during the night, noting his distinctive footprints, the one leaving only three claw marks. Each time he came, he brought his bitch; her smaller, finer tracks mingled with his right up to the back door.

Once, when I was walking through the wilderness, I became aware that I was being followed, and on turning around quickly, I *thought* I saw movement some yards to my rear. Later, on my return, I found his tracks in the snow, and those of his mate. It was evident that he was still drawn to me, but that his bitch would dare only approach just so near to man, and she now exerted greater influence on him than I did.

The next morning I left the house at sunrise, determined to follow Yukon's trail, secretly hoping that he would come to me, but telling myself that I merely wanted to make sure that he was all right.

At first I was bemused by the many tracks within the shelter of the forest on the other side of the clearing, but after a time a definite trail emerged inside a heavy stand of cedars. Following it, I was led deeper and deeper into the forest. By early afternoon I was in country new to me. The trail now aimed directly northward—that is, whereas earlier it had been used repeatedly by Yukon and his mate, now it showed only two sets of tracks and there were few urine stains and only occasional detours. It seemed that the two were marching purposefully, Yukon's distinctive tracks leading his mate's.

I gave up following them at three o'clock, by which time the sun was almost hidden behind the western tree line. It was by now clear to me that the two were moving out of the country, seeking a new range of their own in the deep wilderness away from the other packs and, more important to me, away from the haunts of man.

The journey back to the homestead was gloomy. Try as I might, I could not reconcile myself to his going; it was depressing to realize that we would never run the north woods together.

During the last week of my stay at the homestead Yukon's trails became buried by new snow, erased as though he and his mate had never walked across the clearing. By now the forest was silent; the pairing-off was over.

Yukon was gone. He and his mate would even now be engaged in the rituals that would lead to a new dynasty of wolves.

I was happy for Yukon the day I got into the car to drive back to Winnipeg. But I was sad also. I would always miss him, yet in my heart I knew that I had done the right thing, for he was free at last.

Yukon would continue to live in my memory; just as his great spirit would continue to roam the north woods so long as these remained.